CAMBRIDGE TEXTS IN
HISTORY OF POLITICAL THOU...

*Early Greek Political Thought from
Homer to the Sophists*

CAMBRIDGE TEXTS IN THE
HISTORY OF POLITICAL THOUGHT

Series editors

RAYMOND GEUSS
Lecturer in Philosophy, University of Cambridge

QUENTIN SKINNER
Regius Professor of Modern History in the University of Cambridge

Cambridge Texts in the History of Political Thought is now firmly established as the major student textbook series in political theory. It aims to make available to students all the most important texts in the history of western political thought, from ancient Greece to the early twentieth century. All the familiar classic texts will be included, but the series seeks at the same time to enlarge the conventional canon by incorporating an extensive range of less well-known works, many of them never before available in a modern English edition. Wherever possible, texts are published in complete and unabridged form, and translations are specially commissioned for the series. Each volume contains a critical introduction together with chronologies, biographical sketches, a guide to further reading and any necessary glossaries and textual apparatus. When completed the series will aim to offer an outline of the entire evolution of western political thought.

For a list of titles published in the series, please see end of book

Early Greek Political Thought from Homer to the Sophists

TRANSLATED AND EDITED BY

MICHAEL GAGARIN

University of Texas

PAUL WOODRUFF

University of Texas

 CAMBRIDGE
UNIVERSITY PRESS

HE UNIVERSITY OF CAMBRIDGE
lambridge, United Kingdom

TY PRESS
The Edinburgh Building, Cambridge CB2 2RU, UK
40 West 20th Street, New York, NY 10011–4211, USA
10 Stamford Road, Oakleigh, VIC 3166, Australia
Ruiz de Alarcón 13, 28014 Madrid, Spain
Dock House, The Waterfront, Cape Town 8001, South Africa

http://www.cambridge.org

© Cambridge University Press 1995

First published 1995
Reprinted 1997, 2000

Printed in the United Kingdom at the University Press, Cambridge

A catalogue record for this book is available from the British Library

Library of Congress Cataloguing in Publication data
Early Greek political thought from Homer to the sophists / translated and
edited by Michael Gagarin, Paul Woodruff.
p. cm. – (Cambridge texts in the history of political thought)
Includes index.
ISBN 0 521 43192 1. – ISBN 0 521 43768 7 (pbk.).
1. Political science – Greece – History. I. Gagarin, Michael.
II. Woodruff, Paul, 1943– . III. Series.
JC73.N67   1995
880.8′0358′0901 – dc20   94-36323 CIP

ISBN 0 521 43192 1 hardback
ISBN 0 521 43768 7 paperback

WV

Contents

Contents

Preface

The passages printed in this book are for the most part short, and many of them are fragmentary. They have all been the subject of far more scholarly research than can be aired in this format. We have tried to provide sufficient explanatory material for students to reach a basic understanding of the texts. Those who wish to go further may consult the Bibliographical Note. All readers should be warned that nothing presented here is beyond controversy.

We have been generous in our selection of texts. Some texts of doubtful authenticity that nevertheless represent pre-Platonic political thought have been included. Some texts have been chosen not because of what they say about political theory, but for the light they shed on other texts that are directly relevant to our themes. Questions of authenticity are mentioned in the notes when they arise. We have arranged our texts by genre, with the sophists at the end. We exclude texts representing the thought of Socrates, who will be the subject of another volume in this series. For a chronology of authors and events, see below, pp. xxxii–xxxv. Unless otherwise indicated, all our dates are BCE.

The translations aim at clarity and accuracy, and for the most part follow the structure of the original Greek. Translations of Greek verse are roughly line-for-line, and verse passages are provided with the Greek line numbers for convenient reference. Important words such as *dikē* ("justice") are translated as consistently as possible throughout. Technical Greek words that do not have close English equivalents and words such as *aretē* and *hubris* that have developed a history of their own in modern discussions are transliterated in the text and discussed in the Glossary. Generally we use square brackets, [ ], for explanatory material inserted in the text and angled brackets, ⟨ ⟩, for material that is not in the preserved Greek text but that (in our view) must have been in the original. We have generally adhered to a thematic arrangement of the material, but the arrangement may vary from author to author. In cross-references we identify passages by bold-face numbers usually preceded by "fr." even if the passage is not technically a fragment.

We have furnished new translations for all of the texts in this volume. Gagarin was primarily responsible for the *Hymn to Hephaestus*, Aeschylus, Sophocles, the minor tragedians, the Old Oligarch, Democritus, Antisthenes, Gorgias, Prodicus, Antiphon, Thrasymachus, Evenus, Critias, Lycophron, Alcidamas, *Anonymus Iamblichi*, and *Dissoi Logoi*. Woodruff was primarily responsible for Homer, Hesiod, Archilochus, Tyrtaeus, Solon, the Theognid corpus, Simonides, Xenophanes, Pindar, Euripides, Herodotus, Thucydides, Aesop, Heraclitus, the medical writers, Protagoras, Hippias, and the unknown sophist authors. Dr. Michael Nill prepared a translation, which we followed extensively, of the following texts: Democritus, Gorgias, and the Old Oligarch. Mark Gifford contributed to the translations of Aesop, the Old Oligarch, the medical writers, and the tragic fragments. He also provided useful comments on the Thucydides translation; this began as a revision of the Hobbes version of 1626 but in the process of modernization took on a life of its own. Both Gagarin and Woodruff have reviewed and edited all the translations.

Introduction

Western political thought begins with the Greeks – not just with recognized masterpieces, such as Plato's *Republic* and Aristotle's *Politics*, but with a host of earlier thinkers who are less well known. The purpose of this volume is to present the broad range of ideas about politics and the nature of human society that were proposed and debated before the more formal works of Plato and Aristotle began to dominate and control the expression of political theory.

Greek political thought before Plato comprises everything the Greeks deemed important to the functioning of the city-state, or *polis*: political theory, sociology, anthropology, ethics, rhetoric, and more. These issues come together in the last half of the fifth century in the teaching of the sophists, whose profession it was to prepare young adults for participation in public life. Long before the sophists, however, such issues were central to the poetry that served as the cultural memory of the Greeks. Accordingly, the texts in this volume represent more than thirty authors, including poets, philosophers, playwrights, historians, medical writers, and, of course, sophists. Because the sophists made the most striking contribution to political theory in this period, their surviving works are translated here in their entirety. In the case of other writers, we have included texts that reflect sophistic influence, as well as earlier texts with themes relating to the political thought of the time on such matters as human nature, the origin of human society, the origin of law, the nature of justice, the forms of good government, the distribution of wealth, and the distribution of power among genders and social classes.

Accounts of the sophists have too often assumed the perspective of Plato and later thinkers, who ask in what ways the sophists do or do not address the issues of concern to classical philosophy. In presenting the sophists in this volume together with their predecessors and contemporaries, we hope to foster the view that the sophists are the culmination of a long tradition of inquiry into these matters, and not merely precursors of classical political theory. The latter tradition was inaugurated by Plato and Aristotle and has had so much influence on modern thinking that it has largely eclipsed earlier contributions to political thought. This is regrettable. Political thinking had advanced long before Plato to provide foundations for the development of democracies in Athens and elsewhere. Greek authors as early as Homer and Hesiod understood the importance of procedural justice in communities, and the sophists gave this view theoretical support. By the late fifth century, moreover, perceptive writers such as Thucydides had learned from bitter experience that all elements of a community must be represented in government, and that no class – not even the ordinary people or *dēmos* – should be allowed to tyrannize over others. Thucydides' political thoughts, which anticipate Aristotle's in many respects, are clearly a product of the innovative thinking of the sophistic age – an age that still has considerable indirect influence on modern thinking.

Historical background

The political history of Greece before the fifth century has to be reconstructed from later sources supplemented by evidence from poetry and archaeology. The Homeric epics look back to the Bronze Age (which ended in the twelfth century), when there was a great king in Mycenae; but at the same time the epics reflect the realities of life in the eighth century – Greece fragmented into small communities presided over by hereditary aristocrats known as kings. Book 2 of the *Iliad* shows an assembly of the Greek army in which only kings are permitted to speak. Homer is probably responding to some popular resistance to this system when he introduces a caricature of a common man, Thersites, who attempts to speak in the assembly of the army. Thersites does not stand a chance: Odysseus drives him away, to the laughter of the assembly.

Hesiod's political landscape is similar, but seen from the perspective of a small land-owner and farmer. Power is in the hands of kings, and justice is fragile and easily subverted. Hesiod is passionate in his advocacy of a fair and effective judicial process, but pessimistic about the chances of justice being realized in the community as he knows it. Political change is a remote possibility.

After Homer and Hesiod the seventh and sixth centuries saw the rise of the Greek city-state or *polis* along with the development of constitutions and the codification of statute law. The *polis* was a tightly knit community bound by cultural and religious ties and sharing certain military and economic goals. The development of disciplined heavy infantry (hoplites) gradually eroded the dominance of the cavalry and the aristocrats, whose power had come from their ability to afford horses. This forced the leaders of a city into a sense of community with the middle class who could afford armor and weapons. Power now depended on the ability of a city to field a well-trained phalanx of hoplites who had enough in common to be willing to stand together and fight, each protecting with his shield the sword arm of the man to his left. Leaders and their troops had to work together in the interests of the community as a whole, and there was no place for the individualism of an Achilles. This is the world of Archilochus and Tyrtaeus, the world in which Athens and Sparta came to evolve as the paradigmatic city-states of classical Greece.

The seventh and sixth centuries are also the time when laws begin to be written down in cities all over Greece. Often the laws of a city are attributed to a specific lawgiver; Lycurgus in Sparta and Solon in Athens are the most notable of these. We are told that Lycurgus received his laws from an oracle in Delphi and that Solon rewrote almost the entire set of laws written by his overly harsh predecessor, Draco. The laws and political institutions of this period reflected the interests of those who served in the army – a middle class of farmers, artisans, and merchants. Calls for political reform now had to be taken more seriously, and compromise between the classes was more likely to succeed than total victory for one side or the other.

At the same time, population growth and an increase in commerce created pressure for new forms of political and social organization to replace traditional land-based aristocracies. In many cities nontraditional rulers known as *tyrannoi* came to power in relatively peaceful coups. Even Solon's reforms in Athens in the sixth century did not suffice to preserve the old order or prevent the rise of Peisistratus, who together with his sons ruled Athens for half a century (561–510). Such rulers often had the support of the people and rarely had to resort to force to maintain their positions. Still, the name for such a ruler, *tyrannos*, acquired a bad connotation in the later fifth century, and by Plato's time the word "tyrant" conjured up images of unbridled rapacity supported by unlawful violence. The image does not fit what we know of early tyrants, however, and Thucydides was probably right to insist, against the grain of Athenian opinion, that Peisistratus and his sons had actually been good rulers.

Starting in the eighth century, Greek cities had been sending out surplus population to found colonies in places accessible to their ships. Although politically independent, colonies often maintained close cultural ties with their mother cities, and in some cases economic ties as well. Almost all the Greek cities of Sicily and southern Italy had been founded as colonies by the end of the sixth century. The founding of colonies continued in the fifth century, and provided a practical context for discussions of ideal laws and constitutions. The sophist Protagoras, for example, was called upon to help draft the constitution for Thurii, a colony in Italy founded by Pericles and Athenian allies in 443.

A chief activity of the citizen class of Greek cities was war, and this accounts for the importance of military classification in the social and political orders that emerged in our period. By the fifth century, in Athens, clear lines were drawn between sailors, infantrymen, and cavalry. The rich could supply horses and join the cavalry, while the merely well-off could furnish their own heavy armor and weapons for service as hoplite infantry. The poor, having nothing to offer but themselves, usually saw service in the navy. The practical problem for Greek politics was to keep these groups in a cooperative balance.

In the fifth century, Greek cities were generally ruled by oligarchies or democracies. Oligarchies served the interests of the aristocrats, but some aristocrats such as Pericles held leading positions in democracies as well. Oligarchy was often said to be characterized by its supporters as having *eunomia* (literally, "good law"), but in fact democracy was as dependent on the rule of law as any other form of government, and democratic Athens soon became famous for its litigiousness.

Rather than generalize further about Greek forms of government, we will describe the systems of Athens and Sparta, which became models for the debate about constitutions in the fifth century and afterwards.[1] They were the two most important city-states in fifth century Greece and the two main adversaries in the Peloponnesian War (431–404). Thucydides, who records the history of this war, describes the clash of their two political systems as a clash of two entirely different cultures, and many of the other authors in this volume refer explicitly or implicitly to one or both of these cities.

Athens and Sparta

The government of Athens in the fifth century was the paradigm of Greek democracy. The Assembly (*Ecclēsia*) was open to all citizens, and combined legislative authority with considerable power over the policies and actions of the state. Business for the Assembly was prepared by the Council (*Boulē*) of Five Hundred, whose members were selected annually by lot and could serve no more than two (separate) terms. Managerial responsibility was in the hands of the ten *archōns* ("rulers") and a host of minor officials, who were also selected annually by lot. Most judicial decisions were reached in the popular courts, whose large panels of jurors (sometimes as many as five hundred) were completely autonomous. Judicial service was open to all citizens, and jurors were selected by lot for each trial. The judicial panels were subject to no higher opinion and their verdicts could not be appealed to any higher authority. Compensation for service as a juror or assemblyman was small, but enough for basic sustenance.

Almost all public decisions in Athens were thus made by amateurs, who did their jobs and then returned to private life, and it

---

[1] Among the many good books about these cities, we recommend as starting points R. K. Sinclair, *Democracy and participation in Athens* (Cambridge, 1988), Mogens Herman Hansen, *Athenian democracy* (Oxford, 1991), and Paul Cartledge, *Sparta and Lakonia: A regional history, 1300–362* BC (London, 1979). For Athens one may conveniently consult the most important source, Aristotle's *The Athenian constitution* in P. J. Rhodes' translation, with introduction and notes (Penguin Books, 1984).

was virtually impossible to become a professional politician except by continually persuading the citizens, gathered as assemblymen or jurors, to approve one's recommendations. The only offices not left to the chance of selection by lot and not limited in the term of service were military commands. The most famous Athenian leader, Pericles, maintained his leadership (as Thucydides reports) both by his ability to persuade the Athenians to follow his lead in the assembly and by being elected general year after year.

Athenian democracy (*dēmokratia*) was a form of government in which power was in the hands of ordinary people (the *dēmos*). In ancient Greece, however, *dēmos* referred only to adult male citizens. Women and slaves were never considered full citizens or allowed to participate publicly in political activity. As in the case of most democracies until quite recently, therefore, power was in the hands of less than a quarter of the population.[2]

We have less information about Spartan government. The sources we have are mostly non-Spartan and the reliability of their reports is in most cases questionable.

Sparta had two hereditary kings, whose primary duties were military leadership. There was also a Council of Elders and an Assembly, the relationship between which is uncertain. All judicial affairs were in the hands of five Ephors ("overseers"), elected annually by the Assembly.

A crucial feature of Spartan government and life was that the large majority of inhabitants of the territory were not Spartan citizens but a native people called Helots. Sparta had conquered these people in wars during the eighth and seventh centuries, and thereafter most aspects of Spartan life were organized with a view to keeping the Helots in a serf-like status and preventing their uprising. Thus military considerations were prominent in almost every aspect of Spartan life. The training of young men was well organized and involved a famously high level of discipline that was envied by many conservative Athenians. Full Spartan citizens were highly valued by the state. Each citizen held an allotment of land, which was farmed by serfs, and the citizens were supposed to be more or less equal in social and economic status. In fact, however,

---

[2] As best we can tell, the share of the population eligible to participate in political decision making was almost the same in ancient Athens as in the United States before the Civil War.

Introduction

some were wealthier or more aristocratic than others, and this
seems to have affected Spartan political life, which was essentially
oligarchic.

Early poetry

Poetry was the main cultural medium in early Greece. Easily
committed to memory, it served as a vehicle for views on many
subjects, including ethics, statecraft, and law, until the rise of prose
literature in the fifth century. Part I of this volume covers poetry
from the Homeric poems in the late eighth century to the works
of Simonides and Pindar in the fifth century. These poets express
or imply interesting views on social and political issues, and many
of our passages are quoted widely by later writers and are taken
up in their discussions of political theory. Generally, early Greek
poets stress the importance of *themis* ("right"), *dikē* ("law, justice"),
or *aidōs* ("respect"), and support either monarchy or aristocracy.
They tend to see agitation for a greater share of power on the
part of common citizens (the *dēmos* or *hoi polloi*) as a threat to
public order. On the other hand, Homer's "kings" do not consider
themselves absolute monarchs: both the *Iliad* and *Odyssey* portray
assemblies, primarily composed of aristocrats (also called "kings"),
who advise their leader (who is the "most kingly"). Homer's younger
contemporary Hesiod questions whether the procedure for submit-
ting disputes to these lords for judicial settlement is fair and
effective; he also fashions myths about the origins of social and
cultural institutions, most notably those of Prometheus and Pandora,
that present a broadly pessimistic and regressive view of human
civilization.

Other poets, especially Theognis and Pindar, express a more
strongly aristocratic view: they emphasize the hereditary nature of
virtue and the desirability of having the "better men" rule, and
they bemoan the social mobility of their time. More moderate is
the Athenian reformer Solon, who, as he tells us, did much to
alleviate the sufferings of the common people without giving way
to democracy or to a redistribution of land. Solon explicitly resists
(as he says in passages **2–5**)[3] the attempts of the poor to acquire

[3] Numbers in boldface refer to the numbering of the selections in this volume.

the land of wealthy aristocrats. In his poetry Solon forcefully asserts a traditional moral outlook based on moderation, and against this moral background he sets his political and legal reforms and theorizes about the operation of society. These sentiments of Solon and other early poets are often directed at very specific historical situations, but they provide evidence for the more general theoretical dialogue that must have occurred at the same time.

The works of these early poets provide a crucial background for understanding the rapid innovations of the fifth century – innovations not only in the ideas expressed but also in the forms of expression. One major development is the Athenian institution of tragic drama, which is said to have begun in 535.

Tragedy

Athens' most famous contribution to poetry was tragedy. Each year poets competed for a prize at the largest and most important public festival in Athens, the Greater Dionysia, a setting that in itself underscored the public, political significance of tragedy. A few early tragedies such as Aeschylus' *Persians*, which dramatizes the defeat of Xerxes' forces in 480, were based on historical events and thus had a direct political impact, but even tragedies based on traditional myths must have been understood in the context of contemporary social and political issues. This is especially true of works such as Sophocles' *Antigone* – which presents the bitter conflict between Creon, ruler of the state and upholder of law and order, and Antigone, whose devotion to her family leads her to reject the law and bury her brother in defiance of Creon – or the three plays constituting Aeschylus' *Oresteia* – which portray a series of family murders raising pointed questions about justice and legitimate retribution. These ought to be read in their entirety by anyone studying fifth-century political thought. We have confined ourselves in Part II to a limited number of passages which can be understood when excerpted from their contexts. Most of these passages show direct influence of the sophists in style or content – in the structure of paired speeches and debates, and in themes such as the rule of law, the status of women, the ideal constitution, and the origins of law in human society.

Comedy, which was produced at the same festival as well as at smaller celebrations, was also engaged in the social and political issues of the day. Most of Aristophanes' plays treat political and social themes that were timely when the plays were produced around the end of the fifth century. The material is not readily excerptable, however, and so rather than include an occasional isolated verse, we urge the reader to read entire plays such as Aristophanes' *Clouds* (with its famous portrait of Socrates as a sophist), *Lysistrata* (in which the women take over the government), and *Ecclesiazousai* (which proposes a radically new form of government in which women rule and private property is abolished).

History and folklore

Another major development in this period was the rise of prose writing. Through the first half of the fifth century, most pre-Socratic philosophers wrote poetry, and the style of prose writers like Heraclitus was aphoristic and still quite poetic. Other prose writers used a very simple, direct style. But after the middle of the century various writers and speakers began to mold prose into an artistic medium – a more sophisticated style capable of expressing more complex views. Gorgias and Thucydides were the most notable results of this development, but Herodotus, "the father of history," is also a key figure.

Part III is given over to passages from prose writers of the fifth century who dealt with history or folklore. Herodotus and Thucydides both belong to the revolution of the new learning and both writers reflect in important (though quite different) ways the influence of the sophists. Each writer mingles historical fiction with history, frequently in order to develop points in political theory. Herodotus' fictional dialogue on constitutional forms and most of the speeches in Thucydides are examples of this device. We have excerpted the most important passages of these two *Histories*, but as with Greek tragedy, any serious student of fifth-century political thought ought to read these texts in their entirety.

The information Herodotus gathered may seem to us loosely organized, but when measured against the few rather simple prose works that preceded him, his *History* is remarkable for presenting a unified view of the entire known world and for attempting to understand some of the underlying forces that brought Greeks and

Barbarians (as he divided the world) into conflict. The Persian Wars may have helped Herodotus see all history as part of a single overall struggle between Greeks and others, but the contemporary discussion of social and political issues both stimulated Herodotus' work and also benefited from his inquiries (*historia*) into the customs and beliefs of other cultures.

Thucydides was a political thinker of great power and originality, who constructed a complex account of the moral, social, and political forces at work in Greek society during the Peloponnesian War from its beginning in 431 to 411 when his history breaks off, seven years before the end of the War. Besides recounting events, Thucydides explores the reasons and excuses people give for acting as they do through a series of set-piece debates. The speeches he supplies in the course of this are more reconstruction than history: they reveal what Thucydides thinks were the motives of the speakers. A frequent theme is the conflict between the requirements of justice on the one hand and the needs of imperial power on the other. Although the arguments he reports bear reference to particulars of the war at hand, Thucydides intends his history to have a timeless relevance for human political decisions: human nature being what it is, similar patterns of conflict are bound to recur.

In addition to the speeches and debates, Thucydides' descriptions of certain events – most famously the plague in Athens and the civil war on Corcyra – are virtually essays on human nature. As a result, his book does more than tell the story of one war; it illustrates how Thucydides believes human beings think and act under the stress of war and disaster. His sour view of human nature and his reasoned repugnance to the amoral conduct of empire by the Athenian democracy make him one of the most sophisticated of the political thinkers before Plato. He was a major influence on Hobbes, who translated the *History* as a young man; and he has continued to affect modern discussions of politics. He tells his story from an unmistakably anti-democratic perspective, and his testimony has been noticed especially whenever the idea of democracy is under trial.

The treatise commonly referred to as the Old Oligarch may be the earliest work in this section. This essay on the Athenian constitution was written by an unknown author of the period and has come down to us among the works of the fourth-century historian Xenophon. The writer reveals a mixture of bitter dislike and reluctant admiration for the Athenian political system, and his work has been seen by some as an attempt to present at least some of the points on both sides of what was clearly a heated debate at the time.

To these three writers we have added a few fables of Aesop that represent the folk wisdom of the period on political themes.

Philosophy and science

In Part IV we include prose authors in philosophy and science whose work bears on political themes. The early pre-Socratic philosophers were apparently most interested in cosmogony and cosmology; but questions of ontology and logic came to the fore in the fifth century under the influence of Parmenides. Socrates is the most famous of those who turned philosophy from heaven to earth – from cosmology and ontology to moral and social issues – but he was not alone. Heraclitus and Democritus combine views about logic and epistemology with a strong interest in social, political, and ethical issues. A historian writing in Roman times, Dionysius of Halicarnassus, provides a text that is a direct reflection of fifth-century anthropological views, and we have included this as well. As the most likely author of this piece is Democritus, we have printed it as the first selection under his name. Medical writers often treat their subject against a broad background of views about society and human nature. At the end of this section we translate two short speeches of the Cynic philosopher Antisthenes which clearly belong to the tradition of mythological debate that we see in the work of Gorgias and other sophists.

The sophists

The largest and most important set of passages we translate are the writings of the sophists, who came to prominence around the middle of the fifth century. After the Persian Wars Greece was swept by a wave of confidence, which the Athenians in particular gained from their successes at Marathon (490) and Salamis (480) and from the decisive allied victory at Plataea (479). At this time there arose a new spirit of inquiry and innovation in many fields and in many parts of Greece, which has often been compared to the eighteenth-century Enlightenment. During this period Herodotus traveled to the far corners of the known world conducting his inquiries; in Sicily in the mid-fifth century (we are told) Corax and Tisias invented the art of words, the forerunner of rhetoric; Athenians debated in the Assembly, as well as through their tragedies, the extent and ways in which they should democratize their society; and throughout the Greek world there came to prominence intellectuals who traveled from city to city to discuss, debate, teach and generally display their new approaches to traditional ways of speaking and thinking.

These teachers came to be called sophists, though it is only after Plato, and under his influence, that sophists were considered as a class apart from other intellectuals. The term "sophist" is now used to name certain thinkers who became prominent in Greek intellectual life in the second half of the fifth century, and scholars often speak of them as a school or movement, but such language is misleading. The sophists undoubtedly knew each other's work and some must have been acquainted, but there are significant differences in their interests and ideas. Plato even alludes to their professional rivalry. Certainly they did not in themselves constitute a philosophical school or even an intellectual movement.

Because the name "sophist" has had a uniformly negative connotation since Plato's time, it is worth noting that the first occurrence of the word *sophistēs* ("wise man," from *sophos* = "wise") is in an ode of Pindar (*Isthmian* 5.28) early in the fifth century (478), where it clearly means "poet." Other fifth-century occurrences also show no pejorative connotation until Aristophanes' *Clouds*, our version of which was written around 420. It thus appears that the name was first used as a sign of respect that placed the person so designated in the tradition of wisdom which before the sophists had been dominated by poets. This is the tradition to which Protagoras appeals (passage 1), when he traces his profession back to Homer and Hesiod. The word "sophist" was also used well into the fourth century for people we would now designate as orators or philosophers.

Those who are commonly designated sophists have these distinct features: they traveled widely throughout the Greek world, and gave lessons and lectures to young and old for substantial fees, frequently on ethical, social, and political issues. In addition, various sophists taught all the subjects that were of interest to those who could afford their fees, including history, literature, mathematics, science, and the art of words. Hippias claimed to have taught everything, and indeed exhibited practical skills such as shoemaking, but most sophists steered clear of handicrafts. At the same time, they tended to avoid highly abstract subjects such as metaphysics and cosmology.

Socrates shared the sophists' interest in ethics. In his methods too, and even in some of his doctrines (such as his theory of punishment), he had much in common with the sophists. The most objective feature (emphasized by both Plato and Xenophon) in which Socrates differed from the sophists was his not charging fees for instruction: except for Socrates, other orators and philosophers all charged fees – even Plato. There is no evidence that anyone before Plato criticized the sophists for charging fees; in the *Clouds* Aristophanes stresses the poverty of Socrates' "thinking school" and its pupils. The fees charged by the sophists did mean that their pupils tended to come from the wealthier families, and this may have bred some resentment in democratic cities such as Athens. On the other hand, Socrates, who charged no fees but was probably considered a sophist by his contemporaries (as he is in the *Clouds*), also drew his pupils largely from the wealthy. Indeed, the oligarchic activities of several of Socrates' pupils and associates are often considered a prime cause of his trial and execution in 399.

The other practical difference between Socrates and the sophists is that he spent virtually his entire life in Athens (as Plato tells us), whereas they were itinerant teachers who came from cities all over the Greek world. The only well-attested Athenian sophist was Antiphon, who, to judge from the variety of clients for whom he wrote speeches, had many ties to other cities and probably traveled frequently outside of Athens. It is apparent from Plato's *Protagoras* that the visits of sophists to Athens could generate great excitement, though their itinerant nature may also have aroused hostility against them as outsiders.

Teachings of the sophists

The sophists were the chief representatives of what is appropriately called the new learning. It is largely to them that we owe the ideal of a broad education for mature students, such as exists in the modern university. Their curriculum included history, literature, science, and social science, as well as the art of language or rhetoric.

Many sophists were interested in the origins of justice and law in human society. Although Protagoras and the earlier sophists saw no great tension between human nature and the morality adopted by society, some later sophists came to believe that Greek customs and laws (*nomoi*) ran against the grain of nature (*phusis*); they contended that it was nature, rather than law or custom, that should receive our primary allegiance. Certainly some sophists argued against conventional morality, but it is unlikely that any real sophist took the extreme position of Plato's Callicles in the *Gorgias*, who inveighs against any law or moral code that does not encourage the strong man to promote his own interests and satisfy his own inflated desires. In fact, the sophists' discussions of the tension between *nomos* and *phusis* were part of a larger effort to examine traditional views of morality and justice in a critical but positive spirit.

Relativism is the doctrine most commonly associated with the sophists in modern times. Plato sometimes presents the sophists as holding a view that would deny altogether the existence of truth and would undermine any claim of one person to know more than another. It is unlikely, however, that any of the sophists was an extreme relativist of this sort. To be sure, the sophists' travels stimulated their comparative study of political, legal, social, ethical, and religious ideas, and this may have led some to positions that belong to relativism broadly construed; but (as in the Enlightenment) acquaintance with other cultures helped stimulate many new ideas about human nature and social organization. In the *Theaetetus* Plato represents Protagoras as an extreme relativist, but Plato's fictions are not reliable as history of philosophy, and we have evidence that Protagoras held views incompatible with the position attributed to him in the *Theaetetus*. Protagoras believed, for example, in the existence of human nature (passage 8) and of individual natural talent (passage 5); he also taught students to use language correctly, and his standard of correctness was not merely conventional (passages 28, 32, 33).

On political questions, the main issues were constitutional and concerned the justice and viability of democracy. The training most sophists provided in public speaking as preparation for public life would have been more valuable to young men in democratically ruled cities, although public speaking had been important in Greece long before the birth of democracy. While teaching the art of public speaking, many sophists tended to criticize tradition and to promote innovation, and these tendencies would have been consistent with support of the new democracies. Indeed, we are told that in the Greek world the teaching of rhetoric began after the tyranny at Syracuse was overthrown and replaced by a democracy, and the sophists were more welcome in democratic cities such as Athens than in Sparta.

Nevertheless, the sophists were not especially pro-democratic as a group, and most likely held as wide a range of opinions on politics as they did on other matters. Their clients had to be wealthy enough to afford their fees, and this may have tilted some of their teaching against democracy. We must keep in mind, how ever, that the political sympathies of individual sophists can rarely be determined from the evidence we have. In most cases we do not even know enough to speculate, while the sophists whose sympathies we can identify fall on both sides of the major political issues of the day. Protagoras, for instance, gives support for democratic practices (see esp. fragment 10), but his views could be adapted to support other systems too. Gorgias served as ambassador to Athens from the Sicilian city of Leontini in 427 when it was a democracy. (This is the only indication we have of his political preferences, as the surviving texts do not bear on the matter.) On the other hand, the sophist Antiphon was one of the leaders of an oligarchic coup in Athens in 411 and was tried and executed when democracy was restored a few months later; and the views of Thrasymachus and Callicles, as Plato represents them, seem antithetical to democratic systems.

Methods of the sophists

The sophists' greatest impact may have come less from the specific new doctrines they developed than from their approach and methods. Their starting point is often an aggressive questioning of tradition: Protagoras questions the texts of Homer and Simonides and substantially revises one of Hesiod's myths; Gorgias explicitly challenges the poets who present the traditional view of Helen; and the others all contribute in different ways to the challenging of traditional views. Criticism of one's predecessors was not altogether new, of course: archaic poets and early philosophers had vigorously criticized each other (explicitly or implicitly), and poets had boldly invented new versions of old myths. The competitive setting of much early poetry (see below) surely fostered such rivalry and criticism. For some sophists, however, criticism of traditional culture was so prevalent that it sometimes seemed to become an end in itself. Whatever their intention, the popular view of the sophists (as ridiculed, for example, by the comic poets) was that they sought novelty merely for its own sake.

This is unfair, for the sophists went beyond the questioning of tradition to develop a new form of intellectual inquiry, whereby two passages or views were juxtaposed and arguments made in favor of each. Indeed, the sophists made an art form of formulating positions that compete with one another, both to teach the skill of argument and to bring out the different strengths of contrasting views. Although this process could lead to nihilistic absurdities (as it does in the *Dissoi Logoi*), it could also serve as a constructive means to understanding, as it clearly did for Thucydides in the great paired speeches of his *History*, and probably did also for Protagoras (though nothing survives of his *Contrasting Arguments*). Antiphon's *Tetralogies* argue for competing positions in hypothetical cases at law, thus illustrating methods of argument and at the same time bringing out the moral complexities of the sort of cases that are in question. But even works that do not explicitly involve the juxtaposition of opposed positions often do so implicitly by presenting a strong statement of the "weaker argument," namely the argument that runs contrary to the traditionally accepted position. One example is Gorgias' *Helen*, which defends Helen of Troy against the traditional charge that her willingness to run away with

Paris brought about the Trojan War. Gorgias' argument for the weaker position challenges the traditional, stronger case in language that explicitly echoes that of a legal defense. Whether or not the audience accepted his argument for Helen's innocence, his detailed examination of the influence of external factors on human behavior would lead them to a better understanding of issues that lie at the heart of many judicial cases. Thus the arguments of the sophists, though not as sophisticated as those of Plato and Aristotle, represent a significant advance over, say, the choral passages of Aeschylus or Pindar, or the aphorisms of Heraclitus.

Selection of texts

Most works of the sophists have been lost in the passage of time, and much of what remains is in the form of fragmentary quotations. For completeness we have included in Part V all the surviving works of the sophists, whether or not they deal with political themes, with some exceptions: we have omitted a few poetic fragments of Critias that bear no relation to his thought or practice as a sophist. We have also omitted a few one- and two-word fragments that carry no meaning on their own. In addition we have translated two substantial texts of uncertain authorship that are certainly products of sophists or their students, the *Anonymus Iamblichi*, and the *Dissoi Logoi*.

We have treated Protagoras as a special case. So little of his own writing survives that we are especially dependent on Plato's testimony and on what is called imitation – on Plato's representation of Protagoras in his historical fictions. Accordingly, our section on Protagoras includes substantial passages from Plato that are not exact quotations from the sophist.

We must keep in mind that Plato is not a friendly witness, and that his aim is not an accurate transmission of the history of thought. The sophists were controversial but influential figures in their own day, and Plato saw their work as an integral part of a corrupt enterprise that included two of his other favorite targets, forensic oratory and poetry. Plato proposed in the *Republic* to replace virtually all existing Greek culture with studies that were either preparatory to, or derived from, the pursuit of Platonic dialectic. This course of study would exclude most of what the sophists taught, along with traditional poetry and drama. Scholars who wish to understand the sophists must therefore keep in mind that Plato is no more just to the sophists than he is to the poets, and must filter out Plato's influence by focusing on what the sophists were doing in their own terms rather than what they were not doing in Plato's.

Principal themes

Of the many themes in this volume, justice and rhetoric are the most pervasive and the most important in terms of the influence of Greek ideas on modern political thought.

Justice

In Homer justice (*dikē*) and the related concept of right (*themis*) are used to mark the difference between the civilized human beings who observe them and savages who do not, such as the Cyclopes encountered by Odysseus. Evidently *dikē* indicates a commitment to the peaceful settlement of disputes in a community, while *themis* requires a level of social organization in which each man is not a law unto himself and his immediate family.

Hesiod is our earliest writer to make justice a central theme. He does this, apparently, on account of the injustice he believes he has suffered at the hands of his brother. Justice for Hesiod has to do with the proper distribution of wealth (which in his society consisted mainly of agricultural land) and with giving honest testimony and fair judgments in court. Homer's gods are sometimes oblivious to right and wrong, though they occasionally reward and punish mortals on moral grounds; but Hesiod's gods are primarily protectors of justice against its abuse by rulers who foster *hubris* (an insolent disregard for what is right) by looking only to their own advantage.

Solon largely follows Hesiod in his conception of justice and the importance he attaches to it, although Solon's justice is beginning to moderate the distribution of power among classes, as well as the distribution of wealth among individuals. In classical times the concept comes to have a range of meanings approaching that of "justice" in modern-day discussions; in Greek thought, however, *dikē* generally retains a strong sense of judicial procedure, in addition to distributive and retributive justice, and is sometimes distinguished from fairness. In the poets, divine justice is usually retributive. In Thucydides, justice (as opposed to self-interest) is something an imperial power can rarely afford to observe, and his Athenian spokesmen frequently argue that they must use force to retain their empire whether or not it is just to do so. In an ironic twist, however, Diodotus (Thucydides, fr. 5a) argues that clemency for the Mytileneans is consistent with the Athenians' self-interest despite the contrary requirements of justice.

The teaching of some sophists (notably Antiphon) includes the art of persuasive speaking in court, and this gives them a practical, legal interest in justice. Protagoras sees justice as a condition of survival, and therefore as a second nature in human beings. Justice is part of the package of learned skills and virtues that allow human beings to survive without the claws, armor, or speed that give other animals a measure of protection. Elsewhere, however, Protagoras observes that justice is different in different cities. We do not know exactly how he would reconcile the relativism of this observation with the naturalism of his explanation for the origin of justice; but he may have felt that all men have a natural need for *a* system of justice, but that the actual judicial systems of different societies may vary. Herodotus too notices that different cultures have different moral rules, but neither Herodotus nor Protagoras thought that for this reason traditional morality was entirely groundless.

Later sophists take a more radical turn. Some of them follow Protagoras in thinking of justice as a product of human learning, but differ from him in seeing it as fundamentally opposed to nature. In the end, the sophists come to be seen by traditionalists as dangerous critics of justice and of all ancestral moral codes. Justice, some sophists were accused of saying, is never more than the best of a bad bargain, the result of a social contract that strong men should either avoid or betray. Views of this sort are attacked by Plato in the *Gorgias* and in Books 1 and 2 of the *Republic*.

In the debate over the perceived conflict between nature and justice, however, justice often shows its value – as salvation or bane – through the role it plays when organized society emerges from social chaos. Interest in the origin of society is first apparent in Hesiod, primarily in his two versions of the Prometheus myth

(1, 2), which is taken up later by Aeschylus (1–3) and then by Protagoras (8). Herodotus devises an account of the origin of law in Persia (2), Sophocles offers up a hymn to human progress in the *Antigone* (1), and the *Anonymus Iamblichi* has his story on this theme as well. Thus, for better or worse justice as an organizing principle of society becomes a central concern of the sophists and remains central to the political theory of their successors and detractors, including Plato and Aristotle.

Rhetoric

Although the sophists were only part of a broad development of learning in the fifth century and taught a variety of subjects from mathematics to history, their best known common interest was in the theory and practice of speaking, which Plato was later to stigmatize as "rhetoric."[4] The sophists' experiments in methods of inquiry and argument coincided with and helped stimulate a strong interest in everything comprehended by the word *logos*, which could mean "word," "speech," "argument," "reasoning," and "discourse." This interest in *logos* did not come in a vacuum: public oratory had played an important part in Greek life from the beginning. Oratorical skill was recognized in Homer, Hesiod, Tyrtaeus, and many other early poets; historians wrote of the oratorical ability of Athenian statesmen such as Themistocles; and oratory in the form of long, set speeches was probably an important feature of tragedy from the beginning.

Also fundamental to Greek culture from the beginning was the institution of the contest or *agōn*. The contest may first have evolved out of military combat, but even in the time of Homer and Hesiod the Greeks were engaging in contests in non-military settings. Our earliest references are to athletic contests, such as those in Book 23 of the *Iliad*, and poetic contests, such as Hesiod's victory at the funeral games of Amphidamas. But by the fifth century the basic pattern of the *agōn* could be found in many other areas. Gorgias (1, section 13) refers to astronomical and philosophical debates in addition to legal disputes, and a relatively formal debate, or *agōn*, was a well-established feature of fifth-century tragedy and comedy.

[4] For Plato's misrepresentation of his predecessors on this point, see Thomas Cole, *The origins of rhetoric in ancient Greece* (Baltimore, 1991).

Interest in rhetoric was also stimulated in Athens by the nature of debate in the democratic Assembly and the increasing activity of the popular law courts, which required that any young man seeking to make his mark and attain influence in the city needed to be an effective speaker and debater. The sophists taught their students to be effective speakers by introducing them to persuasive forms of argument and expression, and to the substantial questions in ethics and politics that related to the appropriate content of a speech in a court or assembly. Protagoras supplemented his teaching of rhetoric with an inquiry into what is recognizably a precursor of speech–act theory. Gorgias extolled the power of persuasive speech while attacking the philosophers' concepts of pure being, truth, and knowledge.

One new form of argument perhaps came with Gorgias from Sicily to Athens and took the leading role in some works of the later sophists and orators, as well as in the speeches of Thucydides' *History*. Its strategy is to appeal to what is likely, reasonable, or natural (*eikos*), rather than to what can be grounded in evidence. If a rich man is accused of theft, his wealth alone affords him a defense on this basis: since he would have no reason to steal, he is unlikely to have done so. Such arguments can easily be abused, but the surviving speeches show that arguments involving likelihood (*eikos*) were generally used either to supplement direct evidence or to frame a reasonable hypothesis in a case in which direct evidence was missing or insufficient. We have no reason whatever to believe Plato's characterization of sophistic rhetoric as preferring likelihood to truth (*Phaedrus* 267a).

In addition to speeches composed for actual use in assemblies and law courts, sophists prepared display speeches to entertain and instruct their students and paying audience. The two speeches of Gorgias are of this sort. Both use situations taken from myth, and both illustrate techniques of argument in a manner that is both playful and serious. Mythical situations also are addressed in speeches composed by Antisthenes and Alcidamas, and many speeches in tragedy, especially in the plays of Euripides, belong to this same genre. The speeches in the *Tetralogies* of Antiphon were written for hypothetical cases and show how prosecution or defense could make a persuasive case in such situations.

Plato caricatures rhetoric as he did relativism, treating it as a device for manipulating people's minds (*psychagogia*) and arguing that it should therefore be taught only along with a well-grounded moral theory that would ensure the proper use of so powerful a weapon. But although the sophists understood the power and importance of rhetoric, they say nothing that supports Plato's charge that they were interested merely in manipulation. Rather, they taught (among other things) what many people, including philosophers, have always wanted to know: how to make the best of a case, even one that seems *prima facie* unlikely or that is out of favor at the moment, and how to see the strengths on both sides of an issue.

Their art had its primary use in a society that delighted in open debate and in contests of verbal skill. In fact, the oratory taught by sophists was never the weapon of tyrants; after all, tyrants had a more powerful tool of persuasion in the form of armed men. In Thucydides' *History* only one Athenian regularly uses oratory effectively, and that is Pericles, who needs it precisely because he wields power through democratic institutions. Later politicians like Cleon are depicted by Thucydides as failures at public speaking; and even Nicias, who easily traps Cleon in a debate over Pylos, is later cornered in debate with Alcibiades and put in command of an expedition he believes (but is afraid to say) will surely fail. Although both Pericles (in the funeral oration) and Diodotus (in the Mytilenean debate) argue that there is a necessary connection between rhetoric and action, rhetoric in Thucydides generally turns out to be (as Cleon argues in the Mytilenean debate) ineffectual, a device for masking intentions or delaying action.

The many passages in which Thucydides contrasts speech (*logos*) against action (*ergon*) are complex and laced with irony, but on the whole they show that a person's actions reveal character more truly than his speeches. Still, words affect the way actions are perceived, both by the actors in the *History* and by its readers. The revolutionaries on Corcyra knew that the language they used to disguise their crimes was essential to their success. More to the point, Thucydides knows how much style matters in the telling of his *History*. Generations of historians have been won over to his view of Athenian history by the grace of his prose and its powerful combination of vivid battle narratives with thoughtful debates. The *erga* of the war are interesting and important in their own right, of course, but it is Thucydides' *logoi* that have made his *History* "a possession for all time."[5]

Indeed, words – *logoi* – are always at the center of the sophists' interests. Protagoras' "correct diction," Gorgias' "art of words," Prodicus' careful distinctions between synonyms, Antiphon's legal subtleties, these are but some of the ways in which a primary interest in language and its relation to human action and human nature were central to the sophistic period. Most of the sophists' words have perished, but even the few we have recovered show the vitality and importance of their enterprise.

[5] For a fine study of the complex tension between word and deed, see Adam Parry, *Logos and* Ergon *in* Thucydides (Harvard diss., 1957; reprint 1981, 1988).

Principal dates

Authors are placed roughly when their careers were at their peak. The birthplace or place of principal activity is given for each author when known.

Dates	Events	Authors
776	Founding of the Games at Olympia.	Homer (8th century). Hesiod (8th century), Boeotia. Archilochus (8th–7th centuries), Islands (Paros, Thasos).
675–650?	Constitutional reform in Sparta, attributed to the legendary lawgiver Lycurgus.	
	2nd Messenian War: Spartan subjection of the Helots.	Tyrtaeus (7th century), Sparta.
c. 590	Solon's reforms in Athens.	Solon (6th century), Athens. Theognis (6th century), Megara.
561	The beginning of Peisistratus' first period of rule as a "tyrant" in Athens.	

546–5	The Persian king Cyrus seizes Asia Minor, including the Asiatic Greek cities.	Simonides (556–468), Islands (Ceos).
527–510	The sons of Peisistratus rule in Athens.	Xenophanes (*c.* 570–475), Colophon.
508/7	The reforms of Clisthenes; democratic institutions in Athens.	Heraclitus (6th–5th centuries), Asia Minor (Ephesus).
499–494	The Asiatic Greeks rebel against the Persian empire.	
494	The Persians sack the Greek city of Miletus.	
490	The Persian king Darius sends an army against Greece, which is defeated by the Athenians at Marathon.	
482	Athens builds a fleet that will defeat the Persians at Salamis.	
480	The Persian king Xerxes invades Greece by land and sea; battles of Thermopylae and Salamis.	
479	The Greek allies defeat the Persian army at Plataea.	Pindar (518–*c.* 440), Boeotia. Aeschylus (525–456), Athens.
477	Foundation of the Delian League under the leadership of Athens.	
461	Further democratic reforms by Ephialtes.	
460?–429	The age of Pericles in Athens.	
454	The treasury of the Delian League is transferred to Athens.	

Dates	Events	Authors
447–433	Construction of the Parthenon (the chief temple to the goddess Athena on the Athenian acropolis).	
446–445	Athens and Sparta conclude a thirty-year peace.	Sophocles (496–406), Athens. Protagoras (*c.* 485–425), northern Greece (Abdera).
432	The "Megarian Decree" is passed in Athens.	Herodotus (b. *c.* 485), Asia Minor, southern Italy. Euripides (*c.*485–*c.* 406), Athens.
431–421	Peloponnesian War, first phase (Archidamian War).	
430	The plague breaks out in Athens.	
429	Death of Pericles.	
427	Surrender of Mytilene to Athens.	Democritus (*c.* 460–380), northern Greece (Abdera).
427	Embassy from Leontini (in Sicily) to Athens.	Gorgias (*c.* 480–375), Leontini.
427	Civil war (*stasis*) in Corcyra.	The Old Oligarch.
425	Capture of 120 Spartan soldiers on Sphacteria.	Prodicus (*c.* 470–400), Islands (Ceos). Hippias (5th century), Elis. Antiphon (*c.* 480–411), Athens.
424	Exile of Thucydides.	Thucydides (*c.* 460–400), Athens. Thrasymachus (later

5th century),
Chalcedon.
Evenus (later 5th
century), Islands
(Paros).
Critias (died 403),
Athens.

421–414	Peace of Nicias.	
416	Destruction of the Melians.	
415	Athenian expedition to Sicily.	
414–404	Peloponnesian War, second phase.	
413	Destruction of Athenian army and navy outside Syracuse.	
411	Short-lived oligarchic takeover by the Four Hundred.	
411	Thucydides' *History* breaks off.	
405	Battle of Aegospotami (last major battle of the war).	
404	Surrender of Athens to Sparta; establishment of the Thirty Tyrants.	
c. 400		*Anonymus Iamblichi.* *Dissoi Logoi.* Lycophron (5th–4th centuries). Alcidamas (5th–4th centuries), Elaea, Athens. Antisthenes, (c. 455–360) Athens.

Bibliographical note

A Further reading

The aim of this section is to give students and general readers suggestions for further reading. We have limited ourselves to a small selection of recent books and articles in English. Many of these have full bibliographies and almost all include references to additional work on the subject.

A.1 Ancient political thought

Barker, Ernest, *Greek political theory*. London 1918. An old standard, but still worth consulting.

Farrar, Cynthia, *The origins of democratic thinking: The invention of politics in classical Athens*. Cambridge 1988. Stimulating views, with special attention to Protagoras, Thucydides, and Democritus.

Havelock, Eric A., *The liberal temper in Greek politics*. New Haven 1957. A polemical work that discusses many of our passages.

Ostwald, Martin, *From popular sovereignty to the sovereignty of law: law, society, and politics in fifth-century Athens*. Berkeley 1986. A study of Athenian history and politics in the fifth century with considerable attention paid to intellectual life.

Patterson, Orlando, *Freedom*. Vol. 1: *Freedom in the making in western culture*. New York 1991. In the first half of this study a contemporary sociologist explores the origins of freedom and its relation to slavery in ancient Greece.

Sinclair, T. A., *A history of Greek political thought*. London 1959.

A good survey, although most of the book concerns Plato and Aristotle.

A.2 *Ancient moral thought*

Adkins, Arthur W. H., *Merit and responsibility*. Oxford 1960. Studies especially the ethical vocabulary of authors from Homer to Aristotle, tracing the general shift from competitive to cooperative values.

Lloyd-Jones, Hugh, *The justice of Zeus*. 2nd edn. Berkeley 1983. Primarily a study of archaic and classical poets, beginning with Homer.

Nussbaum, Martha, *The fragility of goodness: Luck and ethics in Greek tragedy and philosophy*. Cambridge 1986. A study of ethics in the broad sense of what it means to have a good life; Nussbaum discusses both literary and philosophical texts.

A.3 *Early society*

Finley, Moses I., *The world of Odysseus*. 2nd edn. New York 1977. A concise digest of the economic, social, and political world depicted in the Homeric poems.

Gagarin, Michael, *Early Greek law*. Berkeley 1986. A survey of the major evidence, some of which is included in this volume.

A.4 *History and folklore*

Helpful discussions of Thucydides are to be found in Ostwald and also in Farrar (above, § A.1). See also John H. Finley, Jr., *Thucydides* (Oxford, 1942), W.R. Connor, *Thucydides* (Princeton, 1984), and Simon Hornblower, *Thucydides* (London, 1987).

More fables of Aesop can easily be found in Handford's translation of Aesop in the Penguin series.

A.5 *Philosophy and science*

Most of the fragments of Heraclitus and Democritus are also translated in *Early Greek Philosophy*, ed. Jonathan Barnes (Penguin Books, 1987). Many of the early medical treatises are translated in *Hippocratic writings*, ed. G. E. R. Lloyd (Penguin Books, 1978); and Heraclitus and Democritus are translated in *The presocratic philosophers*, 2nd edn. by G. S. Kirk, J. E. Raven, and M. Schofield (Cambridge, 1983), which includes Greek texts.

A.6 *The sophists*

Sprague, R. K., ed., *The older sophists*. Columbia, SC 1972. A translation by different hands of all the *Testimonia* and fragments in Diels–Kranz (below § B.5). The section on Antiphon by J. S. Morrison has additional material.

Classen, C. J., *Sophistik*. Darmstadt 1976. A collection of articles in their original languages (some are in English); useful also for its very thorough bibliography.

Guthrie, W. C. K., *The sophists*. Cambridge 1971. The standard reference work on the sophists. This is the first half of vol. 3 of *A history of Greek philosophy* (Cambridge, 1969), which was then published as a separate volume.

Kerferd, George, *The sophistic movement*. Cambridge 1981. A comprehensive interpretation of the whole movement.

Solmsen, Friedrich, *Intellectual experiments of the Greek enlightenment*. Princeton 1975. A discussion of several key issues drawing on the evidence of the sophists and other writers, especially Euripides and Thucydides.

B Textual details

In this section we identify the texts we have used for each author, together with additional texts or commentaries we have found particularly useful.

Abbreviations

DK	H. Diels and W. Kranz, *Die Fragmente der Vorsokratiker*. 6th edn. Berlin 1952.
M	J. S. Morrison, in R. K. Sprague, ed., *The older sophists*. Columbia, SC 1972.
N	A. Nauck, ed., [Euripides fragments]. *TGF*, 2nd edn. Göttingen 1889.

OCT	Oxford Classical Text (the standard modern edition of many Greek authors).
P	A. C. Pearson, *The fragments of Sophocles.* 3 vols. Cambridge 1917.
PMG	D. L. Page, ed., *Poetae melici graeci.* Oxford 1962.
S	B. Snell, ed., [Minor tragedians]. *TGF*, vol. 1. Göttingen 1971.
TGF	B. Snell *et al.*, eds., *Tragicorum graecorum fragmenta.* Göttingen 1971–.
W	M. L. West, ed., *Iambi et elegi graeci,* 2 vols. Oxford 1971–1972.

B.1 *Early poetry*

For Homer and the Homeric *Hymn to Hephaestus* we use the OCT in five volumes (Allen).

For Hesiod we use the two editions with commentary of M. L. West (*Theogony*, Oxford, 1966; *Works and Days*, Oxford, 1978), although we often adopt the interpretations of W. J. Verdenius, "Hesiod, *Theogony* 507–616: Some comments on a commentary," *Mnemosyne* 24 (1971) 1–10; and *A Commentary on Hesiod: Works and Days*, vv. 1–382. (Leiden, 1985).

For Archilochus, Tyrtaeus, Solon, Theognis, and Xenophanes 1 we use W. For the rest of Xenophanes we use DK.

For Simonides we use *PMG*. We have also consulted the Loeb edition of *Greek lyric* (vol. 3) by D. A. Campbell (Cambridge, MA, 1991).

For Pindar we use the Teubner text, vol. 2 (ed. B. Snell and H. Maehler, Leipzig, 1975). There are useful notes and a brief bibliography in Gordon Kirkwood, *Selections from Pindar* (American Philological Association Textbook Series, No. 7, 1982) 347–349. See also Martin Ostwald, "Pindar, Nomos, and Heracles," *Harvard Studies in Classical Philology* 69 (1965) 109–38.

B.2 *Tragedy*

We use the OCT for Aeschylus (Page, 1971), Sophocles (Wilson and Lloyd-Jones, 1990), and Euripides (Diggle, 1981–1984, for vols. 1–2; Murray, 1909, for vol. 3). In addition, we have found

Mark Griffith's commentary on Aeschylus' *Prometheus Bound* (Cambridge, 1983) very helpful.

For Fragments we use the volumes of the new *TGF*, except for Euripides (see below). In our translations we give parenthetical references to the numbering of *TGF*. Aeschylus: *TGF*, vol. 3, ed. Stefan Radt (Göttingen, 1985). Most of these fragments are conveniently collected (Greek and English) in vol. 2 of the Loeb edition of Aeschylus (Cambridge, MA, 1957). Sophocles: *TGF*, vol. 4, ed. Stefan Radt (Göttingen, 1977). Also helpful is P. Fragments 10–12 from the play *Aletes* are not considered genuine by Radt. They are found in vol. 2 of *TGF* (*Unknown authors*), F 1b. For these we give the numbering of Pearson, who does accept Sophoclean authorship. Euripides: Since there is not yet a new edition of *TGF* for Euripides, we have used N. For the papyrus fragment from *Melanippe* we have used the Loeb edition of *Select papyri*, vol. 3, by D. L. Page (Cambridge, MA, 1941).

Minor tragedians: *TGF*, vol. 1.

Unknown authorship: *TGF*, vol. 2, ed. Richard Kannicht and Bruno Snell (Göttingen, 1981).

B.3 *History and folklore*

For Herodotus we use the OCT.

For Thucydides we follow the OCT except where we prefer readings proposed by recent commentators: Simon Hornblower on Books 1–3 (Oxford, 1991); J. S. Rusten on Book 2 (Cambridge, 1989); K. J. Dover on Books 6–7 (Oxford, 1965); and the five-volume commentary on the entire work by Gomme, Andrewes, and Dover (Oxford, 1945–1981). We have also made use of the anonymous commentator on the Molesworth edition of Hobbes' translation (London, 1843).

For the Old Oligarch we generally follow the text of G. W. Bowersock in vol. 7 of the Loeb edition of Xenophon (Cambridge, MA, 1984). The text is accompanied by a translation and brief notes, introduction, and bibliography.

For Aesop we use Ben Edwin Perry, *Aesopica* (Urbana, 1952), and the Loeb edition of Phaedrus and Babrius, also by Perry (Cambridge, 1965), which uses the same numbering for the fables.

The text of the *Life of Aesop*, a product of the first century CE, is in *Aesopica*.

B.4 *Philosophy and science*

For Heraclitus we use DK and the edition with translation and commentary of Charles Kahn, *The art and thought of Heraclitus* (Cambridge, 1979). For Democritus we use DK. For the authenticity of 1 from Diodorus Siculus, see Thomas Cole, *Democritus and the sources of Greek anthropology* (American Philological Association Monographs, No. 25, 1967).

For the Medical writers we use Hans Diller, *Hippokrates über die Umwelt* (Berlin, 1970) for *Airs, Waters, Places*; and the Loeb edition of Hippocrates, vol. 4, by W. H. S. Jones (Cambridge, MA, 1931) for *On the Nature of Humans*. For the provenance of *Airs, Waters, Places*, see Morrison in *Classical Review* n.s. 6 (1956) 102–103.

For Antisthenes we use the text in *Socratis et socraticorum reliquiae*, ed. Gabriele Giannantoni, vol. 2 (Naples, 1990) 157–61. We also use Radermacher (below, § B.5) and *Antisthenis fragmenta*, ed. F. Decleva Caizzi (Milan, 1966).

B.5 *Sophists*

DK, vol. 2, section C, pages 252–416 ("Ältere Sophistik") contains the standard edition of the Greek texts of fifth-century sophists, called the Older Sophists to distinguish them from the Second Sophistic Period some seven centuries later. Several of these works are also found in L. Radermacher, *Artium scriptores* (Vienna, 1951), a collection of rhetorical texts from this period.

For passages from Plato relating to Protagoras we use the OCT of Plato, vol. 3. For Protagoras 21 see Paul Woodruff, "Didymus on Protagoras and the Protagoreans," *Journal of the History of Philosophy* 23 (1985) 483–497.

For Gorgias we generally follow Thomas Buchheim's recent edition (Hamburg, 1989) with German translation and commentary. For *Helen* MacDowell's text and commentary (Bristol, 1982) is helpful and we often prefer it to Buchheim. *On Not Being* is known to us only through two later summaries or paraphrases: Sextus Empiricus (second century CE), *Against the Mathematicians* 7.65–87; and *On Meslissus, Xenophanes and Gorgias*, a work attributed to Aristotle but almost certainly written after his death by someone in his school. Each version is deficient in different ways. We use *MXG* as the basis of our translation (DK use Sextus), indicating with italics passages that appear to be later comments and using angled brackets ◊ for significant material we have inserted to help make sense of the Greek. We do not discuss textual problems, which are ubiquitous, especially in argument (b).

For Prodicus, Hippias, Thrasymachus, Critias, Lycophron, and *Anonymus Iamblichi* we use DK.

For Thrasymachus 1 we have often followed the texts of Rader-macher (above) or S. Usher in the Loeb edition of Dionysius of Halicarnassus, *Critical essays* (Cambridge, MA, 1974) rather than DK.

For Critias we translate all the fragments in DK except for those that relate specifically to a dramatic context or present no relevant general reflections. For fragments from tragedy we have also consulted the text in vol. 1 of *TGF* (above, § B.2) and include Snell's numbering (S) in addition to that of DK. Some ancient sources ascribe Critias 5 to Euripides, whose satyr play *Sisyphus* was produced in 415. We follow the most recent text and commentary of M. Davies, *Bulletin of the Institute of Classical Studies* 36 (1989) 16–32.

Critias 26 is part of a speech found in a single manuscript containing other speeches of fifth- and early fourth-century orators and sophists. Although there are a few words on the subject of oligarchy in sections 30–31, the title is clearly inappropriate to the work as a whole, and the ascription to Herodes Atticus, a "sophist" of the second century CE, has frequently been doubted. Either the speech was written for the actual situation in about 404, or it is a later exercise pretending to address this hypothetical audience. The argument for Critias' authorship is made by H. T. Wade-Gery, "Kritias and Herodes," *Classical Quarterly* 39 (1945) 19–33 (= *Essays in Greek history* [Oxford, 1958] 271–92). Some scholars have assigned it to Thrasymachus, who also wrote a speech for the Larissaeans (fr. 2). We generally follow Albini's text (Florence, 1968), but in several places where he emends we retain the ms. reading.

For the *Anonymus Iamblichi* we have also consulted the Budé edition of Iamblichus' *Protrepticus* by Edouard des Places (Paris, 1989). A useful study is A. T. Cole, "The *Anonymus Iamblichi* and his place in Greek political theory," *Harvard Studies in Classical Philology* 55 (1961) 127–163.

For Antiphon 1 we use the text in *Corpus dei papiri filosofici greci e latini*, vol. 1 (Florence, 1989), in which all the papyrus fragments of Antiphon are edited by F. Decleva Caizzi, pp. 176–222. For 2–4 we generally follow *Antiphontis Tetralogiae*, edited, translated, and commentated by F. Decleva Caizzi (Milan, 1969). For the remaining fragments of Antiphon we include, in addition to DK numbers, the numbering of J. S. Morrison (M) in Sprague, ed., *The older sophists* (above, § A.6). For 5 we translate the text recently proposed by Morrison (*Phronesis* 8 [1983] 40), which differs significantly from that of DK. Fragment 6 is often assigned to a courtroom speech (fr. 35 in the Teubner text by Th. Thalheim [Leipzig, 1914]). Morrison's arguments for including it in *Truth* are not strong, but there is no reason to doubt the genuineness of the fragment, and its content is appropriate to this work. For 7 a papyrus discovered since DK's text and M's translation has added some new text and led to a rearrangement of the previously known fragments. We follow Decleva Caizzi (above), whose text reverses the order of 7a and 7b given in DK and M. The length of the gap between 7a and 7b is unknown. Fragment 7c is from a different papyrus altogether, but is generally assigned to the same work because of similarities of content and style.

For Evenus we use W.

For Alcidamas, 2 and 3 we generally follow Blass' Teubner text (Leipzig, 1908); we have also consulted Radermacher (above, § B.5) and the recent text and (Italian) translation of Guido Avezzù (Rome, 1982); see also LaRue Van Hook, "Alcidamas versus Isocrates; the spoken versus the written word," *Classical Weekly* 12 (1919) 89–94. Many scholars have doubted, primarily on the basis of its supposed poor quality, that passage 3 was composed by Alcidamas. If he did write it, it is probably an earlier work than passage 2. See in general Guthrie (above, § A.6), 311–313.

For the *Dissoi Logoi* we use T. M. Robinson, *Contrasting arguments* (New York, 1979), which also has a helpful commentary.

For the unknown sophist authors we use the OCT of Plato.

Glossary

This Glossary provides information about the Greek words and technical terms that occur in the text and about some of the people and places that may not be familiar to readers. Where relevant we give forms for the plural in parentheses.

adēlon: "non-evident," "not clearly known."

adikia: usually rendered as "injustice," although "wrong" is sometimes more accurate (cf. *dikē*).

adikos: "unjust" or "in the wrong."

agathos (agathoi): "good," "noble." Such words tend to conflate social and moral evaluation: the upper class made special claim to being *agathoi* and *kaloi* and *esthloi* and *chrēstoi;* they tended to look down on the lower class as being *kakoi* and *ponēroi* and *aischroi.*

agōn (agōnes): "contest(s)." Any sort of competition among athletes, speakers, or poets is considered an *agōn*; the word sometimes implies a legal trial.

agora: the marketplace or meeting place in a town.

aidōs: "shame," "respect" for the moral opinions of others.

aischros: "shameful," "bad"; see *agathos.*

akrasia: "lack of self-control."

anankē: "necessity" or "compulsion." *Anankē* is often contingent on human factors.

anomia: "lawlessness," or the absence of law and order.

archē: in Thucydides it is translated "empire" throughout. Elsewhere it can mean "rule," "reign," "cause," "origin," "beginning," or "first principle."

xliv

archōn: a high magistrate in Athens; see p. xiii.

aretē: "virtue," "courage."

atē: "madness" or "ruin": the madness that leads inevitably to disaster.

basileus (basileis): "king" is the traditional English translation, but in most of our passages the "king" is not a sole monarch but a lord or chief, usually one of many. One of the main functions of the *basileus* was judicial. In reference to Persia and other Near Eastern cultures, *basileus* did mean the King.

Boeotia: the country bordering on Athens to the west, with its main city at Thebes.

chrēstos: "good"; see *agathos*.

colonies: city-states founded by older Greek cities beginning in the eighth century. They were usually independent politically, but maintained friendly relations with their parent cities.

Corcyra: an island off the west coast of Greece. Corcyra was a colony of Corinth, but it sided with Athens in the Peloponnesian War.

Corinth: a city and important commercial center on the isthmus between Athens and the Peloponnesus.

cottabus: a game played by tossing wine lees into a cup.

deinos: "clever," "skillful," "terrible." The word may carry negative connotations of inspiring awe or dread.

Delian League: the alliance of Greek city-states against Persia led by Athens in the decades following the Greek victories at Salamis and Plataea (480 and 479).

dēmos: literally "people," usually the common people as opposed to the upper classes, and sometimes the popular party in politics. *Dēmokratia* is literally "rule by the people."

dikaion: "just," "justice," "right" (as opposed to wrong).

dikaiosunē: "justice," conceived abstractly as a virtue; *dikaiosunē* replaces *dikē* in the sense of "justice" in the fourth century.

dikē (dikai): "justice," or "case" at law. The word is also used for private suits, similar in some ways to our civil cases. But many offenses that we treat as crimes (theft, homicide, etc.) were normally treated as *dikai*, or private suits. See *graphē*.

drachma: a unit of money which would pay for one day's labor by a skilled man, roughly equivalent to $75–100 in 1993 U.S.

currency; a citizen's pay for a day of jury duty was half a drachma (3 obols).

eikos: "reasonable expectation," "likelihood." Greek orators frequently built arguments around what was *eikos*, or what could reasonably be expected.

epieikeia: "fairness," or "decency."

ergon: "action"; frequently contrasted with *logos*, "word" or "speech."

esthlos (esthloi): "noble"; see *agathos*.

euboulia: "good judgment."

eunomia: literally, "good laws" or "good order." *Eunomia* was widely considered a special virtue of the Spartan constitution, and more broadly of any system of government that was not democratic. The opposite is *kakonomia*, literally "bad laws."

euthunai: the formal examination of their conduct in office that was required of all Athenian public officials when their term expired.

Four Hundred: the oligarchy that seized power in Athens and held it for a few months in 411.

graphē: "indictment"; a procedure used in many criminal cases; see *dikē*.

Helots: the indigenous serf-like population that cultivated the land of Sparta; see "Messenians."

historia: "inquiry," "research"; first applied to "history" in the first sentence of Herodotus.

hoplites: heavily armed infantry who formed the backbone of Greek armies in this period. As they were expected to pay for their own arms and armor (*hopla*), they had to be moderately well-off citizens.

hubris: aggressive wickedness, as manifest either in physical violence (assault or rape) or as insulting behavior. Sometimes used of a human who claims divine prerogatives.

ison, isotēs: "equal," "equality," often with the sense of fairness (rather than strict equality).

isonomia: a system of law or distribution that is fair or equal; *isonomia* was a fundamental principle of Athenian democracy and an older term than *dēmokratia*.

kairos: "opportunity"; in rhetoric *kairos* designates the occasion and the spirit of the audience, which public speaking should fit.

kakonomia: "bad laws," the opposite of *eunomia*.

kakos (kakoi): "bad," "evil"; see *agathos*.

kalos: "beautiful," "noble," "good"; see *agathos*.

kreissōn: "better"; see *agathos*.

liturgies: specific financial obligations underwritten by wealthy individuals for the public good. The main liturgies were the arming of warships and the training of choruses for performances at public festivals.

logos (logoi): "speech(es)"; *logos* may also mean "word," "argument," "principle," or "ratio."

Messenians: inhabitants of Messenia, a district west of Sparta. Conquered by Sparta in the eighth and seventh centuries, most Messenians were forced to work their land for Spartan landlords. A cross between serfs and share-croppers, they were known as "Helots."

metics: resident aliens in Athens; *metics* were a large and economically important group.

mina: a weight and an amount of money, equal to one hundred drachmas or a sixtieth of a talent.

nemesis: punishment, public disapproval, the righteous anger of the gods.

nomimon (nomima): "customs," "convention(s)"; *nomimon* covers the broader meanings of *nomos* but cannot mean "law" or "statute."

nomos (nomoi): "law(s)," "custom(s)," "convention(s)," or "common opinion(s)." The relationship of *nomos* and *phusis* was discussed by some sophists.

oligos (oligoi): "few"; *oligarchia* is literally, "rule by the few."

orthōs: "correctly"; the adjective *orthos* means "straight" or "correct" in either a technical or a moral sense (or both).

Peisistratus: tyrant of Athens from about 561 to his death in 527. During his rule and that of his sons, Athens emerged as a military and commercial power in Greece and began its rise to cultural ascendancy.

phalanx: the line of battle formed by the heavy infantry, or hoplites.

phusis: "nature"; in human beings, *phusis* is contrasted with training and education; see *nomos*.

Piraeus: the main port of Athens, on the coast about seven miles away. A road protected by the Long Walls (built in 458) joined Piraeus to Athens.

plēthos: a large number; in political contexts it means "the multitude," "the common people," or "the majority."

poiēsis: any productive process; specifically, the making of poetry.

polis (poleis): "city (cities)"; in classical Greece a *polis* such as Athens was a political, cultural, and social unit. The word for constitution (*politeia*) is derived from *polis*, and Protagoras (in Plato's representation) calls the science of statecraft *politikē technē*.

ponēros: "bad"; see *agathos*.

psuchē: "life-breath" or "life-force"; later "mind" or "soul."

sophia: "wisdom," either the abstract wisdom of a philosopher or the applied knowledge of a craftsman.

sophos (sophoi): "wise," "clever," "skilled."

sōphrōn: "sound of mind," "prudent," "sensible," "clear-headed."

sōphrosunē: the virtue of being *sōphrōn*: "self-restraint," "moderation," "prudence." *Sōphrosunē* is opposed to madness (*atē*) and arrogant wickedness (*hubris*); it often suggests obedience to the law or to one's superiors and was considered a virtue of oligarchic cities and of Sparta in particular.

stasis: "faction," "factionalism," or "civil strife"; *stasis* ranges from political conflict to all-out civil combat.

sumpheron: "advantage" or "what is advantageous," often contrasted with *dikaion* ("just").

talent: a weight and an amount of money, equal to 60 *minas* or 6,000 drachmas; roughly equivalent to $500,000 in 1993 U.S. currency.

technē (technai): "specialized knowledge," "craft," or "skill."

themis: "what is right"; mostly found in early poetry, *themis* is a precursor of later Greek ideas of justice.

thesmos (thesmoi): the early Athenian word for "law" or "statute," replaced by *nomos* in the fifth century.

tuchē: "chance," "luck," or "fortune"; what happens by *tuchē* is contrasted with what comes about as a result of planning or *technē*.

tyrannos: "tyrant" – a sole ruler without the legitimacy of a traditional monarch. Tyrants were established in many Greek cities during the seventh and sixth centuries; the word *tyrannos* did not have a pejorative connotation until well into the fifth century.

Table of equivalents

Here we list those authors whose works are usually known by the text or fragment numbers in standard editions. Heraclitus B102 (DK), for example, is numbered 14 in this edition.

Antiphon

Diels–Kranz	Gagarin–Woodruff	Morrison	Gagarin–Woodruff
1	5	67	5
2	8	68	6
10	10	70	8
14	11	78	10
15	9	82	11
29	12	83	9
30	13	91	7
44	7	101	12
48	14	102	13
49	17	117	18
50	22	118	20
51	15	119	19
52	16	123	17
53	24	124	30
53a	23	125	26
54	25	127	31

1

Diels–Kranz	Gagarin–Woodruff	Morrison	Gagarin–Woodruff
56	31	128	32
57	32	129	22
58	30	130	15
59	26	131	16
60	18	132	24
61	20	133	23
62	19	134	25
63	33	135	14
64	28	136	33
65	29	137	28
66	21	138	29
70	27	139	21
		144	27
		159	34
		160	35
		161	36
		162	37

Archilochus

M. L. West (1971)	Gagarin–Woodruff
14	1
19	3
174	2

Critias

Diels–Kranz	Gagarin–Woodruff	Snell	Gagarin–Woodruff
1	24	10	1
2	22	11	2
6	21	12	3
7	18	17	4
9	13	19	5
12	6	21	6
15	4	22	10
21	1	23	8
22	2	24	7
23	3	25	9
25	5		
26	10		
27	8		
28	7		
29	9		
31	23		
32	11		
34	20		
37	19		
39	15		
40	14		
42	16		
44	25		
48	17		
49	12		

Democritus

Diels–Kranz	Gagarin–Woodruff
3	31
5	1
33	33
41	24
47	18
49	17
110	20
111	19
157	6
181	21
184	30
242	32
245	22
248	23
249	5
250	4
251	8
252	3
253	13
254	16
255	12
259	25
260	26
261	27
262	28
263	7
264	29
265	14
266	15
267	2
277	35
278	34
279	36
280	37
283	9
287	10
291	11

Gorgias

Diels–Kranz	Gagarin–Woodruff
A8b	14
A21	12
A27	13
3	18
4	20
5	21
5a	5
5b	4
6	3
8	8
11	1
11a	2
12	9
15	7
16	6
19	15
20	17
22	16
23	10
26	19
27	11

Heraclitus

Diels–Kranz	Gagarin–Woodruff
1	1
2	3
5	26
11	19
23	17
28	24
29	11
33	8
43	25
44	7
49	9
52	13
53	20
58	18
61	15
64	28
78	27
80	22
94	23
102	14
104	12
110–111	16
112	5
113	2
114	6
116	4
121	10
Aristotle *EE* 1235a25	21

Hippias

Diels–Kranz	Gagarin–Woodruff
9	1
11	2
16	3
17	4
Plato *Protagoras* 337d–338b	5

Lycophron

Diels–Kranz	Gagarin–Woodruff
1	3
3	1
4	2

Prodicus

Diels–Kranz	Gagarin–Woodruff
A13	1
2	4
4	6
5	5
6	3
7	2

Protagoras		Diogenes Laertius	Gagarin–Woodruff
Diels–Kranz	Gagarin–Woodruff	9.51	24
		9.53	25
1	15	Plato	Gagarin–Woodruff
2	16		
3	5	*Cratylus* 391c3	29
4	20	*Phaedrus* 267c6	31
5	23	*Protagoras*	
6b	27	316d3–317c1	1
10	6	318a6–9	3
68 B 156	26	318d7–319a7	4
		320c7–322d5	8
Aristotle	Gagarin–Woodruff	322d5–324d1	9
		324d2–328c2	10
Metaphysics		334a3–c6	11
997b35–998a4	22	338e7–339a1	28
Poetics		348e6–349a4	2
1456b15	33	351a1–b2	7
Rhetoric		351d4–7	12
1402a23	27	*Theaetetus*	
Sophisticis		152a6–8	17
Elenchis 173b17	32	166c4–6	19
		166d6–8	13
Didymus Fragment	Gagarin–Woodruff	167a7	18
		167c4–5	14
–	21	Plutarch	Gagarin–Woodruff
		Against Colotes	
		4, 1108f.	26
		Life of Pericles	
		36.3	30

Solon

M. L. West	Gagarin–Woodruff
4	1
5 and 6	2
9	6
11	7
13	8
15	9
16	10
17	11
18	12
34	3
36	4
37	5

Xenophanes

Diels–Kranz	Gagarin–Woodruff
2	1
11	4
15	2
16	3
34	5
35	6

Tyrtaeus

M. L. West	Gagarin–Woodruff
4	1
10	2

PART I
EARLY POETRY

Most of the verse translated in this part was originally in dactylic hexameter, the traditional form for epic poetry; elegiac couplets (dactylic hexameter alternating with shorter dactylic lines) are indicated by the indenting of every second line.

Homer

Homer is the name traditionally given to the author of the Iliad *and* Odyssey. *Of the actual composition of the poems we know very little. Many scholars believe the two poems were the work of different authors, and some believe in the multiple authorship of each work. The poems probably took their final form at the end of the eighth century or later, with the* Odyssey *following the* Iliad *by about a generation. Although the poems draw on stories that were orally preserved and passed down over several centuries, the ideas of justice and social order evident in the following passages were probably current in the eighth century.*

1. *The role of common citizens in the assembly (*Iliad *2.188–278)*

As the Achaeans stream from their assembly to the ships, thinking to abandon the siege of Troy, Odysseus calls them back to their seats.

To any king or foremost man he overtook
he would speak softly and restrain him, standing by:
"My friend, a coward's panic does not suit you.   190
You should stop, and bring the rest of the people to their seats,
for you don't yet know what plan Agamemnon has.
Now he is testing you, soon he will frown on you sons of Achaeans.
Did we not all hear what he said in the council?
Pray he won't in his anger do some harm to the sons of Achaeans, 195
for the spirit of Zeus-nurtured kings is great,
their honor is from Zeus, and he loves them in his wisdom."
     But when he saw a man of the *dēmos* and found him shouting,

3

he would herd him with blows of his staff and rebuke him:
"Sit still, my friend and hear the word of the others   200
who are your betters, you unwarlike men, you weaklings –
you don't ever count for anything, in war or in council.
There's no way all of us Achaeans can be kings here.
Multiple leadership is no good; let there be one leader – one king
to whom the son of clever Cronus gave the staff   205
and the rule of *themis*, so that he would take counsel for them."
In this way he took charge of the army, providing leadership,
and they fell back to the assembly (*agora*) from their ships and
    their quarters
with a roar, as when a wave of the thunderous sea
beats on the great beach and the waters crash.   210
    All the rest were sitting now, lined up on their seats,
but loose-tongued Thersites alone was still jabbering;
his mind was full of disorderly things to say,
and he was intent on quarreling recklessly with kings,
saying whatever he thought would be funny   215
to the Argives. He was the most foul man who came to Troy:
bow-legged, one foot lame, his two shoulders
slumped and pulled together at his chest; and sparse wool
grew atop his low-browed pointy head.
He was much the most hated by Achilles and by Odysseus too,   220
for he kept taunting them. But this time it was brilliant
Agamemnon at whom he screamed his harsh abuse.
The Achaeans were quite furious with him, their spirits angry.
But he was taunting Agamemnon with great shouts:
    "Son of Atreus, what's your complaint now? What do you want?   225
Your quarters are full of bronze, and many women
are there in your tents, the choice ones we Achaeans
give to you before anyone else when we capture a town.
Or are you still short of the gold, that one of the Trojans
(those tamers of horses) brings as ransom from Troy,   230
when I catch him and bring him in, I or another Achaean?
Or do you want a young woman, to make love with her,
and keep her all to yourself? It is not suitable
for a ruler to bring evil upon the sons of Achaeans.
O you weaklings, you disgraceful wretches! You Achaeans   235
are women, not men! Let us go home in our ships and leave

4

this man here at Troy to brood on his prizes of war
till he sees whether we were any help to him here or not.
And now he's dishonored Achilles, a much better man
than he, for he seized his prize and took her for himself.   240
But there's not much anger in the mind of Achilles, he's let it go;
otherwise, son of Atreus, this would be your last crime."
   So spoke Thersites, taunting Agamemnon, shepherd
of the people. But quickly came brilliant Odysseus beside him
with a grim frown, and gave him this harsh rebuke: 245
   "Thersites, you babbler, a fine orator you are!
Be quiet, and do not try to quarrel with kings on your own;
for I will say that there is not a worse man than you
among all those who came with the sons of Atreus to Troy.
For that, you may not raise your voice to speak against kings;   250
you may not reproach them, or look after your own homecoming.
We don't know yet at all how this will be worked out
or whether we sons of Achaeans will come home well or badly.
Is this why you are sitting now and finding fault with Agamemnon,
shepherd of the people: because the Danaan warriors   255
give him many things? Your speech is pure mockery.
Now I will tell you something, and it will certainly happen:
if ever again I find you acting as foolishly as you are now
then let Odysseus' head no longer ride on his shoulders,
and may I no longer be called the father of Telemachus,   260
if I do not take you and strip off your very own clothes –
the cloak and tunic that cover your private parts –
and send you weeping to the swift ships,
beating you out of the assembly with blows that bring shame."
   So he spoke, and beat Thersites' back and shoulders   265
with his staff. Thersites writhed, and tears burst from him,
while a bloody welt was raised on his back
by the golden staff. He sat down in terror then,
and grief, and staring uselessly he wiped away a tear.
Though they were in distress, the others laughed in delight,   270
and one would look at his neighbor and say to him:
   "Truly, Odysseus has done thousands of noble deeds,
taking the lead in giving good advice and at the head of battle;
but this now is much the best thing he has done among the
     Argives,

5

to keep this word-shooting scoundrel from making speeches.   275
His proud spirit will surely not rouse him again
to taunt the kings with words of blame."
So said the crowd.

2. *Arbitration by the elders (*Iliad *18.497–508)*

After the death of Patroclus, the god Hephaestus makes new arms for Achilles, including an elaborately engraved shield depicting scenes that would have been familiar to Homer's audience. One scene shows an early form of trial.

Meanwhile a crowd gathered in the *agora*, where a dispute
had arisen: two men contended over the blood price
for a man who had died. One swore he'd paid everything,
and made a public declaration. The other refused to accept
    anything.   500
Both referred the matter to a referee for a decision.
People were speaking on both sides, and both had supporters;
but the heralds restrained them. The old men
took seats on hewn stones in a sacred circle;
they held in their hands the scepters of heralds who raise their
    voices.   505
Then the two men came before them, and in turn pleaded
their cases. In the middle there lay two talents of gold
as a gift for the one among them who would give the straightest
    judgment.

3. *The duties of aristocrats (*Iliad *12.310–21)*

Before attacking to break down the wall erected by the Greeks, the Trojan hero Sarpedon addressed his fellow soldier Glaucon. The speech shows how aristocrats were supposed to earn their privileges.

"Glaucon, what is the point of all this honor we receive –   310
a seat of honor, extra cuts of meat, goblets of wine?
Why do they look on us as gods in Lycia,
and set aside for us great lands along the Xanthus River,
rich for planting and plowing and the bearing of grain?
As we are among the first in rank in Lycia we are obliged (*chrē*) 315

to stand and face the battle where it burns most hot,
so that any of the Lycians, in their close armor, would say:
'There's no lack of fame for these lords of Lycia
who are our kings and who dine on fat sheep
and choice wine that's honey sweet; but, really, their strength   320
is noble, since they fight among the first of the Lycians.'"

4. Life without justice (Odyssey 9.105–115)

Odysseus reaches the land of the giant Cyclopes on his travels, and finds
them living in a pre-civilized state. This passage, which comes from the
story Odysseus tells, reflects Homer's view of human life before civilization.

We sailed on from there, grieving at heart,   105
and came to the land of the Cyclopes, insolent giants who had
no concept of right (*themis*): they trusted the immortal gods,
and neither planted with their hands nor plowed the ground,
but everything grew without sowing or tilling – [1]
wheat and barley and grapes in wide clusters   110
that made wine, and Zeus brought frequent rain for them.
They have no assemblies to give counsel, nor any rules of *themis*,
but they dwell on the heights of lofty hills
in deep caverns, and each one makes his own *themis*
for his women and children, and does not care about the others.   115

5. The importance of themis (Odyssey 18.130–142)

Odysseus, in disguise as a beggar, addresses Penelope's suitors.

"Of all the things that breathe and move on earth,   130
earth nurtures no more frail thing than a man:
as long as the gods give him courage (*aretē*) and put strength in
    his knees
he'll never expect to encounter any evil.
But when the blessed gods bring grievous things to pass,
he bears them unwillingly with his enduring spirit.   135
For the minds of men who dwell on earth are like
the daily fortunes brought by the father of gods and men.[2]

---

[1] Cf. Hesiod, *Works and Days* 117–118.
[2] The "daily fortunes" are mainly changes in the weather.

7

I too once looked forward to happiness among men,
but I did reckless things, gave in to strength and violence,
counting on my father and my brothers.   140
No man, therefore, should ever in any way violate the right (*themis*),
but one should keep in silence whatever gifts the gods may grant."

Hesiod

Hesiod lived in Boeotia in the late eighth century. His two substantial poems in epic verse are the Theogony *("Generation of the Gods"), which is a retelling of traditional myths of origin, and* Works and Days, *which is addressed to his brother Perses over the disputed division of property that followed their father's death. Hence arises Hesiod's concern with justice and the resolution of disputes.*

1. *The origins of evil (*Theogony *507–612)*

Hesiod's versions of the Prometheus myth are translated here as background for later accounts of the origins of human society. See especially Protagoras, *fr.* 8. *"Prometheus" means "Forethought," and "Epimetheus," "Afterthought."*

Iapetus took Clymene, fine-legged daughter of Ocean,
to wife, and went into the same bed with her.
She bore him a son, stout-hearted Atlas, and also
gave birth to Menoitios whose pride soared, to Prometheus   510
with his quick versatile mind, and to wrong-headed Epimetheus,
who was an evil from the beginning to hardworking men,
for he was first to welcome the woman Zeus had formed,
the maiden. Far-seeing Zeus struck wicked Menoitios
with a smoking thunderbolt and sent him down to Erebos   515
for his impudence and his overweening audacity.
By the force of necessity, Atlas stands at the ends
of the earth by the clear-voiced Hesperides, and holds

9

broad heaven on his head and untiring hands,
for Zeus in his wisdom assigned him this lot.   520
And he bound Prometheus of the versatile mind
inescapably with painful chains run through the middle of a column.
And he set against him a long-winged eagle, and this devoured
his immortal liver, which grew back at night, entirely
as much as the long-winged bird had eaten the day before.   525
The bird was killed by the powerful son of fine-legged Alcmene,
by Heracles, who saved him from an evil plague
and released the son of Iapetus from his troubles.
Olympian Zeus who rules on high allowed this,
so that the glory of Thebes-born Heracles would be   530
still greater than it was before on the earth with its many herds.
Thus reverently he gave honor to his well-known son,
and angry as he was he gave up the anger he'd had before,
because Prometheus had contested the wisdom of mighty Zeus.
For when gods and mortal humans were deciding things   535
at Mekone,³ he divided a great ox with forethought
and set it before them, to trick the mind of Zeus.
On one side he set flesh and entrails rich with fat
in the hide and covered them with the ox's stomach;
on the other side he arranged the white bones of the ox   540
with crafty art and covered them with gleaming fat.⁴
Then up spoke the father of gods and men:
"Son of Iapetus, well known among all the lords,
my friend, how one-sided is your division of the shares!"
So Zeus, who knows schemes that never fail, spoke to rebuke him. 545
And crooked-minded Prometheus answered him
with a gentle smile, and did not forget his crafty art:
"Glorious Zeus, greatest of the gods who are forever, choose
whatever share the spirit in your breast moves you to take."
So he spoke, meaning to be crafty. But Zeus, who knows schemes
        that never fail,   550
made no mistake and saw through the trick;⁵ and his spirit brooded
on the evils he would bring to pass for mortal humans.

³ Mekone: said to be an older name for Sicyon.
⁴ Animal fat was rare and highly valued for nutrition.
⁵ Hesiod apparently added these lines to an earlier version in which Zeus was taken
  in by the trick.

But he raised the white fat with both hands;
then he was angry in his breast, and anger surrounded his spirit
when he saw the white ox bones arranged by crafty art.   555
From that time on, human tribes on earth have burned
white bones on fragrant altars in sacrifice to the immortals.
But Zeus who gathers clouds spoke in great anger to Prometheus:
"Son of Iapetus, you who know schemes better than anyone,
My friend, have you still not forgotten your crafty art?"   560
So spoke Zeus in his fury, he who knows schemes that never fail.
He remembered the trick forever after this,
and withheld the power of untiring fire from ash-tree wood
and kept it from the mortal humans who dwell on earth.
But the good son of Iapetus deceived him   565
and stole away the beacon light of untiring fire
in the hollow of a fennel.[6] But this bit deep into the spirit
of high-thundering Zeus, and it angered him in his own heart
when he saw that humans had the beacon light of fire.
So right away, to pay for the fire, he made an evil thing for
      humans: 570
he had the famous god Hephaestus fashion from earth
the likeness of a modest girl, according to the design of Zeus.
Then the pale-eyed goddess Athena dressed her elegantly
in clothes of gleaming white, and with her hands drew
a decorated veil down over her head, a marvelous thing to see,   575
and all around her head lovely wreaths of flowers,
fresh from the meadows, were placed by Pallas Athena;
and she circled her head with a wreath of gold
made by the famous god Hephaestus
as his own handiwork, done to please his father Zeus.   580
This he decorated richly, a marvelous thing to see:
he put on it many of the beasts that are nourished
by land or sea, and delight breathed over it all.
They were marvelous animals – they looked alive and ready to
      speak.
Now when he had fashioned this lovely evil – the price of something
      good –   585
he led her out where the other gods were, and the humans,

---

[6] The fleshy center of a stalk of a giant fennel, known as pith, held fire conveniently.

11

and she was splendid in the elegance of pale-eyed Athena
whose father is mighty. Then they were spellbound, immortal gods
and mortal men alike, to see the trap that was too deep for men.
For from her came the race of female women,[7]   590
who are a great misery when they dwell with mortal men,
for they will not share in terrible poverty but in wealth.
Just as when bees feed drones
in the vaulted nests (their companions in hard times),[8]   595
one group works hard the whole day
till sundown, building with white wax,
while the drones stay inside the sheltered hive
and harvest the toil of others into their own bellies.[9]
That is just the sort of evil high-thundering Zeus   600
set up for mortal men when he made women their companions
for hard times. And he added a second evil as price for the good:
Whoever wants to avoid marriage and the troublesome deeds
of women, and does avoid it, comes to a deadly old age
with no son to care for him then. Although all his needs are met 605
while he is living, his distant kin will divide up his property
when he dies. But then a man whose lot it is to marry,
and has a dear wife who is furnished with good sense –
his life will always be a balance of evil against good;
while a man who draws a wife of the baneful sort   610
lives with constant torment in his breast, in heart
and spirit. And that is an evil without a cure.

2. *The origins of evil* (Works and Days *42–105*)

The same basic material as in Theogony *507–612 takes a different
turn in the* Works and Days. *Here, the woman is given a name by
Hermes.*

The gods keep the means of life hidden from human beings,
for otherwise you'd easily produce enough in a single day

---

[7] We have omitted line 591 as it is unlikely to be genuine.
[8] Drones are companions in hard times because it is then that they need the support
of the worker bees. The same expression is used of women in 601; the point of
593 is that women will not share in the hardship.
[9] Cf Plato's use of this image, *Republic* 552c.

to keep yourself in idleness for an entire year
and straightway hang your steering oar above the smoke[10]   45
while there would be no more labor with mules and oxen.
   But Zeus hid this from us; he was angry
over his deception by Prometheus with his crooked schemes
and therefore he designed painful troubles for humankind
and hid fire away. But the strong son of Iapetus [Prometheus]   50
stole it back for humans from much-devising Zeus
in the hollow of a fennel stalk, fooling Zeus the thunderer.
In his anger Zeus cloud-gatherer spoke to him thus:
"Son of Iapetus, you know better than anyone how to scheme:
you are delighted at stealing fire and fooling me –   55
a great disaster for you yourself and for men to come.
To pay for the fire I shall give them an evil they will all
enjoy in their hearts as they embrace their evil."
So he spoke, the father of gods and men, and burst into laughter.
   Then he ordered Hephaestus who is everywhere famous   60
at once to knead earth with water and place in it a human voice
and strength, and fashion it with the look of the immortal goddesses
and the enticing beauty of a young girl. Next he asked
Athena to teach her the skill of intricate weaving
and golden Aphrodite to pour charm around her head,   65
with painful longing and the passions that gnaw men's limbs;
and he instructed Hermes, guide of the dead and slayer of Argus,
to give her the mind of a bitch and a taste for deception.
   So he spoke, and they obeyed lord Zeus, son of Cronus.
Right then famous Hephaestus fashioned from earth   70
the likeness of a modest young girl, according to the design of
      Zeus.
Then the pale-eyed goddess Athena dressed her elegantly,
while the divine Graces and Lady Persuasion
placed golden necklaces around her and the lovely-haired
Seasons crowned her with spring flowers.[11]   75
All this elegance was adjusted for her by Pallas Athena.
Then Hermes, guide of the dead, set lies in her breast,

---

[10] "Hang your steering oar above the smoke": for safe, dry storage over the fireplace
    when not in use.
[11] The Graces and Persuasion are attendants of Aphrodite. The Seasons belong in
    this context because they bring all things to fruition.

cleverly seductive speeches, and a taste for deception,
according to the design of deep-thundering Zeus, and the herald
   of the gods
gave her a voice, and named the woman Pandora –   80
All-gift – because all those who have homes on Olympus
gave her as a gift – misery for men who eat bread.
   Now when he had completed this trap too deep to escape
father Zeus sent famous Hermes, swift messenger of the gods,
to lead her as a gift to Epimetheus. And Epimetheus   85
did not keep in mind what Prometheus told him, never
to accept a gift from Olympian Zeus, but to send it right
back, so that no evil would come upon mortals.
But he accepted it, and remembered only when he had the evil.
   Before then the human tribes had lived on earth   90
apart from evils and free from harsh toil
and bitter diseases that bring ruin to men.[12]
But the woman took the great lid off the jar,
scattered them abroad, and so devised sad cares   95
for humankind. Only Hope remained in its safe home
inside the lip of the jar and did not fly
outdoors, because she put the lid back first,
as Zeus had planned, he who gathers clouds and wears the aegis.
Now endless miseries wander among men;   100
the earth is full of evils, as is the sea;
diseases visit men by day, and others by night,
coming on their own to bring evils to mortals
in silence, since Zeus in his wisdom took away their voice.
So it is: the purpose of Zeus cannot be evaded.   105

3. *The decline of morals* (Works and Days *174–201)*

Hesiod describes ages of gold, silver, and bronze, after which came the age of heroes. He then turns to the current age of iron.

I wish I had no part in this fifth race of men.
I wish I had died before, or been born after them.   175

---

[12] We have omitted line 93, which is probably interpolated.

For this race now is of iron, and they do not cease
from toil and woe by day or night
in their exhaustion, but the gods give them harsh cares;
but even so their good is mixed with evil.
Zeus will destroy this race also of men who speak language,   180
when at birth they are already grey with old age.
Then a father will not think like his sons, nor they like him,
nor a guest like his host, nor comrade like comrade;
and even a brother will not be as friendly as before.
They will treat their parents with disrespect as soon as they grow
        old,   185
upbraiding them and railing with harsh words,
rough men who know nothing of the gods' punishment,
and do not pay back their aging parents for rearing them.
Their justice is violence,[13] people ruin each others' cities,
they give no thanks to those who keep their oaths   190
or are just or good; instead, they honor the man who works evil,
the man of violence (*hubris*). For them justice will be in violence,
        and respect
will not exist. A bad man will harm his better
by telling a crooked tale and swearing an oath to it.
And hate-faced Envy will dog the wretched feet of every   195
human being, spreading malice and rejoicing in evil.
And then, indeed, Respect and Disapproval[14] will hide
their lovely faces behind white robes, leave the earth
with its wide-reaching roads to join the tribe of immortals
on Olympus, and abandon human beings. These grievous   200
miseries will remain for mortal humans, and there will be no
        defense against evil.

---

[13] Here the context widens to cover people of the current age in general. Many
editors delete line 189, but it is defended by West. "Their justice is violence"
translates one compound word, *cheirodikai*, "handjustices," or, as West has it,
"fist-law men." The point is that violence, rather than law, settles disputes in
this age.

[14] "Respect and Disapproval": *Aidōs* and *Nemesis*. Neither word has an exact English
equivalent. *Aidōs* is the respect one should feel for the disapproval of others, and
is sometimes rightly translated "shame." *Nemesis* is righteous anger, public disapproval, or simply punishment. Together, in Hesiod's world, they form the only
bulwark against human evil.

4. *The value of competition (*Works and Days *11–26)*

Alluding to the quarrel he implies his brother has picked with him,
Hesiod distinguishes two kinds of strife. In the Theogony, *by contrast,*
Hesiod had spoken of strife as always destructive, just as Homer had.

After all, there is not only one kind of Strife (*eris*) on earth,
but two. One of these you may praise once you know her,
the other deserves great blame, and their spirits are opposed.
One kind feeds evil war and fighting; she is rough,
and no mortal loves her, but under compulsion   15
and by design of the immortals all must pay respect
to the heavy Strife. But the other one was born first
to black Night, and lofty Zeus who dwells in heaven
set her at the roots of earth, and she is much better for men:
she rouses them, however lazy, to their work.   20
For when one man who is not working sees another
who is rich and plows and plants with zeal,
a good manager, then neighbor competes with neighbor
zealously for wealth. Now this Strife is good for mortals:
"And potter is envious of potter, builder of builder,   25
Beggar is jealous of beggar, and singer of singer."[15]

5. *The fable of the hawk and the nightingale (*Works and Days *202– 212)*

And now, though kings[16] are wise on their own, I will tell them a
     fable:
Thus spoke the hawk to the bright-throated nightingale
he was carrying high in the clouds, seized in his talons –
she cried piteously, pierced by his hooked talons,   205
but he had her under his control, and spoke this word to her:
"What possesses you to shriek like this? You are being held by
     one
who is much stronger, and you will go wherever I take you, singer
though you are. I will make a meal of you, if I want, or let you go.

---

[15] In these last two lines, Hesiod is probably quoting a proverb widely known in antiquity.
[16] For *basileis* ("kings"), see Glossary.

Only a fool wants to pit himself against those who are stronger
    (*kreissōn*);   210
he will lose the victory and add misery to his humiliation."[17]
So spoke the swift-flying hawk, bird with great wings.

6. *Zeus gives justice to human beings* (Works and Days *213–285)*

But you, Perses, listen to Justice and do not feed *hubris*;
hubris is bad for a poor mortal, and even a worthy one
cannot bear it easily, but it weighs him down   215
when he encounters ruin. The road that goes the other way,
to doing justice, is the better (*kreissōn*) course, and justice comes
    in the end
to triumph over *hubris*. A fool learns this by experience.
For Oath[18] catches up right away with crooked judgments
and there's an uproar when justice is abducted and men   220
take her away in their hunger for gifts, giving verdicts that are
    crooked.
Justice follows them weeping for their city and the habits of their
    people;
clad in darkness she bears evil to the men
who drove her out and gave judgments that were not straight.
But those who give straight verdicts to both foreigners   225
and residents, and do not step outside of justice,
their city flourishes and their people blossom in it.
Peace lies over the land and nourishes their young men; wide-seeing
Zeus does not mark them out for bitter war.
Men of straight justice are not pursued by Famine   230
or Ruin (*atē*); they feast instead on the crops they have tended.
The earth bears a plentiful livelihood for them; on the mountains
oak trees bear acorns on their branches and bees in their hollows;
the woolly sheep are covered with heavy fleeces;
and the women give birth to children who look like their fathers. 235
They flourish among continual blessings, and they have no need
to sail in ships, since the grain-giving plowland bears them crops.

---

[17] Cf. Thucydides' Melian dialogue (fr. 5b).
[18] Oath: here personified as the penalty that falls on judges or litigants who break
    their oaths in giving false verdicts.

But for those who turn to evil *hubris* and to wicked deeds
justice is determined by the son of Cronus, wide-seeing Zeus.
Often even an entire city pays for one evil man   240
if he goes wrong and commits outrageous acts.
Then Zeus brings a great disaster on them from heaven –
famine and plague together, and the people perish;
the women do not give birth, households are diminished,
according to the design of Olympian Zeus. Another time   245
Zeus destroys their extensive army or their wall,
or takes vengeance on their ships at sea.
    O kings, you too should take careful note
of this kind of justice, for there are immortals close by
to human beings, and they take note of all who oppress   250
each other with crooked judgments, heedless of retribution from
        the gods.
Zeus's immortal watchers over mortal men
number thirty thousand upon rich-pastured earth;
they watch, of course, for judgments and wicked deeds.
They are clad in darkness and travel frequently everywhere.   255
And there is the young girl, unmarried Justice, Zeus's daughter,
who is prized and respected by the gods on Olympus;
and so when anyone harms her – offends her with crookedness –
she takes her seat at once by the side of Zeus the father
and tells tales of men whose minds are unjust, so that the people 260
may pay for the outrages of their kings, who, with evil intent,
tip justice off her course, pronouncing crooked verdicts.
Watch for these things, you kings, and keep your words straight;
though hungry for gifts, give up crooked verdicts altogether.
"A man makes evil for himself when he makes evil for another."   265
"An evil plan is most evil to the one who planned it."[19]
The eye of Zeus sees everything and understands everything;
it catches sight of these things too, if it wants to, and does not
        overlook
what sort of justice it is that a city has within it.
Under these conditions[20] I would not wish to deal justly with men, 270
not I or my son, since it is bad to be a just man

[19] These two lines are evidently proverbs.
[20] "These conditions": the conditions in a city ruled by kings who give crooked
    judgment. The wish is ironic.

when the greater injustice leads to the better verdict.
But I don't expect that Zeus in his wisdom is quite finished![21]
  But you, Perses, should take this to heart:
listen to justice, and forget the use of violence altogether.   275
  This was the *nomos*[22] Zeus established for human beings:
for fish and beasts and flying birds he allowed
that one may eat another, since there is no justice among them;
but to human beings he gave justice, which turns out to be
much better. For if someone is willing to speak justly   280
in full knowledge, wide-seeing Zeus makes him prosper;
but if someone lies intentionally under sworn oath
in giving testimony, and so hurts justice, he is incurably ruined.
From that time forth his family will be left in obscurity,
while the family of an oath-keeping man will prosper ever after.   285

7. *The Muses on truth and falsehood* (Theogony *24–28*)

Here is the story that the goddesses told to me first,
the Olympian Muses, daughters of Zeus who bears the aegis:
"You shepherds who live in the fields, foul disgraces, like bellies!
We know how to tell many lies that resemble the way things are,
while we know too (if we want) how to give voice to the truth."

8. *The gifts of the Muses* (Theogony *80–103*)

Hesiod describes the power of speech/song granted to "kings"[23] *(in their capacity as judges) and bards, suggesting that a similar power is at work in both professions.*

Calliope keeps company with kings who are held in awe,   80
and if the daughters of great Zeus should honor and watch
at the birth of one of the kings who are nourished by Zeus,
then they pour sweet honey on his tongue, and the words
from his mouth flow out in a soothing stream, and all
the people look to him as he works out what is right   85

---

[21] "I don't expect that Zeus in his wisdom is quite finished!": i.e. "I don't expect that Zeus will allow the reign of injustice to continue."
[22] Way of life, custom, or law.
[23] For *basileis*, ("kings"), see Glossary.

by giving resolutions that are fair: he speaks out faultlessly
and he soon puts an end to a quarrel however large, using his
  skill.
That's why there are kings with intelligence: so they
can turn things around in the *agora* for people who've suffered
harm, easily, persuading them with gentle words.   90
As he comes to the hearing, like a god they seek his favor
with respect that is soothing, and he stands out from those
  assembled.
Such is the holy gift the Muses grant to human beings.
It's from Muses, you see, and from Apollo far-shooter
that we have men on earth who sing or play the lyre.   95
True, kings are from Zeus, but anyone prospers if he's loved
by Muses: then his voice flows sweetly from his mouth.
And when someone grieves and is newly troubled in spirit,
while pain withers his heart, then, even so, if a singer
who serves the Muses will sing out the glory of bygone men   100
and the joys of the gods who dwell on Olympus,
then he will soon forget his troubles and not remember
his cares, as the goddesses' gifts quickly grant him a change.

Archilochus

Archilochus of Paros, an elegiac and iambic poet, lived in the eighth and seventh centuries, and is said to have taken part in the colonization of Thasos in about 708. Little is known about his life, but a large number of poems and fragmentary quotations survive.

1. The common people (W 14)

If a man listened to the reproaches of the common people,
Aesimedes, he would never have very much fun.

2. The eagle and the fox
2a. (W 174)

This is a fable people tell,
how a fox and an eagle joined
as partners.

2b. (Atticus, quoted by Eusebius in Praeparatio Evangelica 15.4.4)

Do you see where that high rock is,
rough and menacing?
There I sit lightly, planning my fight with you. . .

[Our source continues in paraphrase as follows:]

Up to this high rock it is impossible for this clever wicked animal to climb, so that for the fox to come where the eagle's offspring are, they would have to meet a sad accident and fall to earth, losing their home, or else he would have to grow what it is not his nature to grow, and bend swift wings; then rising from the ground, he could fly up to the high rock. But as long as each stays in his appointed home, there will be no sharing between the creatures of the land and those of the sky.

3. *On the power of Gyges (W 19)*[24]

All the gold of Gyges means nothing to me;
I've not yet been seized by envy, I do not admire
what the gods do, and I do not want to be
a great tyrant. These things are beyond my sight.

[24] Gyges was king in Lydia, *c.* 685–657. Plato's anecdote about his rise to power is told in *Republic*, 359c ff.

Tyrtaeus

A seventh-century poet of Sparta, Tyrtaeus was said to have been a general in the second Messenian War, during which Sparta subjugated Messene. Most of his surviving poetry consists of exhortations to combat, but he also wrote a poem on the Spartan constitution.

1. *The place of common citizens in the assembly (W 4).*

The legendary Spartan lawgiver Lycurgus was said to have received the constitution of Sparta from the oracle of Delphi. These verses describe his reforms. See also Plutarch, Life of Lycurgus *6.*

After they heard Phoebus out they brought home from Pytho[25]
    the god's oracles, the perfect words,
[for this was the proclamation of Apollo, golden-haired lord
    of the silver bow who shoots far, from his rich shrine]:[26]
the Kings whom the gods honor shall lead the council,
    they must look after the lovely city of Sparta,
they and the old men, the Elders; after them the common men   5
    shall respond with decrees that are right,
speaking well and acting with justice in all things,
    never making a judgment that is crooked for the city.
And so victory and strength will attend the mass of people.
    For that is the word of Apollo to the city on these matters.   10

[25] Pytho was the most ancient divinity of the oracle at Delphi; Phoebus Apollo was its presiding god in historical times.
[26] These two lines are omitted in Plutarch.

2. *Dying for one's country (W 10, lines 1–14)*

It is noble for a good man to die, falling in the forefront
    of battle, fighting for his fatherland.
but there is nothing more wretched than leaving
    one's city and rich fields to beg,
and wander with his dear mother, his old father,   5
    his little children and wedded wife.
For he will be hated by those he comes to be among
    in the grip of want and ugly poverty;
he shames his family, he undermines his bright beauty
    and brings every evil and dishonor after him.   10
Thus no one cares for a wandering man,
    and no one gives any respect to him or his descendants.
So let us fight with spirit for this land and for our sons;
    let us die with no thought of our own lives.

Solon

Solon, one of the legendary seven wise men of ancient Greece, was a poet and a lawgiver to his native Athens in the seventh and sixth centuries. He was archōn *with special powers in about 590 and instituted reforms to the economy and to the constitution. He provided for the relief of debts (the* seisachtheia) *and rewrote most of the laws enacted by his predecessor Draco.*

Though a model for later reformers, Solon's laws were not an unqualified success, and in 561 a series of disturbances led to the tyranny of Peisistratus (died in 527), who rose to power on the basis of popular support.

Fragments of Solon's poems have come down to us as quotations in later works. We have translated here all the passages relevant to political theory. For a famous anecdote about Solon see Herodotus, 1.

1. *The importance of good government, or* eunomia *(W 4, lines 1–10, 26–39)*

Our city will never be destroyed by the fate
    of Zeus or the plans of immortal gods,
for Pallas Athena our protector, great-spirited daughter
    of a mighty god, holds her hands over us.
But the citizens themselves, lured by wealth, want to bring   5
    this great city down with their stupidities.
The common people's leaders have a mind to do injustice,
    and much grief is about to come from their great *hubris*,
for they do not know how to hold excess in check, nor to give
      order to

the pleasures of their present feast in peace.   10

. . .

In this way the public evil comes home to each man   26
   and the outer doors can no longer hold it back;
it leaps high over the courtyard wall and finds you
   anywhere, even if you hide in your inmost bedroom.
This is what my spirit tells me to teach the Athenians: 30
   bad government brings the most evils to a city;
while good government (*eunomia*) makes everything fine and orderly,
   and often puts those who are unjust in fetters;
it makes rough things smooth, stops excess, weakens *hubris*,
   and withers the growing blooms of madness (*atē*).   35
It straightens crooked judgments, makes arrogant deeds
   turn gentle, puts a stop to divisive factions,
brings to an end the misery of angry quarrels. This is the source
   among human beings for all that is orderly and wise.

2. *Solon comments on his own reforms (W 5 and 6).*

I gave the common people as much privilege as they needed
   neither taking honor from them nor reaching out for more.
But as for those who had power and were admired for their wealth,
   I arranged for them to have nothing unseemly.
And I set up a strong shield around both parties   5
   by not allowing either to defeat the other unjustly.

. . .

In that way the common people best follow their leaders
   neither giving them too much freedom or too much force.
For excess breeds *hubris*, when great wealth comes
   to people whose minds are not in order.   10

3. *On land reform (W 34)*

But they came for plunder[27] hoping for riches;
each thought he'd find much happiness for himself
and that, though smooth of tongue, my mind would be tough.
Their plans at that time were futile, and now they all are angry

---

[27] Those who wished for a redistribution of land to the poor.

with me and turn their eyes askance as if I were an enemy. 5
That's not right: for what I said I would I did, with the gods'
    help.
But I did nothing without purpose, and it did not please me
to use the force of a tyrant, or to allow the equal division (*isomoira*)
of our rich fatherland among poor and rich alike.[28]

4. *Solon explains why he left Athens without accomplishing a democratic*
revolution (W 36).

Scholars are in dispute about exactly what he accomplished, and what
evil he removed.

Why did I stop before I won any of those things
for which I brought the *dēmos* together?
In Time's court of justice I'll have a most favorable witness
in the great mother of divine Olympians,
black Earth, from whom I once pulled up 5
the boundary stones that were fixed in many places;[29]
and she who was formerly a slave is now free.
I brought many back to Athens,
their god-built fatherland, after they had been sold abroad,[30]
some unjustly, some with justice, and some who had fled 10
under the compulsion of poverty, and no longer spoke
the Athenian tongue, so widely had they traveled.
And others had been shamefully made slaves
right here, trembling at the tempers of their masters.
These I set free. I put these things in force 15
by joining might and right (*dikē*) together,
and I carried through as I had promised.
I wrote laws (*thesmoi*)[31] too, equally for poor and rich,[32]
and made justice that is fit and straight for all.

---

[28] "Poor and rich alike": *kakoi* and *esthloi* ("bad" and "noble") imply both moral
  and social judgments. See Glossary, *s.v. agathos*.
[29] The boundary stones probably showed that the property was mortgaged; if so
  Solon refers to his reduction of debt for poor farmers.
[30] Sold as slaves.
[31] *Thesmos* is the early Athenian word for "law" or "statute," replaced by *nomos* in
  the fifth century.
[32] Literally, "for bad and good." See n. 28.

If another man had taken the goad as I did, 20
but been foolish and fond of wealth,
he would not have held the *dēmos* back.
Had I been willing to please the opposition at first,
and afterwards to do to them what these people asked,[33]
this city would have lost many men. 25
That is why I built strength from all sides,
like a wolf wheeling about among many dogs. . .

5. *Aristotle tells us that the following fragment comes later in the same poem (W 37)*

Line 6, which we have bracketed, is his paraphrase of the verse.

As for the *dēmos*, if I may rebuke them
openly: what they have now they
would never have seen, even in their dreams. . .
And the greater men, superior in might,
may praise me and be friends. 5
[For if someone else had had my position]
he would not have held back the *dēmos*, nor stopped
before he'd stirred up the milk and taken off the fat.
But I, I took my stand like a boundary stone
in the ground between them.[34] 10

6. *The danger of tyranny, a warning against Peisistratus (W 9)*

From a cloud comes the strength of snow and hail,
but thunder comes from bright lightning.
From great men comes destruction of a city, and the people
fall through ignorance under the slavish rule of one man.
It's not easy for one who flies too high to control himself 5
afterwards, but these things should be thought of now.

7. *On who is to blame for the tyranny of Peisistratus (W 11)*

If you have felt grief through your own fault
do not put the blame for this on the gods;

[33] "The opposition": the aristocrats; "these people": the *dēmos*.
[34] The word is used for the ground between opposing armies.

for you increased the strength of these men yourselves when you
    gave them
  the guards,[35] and that is why you are in evil servitude.
Each of you follows the footprints of this fox,   5
  and you all have empty minds,
for you watch only the tongue of the man, his slippery speech,
  but you never look at what he actually does.

8. *Solon prays to the Muses for justice (W 13, known as the "Hymn to the Muses" [lines 1–32])*

Pierian Muses, dazzling children of Memory
  and Olympian Zeus, hear my prayer.
Give me prosperity from the blessed gods, and from all
  people, always, give me good repute,
and let me be as sweet to my friends as I am bitter to my foes, 5
  respected by these, terrible for the others to see.
And I long to have property, but I do not want
  to get it unjustly, for Justice always comes after.
The wealth the gods give stays with a man
  unshaken from the lowest bottom to the top;   10
but that which men value owing to *hubris* comes
  improperly; won over by unjust deeds,
it follows a man reluctantly and soon is coupled with Ruin (*atē*):
  its beginning is small, like that of fire,
meager at first, and awful in the end.   15
  For the products of *hubris* are not with men for long,
but Zeus oversees the ends of all things, and suddenly,
  as the wind in spring quickly scatters
the clouds, stirs the depths
  of the wave-tossed barren sea, lays waste   20
fine crops on wheat-bearing land, and reaches the gods'
  high seat in heaven, making the sky clear again
to see, and the sun's strength shines on fertile fields
  beautifully, and not one cloud can be seen –

---

[35] In 560 Peisistratus persuaded the people that he was in personal danger from his political enemies, and was given an official bodyguard. This soon gave Peisistratus the power to take control of Athens.

just so comes the punishment from Zeus; unlike   25
    a mortal man, he is not quick to anger at each thing,
but he never completely forgets a man who has
    a wicked spirit, and that man is always exposed in the end.
One man pays right away, another later. Others may escape
    in their own lifetimes, and the gods' fate may not catch up   30
with them, but it always comes back, and their blameless children
    will pay for their deeds, or else their descendants after them.

9. *The importance of virtue (W 15)*

Many bad men are rich, many good men poor,
    but we will not exchange with them
our virtue (*aretē*) for their wealth, for virtue is firm forever,
    but property goes from one man to another.

10. *(W 16)*

The measure of judgment (*gnōmosunē*) is unseen and very hard to
    know,
    though that alone grasps the ends of all things.

11. *(W 17)*

In every way the mind of the immortals is unseen by human beings.

12. *(W 18)*

As I grow old I am always learning much.

Theognis

Theognis was an elegiac poet of the sixth century who most likely came from Megara. About 1,400 lines of verse have come down to us under his name. Some of these verses are elsewhere attributed to other poets, and it is likely that the corpus includes lines that are not written by Theognis. Of Theognis' life we know little, but we can infer from the poems that he was concerned to give advice to a young friend Cyrnus, and that he lived in a time of political upheaval.

Various fragmentary passages on different topics are all run together in what has come down to us. We have excerpted several passages that bear on ancient political thought. Some of these are probably complete poems. As all these verses represent upper-class views of the period, we have not taken a position on the question of authorship.

1. *Lines 39–52*

Cyrnus, this city is pregnant; I fear she may give birth to a man
    to straighten out our evil *hubris*,[36]   40
for these citizens are still sound of mind, but their leaders
    have turned towards a fall into great evil.
No city has yet been destroyed by good men, Cyrnus;
    but when it pleases evil men to commit *hubris*,
when they corrupt the common people and give judgment   45
    in favor of the unjust for their own profit or power,
do not expect that city to stay peaceful for long,

---

[36] "A man to straighten out our evil *hubris*": evidently a tyrant is meant.

not even if it now rests in tranquility,
and because these things are dear to evil men
   their profits bring evil to the people.   50
And from them comes civil strife, the killing of kinfolk,
   and dictatorships too. May the city never wish for these!

2. *Lines 145–148*

Prefer living piously with few possessions
   to being rich on unjust acquisitions.
In justice,[37] in a word, is every virtue (*aretē*),
   and every good man, Cyrnus, is just.

3. *Lines 219–220*

Do not be too upset when the citizens are in disorder,
   but, Cyrnus, take the middle of the road, as I do.

4. *Lines 233–234*

Though he be a fortress and tower for empty-headed common
   people,
Cyrnus, little honor is the lot of a good man.

5. *Lines 279–282*

It is natural (*eikos*) that a bad man should think badly of justice,
   and have no dread of the punishment (*nemesis*) hereafter,
for a wretched mortal can take up many things he should not
   touch
   that lie at his feet, and think he sets everything right.

6. *Lines 319–322*

Cyrnus, a good man has a mind that is always steadfast,
   he is brave whether his situation be good or ill.

---

[37] "Justice": *dikaiosunē*. This is the earliest use we know of for this word, which later came to replace *dikē* for the general sense of "justice."

But if god gives a bad man a livelihood and then adds wealth,
  he is foolish, and cannot keep his wickedness in check.

7. *Lines 337–340*

May Zeus grant me the power to repay my friends who love me
  and my enemies, Cyrnus, even more.
This way I will be considered a god among humans,
  if death does not catch me till I have paid my debts.

8. *Lines 363–364*

Chatter nicely with your enemy, but when he comes under your
    power
pay him back, without making any excuse.

9. *Lines 429–438*

It is easier to conceive and raise someone than it is to put good
    sense
  in him. No one has yet found a way   430
to make a foolish man wise or a bad one good.
  But if the god had given this power to the doctors
to cure the wickedness and ruinous minds of men,
  they would have made a great deal of money.
But if it could be done, if intelligence could be put in a man,   435
  then a bad son would never come from a good father;
he would be persuaded instead by his sound advice. But teaching
  will never ever make a bad man good.

10. *Lines 535–538*

A slave never holds his head straight by nature
  but always crooked with neck at a slant;
for no rose or hyacinth ever grows from a sea onion
  and no free child from a slave-woman.

11. *Lines 561–562*

I wish I owned some of my enemies' wealth
  and could give away much of it to my friends.

12. *Lines 847–850*

Grind your heel on the empty-headed *dēmos*, hit them
   with a sharp stick, and put a painful yoke around their necks;
that way you'll never find a people that love their masters more
   anywhere under the sun.

Hymn to Hephaestus

This short piece is preserved with a group of hymns attributed to Homer, but most probably date from the seventh or sixth centuries. Hephaestus is the smith-god; in the Iliad *he forges Achilles' elaborate new armor.*

Sing, Muse with clear voice, of Hephaestus, famed for
    inventiveness,
who together with gray-eyed Athena taught glorious crafts (*erga*)
to mortals on earth. In earlier times they lived
in caves on mountains like wild beasts,
but now they have learned crafts because of Hephaestus, famed
    for skill   5
and thus all year long they pass their lives
easily, without care in their own houses.
Look favorably on me, Hephaestus, and grant me *aretē* and
    prosperity.

Simonides

The life of Simonides of Ceos (556–468) stretched from the age of tyrants through the overthrow of the Peisistratids in Athens, the turning back of the two Persian invasions, and the rise of Athens. Invited to Athens by the tyrant Hipparchus as part of his effort to bring culture to Athens, Simonides left after his fall for various courts in Thessaly. Later, when his patrons sided with the Persians, he returned to Athens where he celebrated the Greek victory. He died while visiting the court of Hieron in Syracuse. His reputation was such that his name was linked with those of Homer and Hesiod as a source of wisdom.

1. Is it hard to be good?

This is an encomium (or song of praise) to Skopas, a king in Thessaly whom Simonides had visited (PMG 542, four strophes in a complex lyric form).

1a. It is hard to be[38] a truly good man
foursquare in hands and feet and purpose,
   made without blame.
[*Seven lines are missing.*]
1b. And Pittacus' proverb does not ring true to me,   11
though it was said by a wise man:
   that it is hard to be noble.[39]

---

[38] "Be": *genesthai*, so in most translations of this line; but the verb may mean "become."
[39] Pittacus was one of the sages of archaic Greece included in a group that was later designated the "Seven Wise Men"; he ruled Mytilene in the early sixth century. The apparent contradiction between Simonides' opening lines and his

Only a god may have that prize; while a man
   cannot but be bad   15
if a hopeless catastrophe brings him down.
For every man who fares well is good,
but he is bad if he fares badly,
and generally those
   the gods love are the best.   20
1c. Therefore I will not throw away my share of life
on an empty, impractical hope, seeking
   what cannot come to be –
an all-blameless human being, out of all of us who take
   the fruit of the wide earth;   25
if I find one I will announce it to you.
But I praise and love all those
who willingly
do nothing shameful. Not even
   gods fight necessity.   30
1d. [*Two lines are missing.*]
I do not tend to find fault. It is enough for me
if a man be not evil or witless,
   but that he know the justice that is good for cities   35
and that he be healthy. With such a man
I will not find fault. For the generations
of fools are infinite.
All things are good,
if nothing shameful is mixed with them.   40

2. *Justice* – *(cited in* Republic *331e3)*

[Simonides said that] justice is giving each man what is owed to him.[40]

verdict on Pittacus' proverb is the starting point for a discussion between Socrates and Protagoras in Plato's *Protagoras* 339a–46d, which is our source for this poem. The discussants do not agree about how to resolve the apparent contradiction, and the issue is still under debate today. The poem is not concerned with moral education (the topic of the *Protagoras*) but with the vagaries of fortune – a familiar theme in ancient Greek literature. "Good" and "bad" are used here mainly in a non-moral sense. The point of the poem, in our view, is that it is easy for a man to be good (i.e. prosper) if he has good fortune, but hard to be secure (foursquare) in his good fortune, since bad luck can bring him down.

[40] The speaker, Polemarchus, explains this a few lines later: giving each man "what is owed him" is a matter of doing good to one's friends and evil to one's enemies (332a–c).

Xenophanes

Xenophanes of Colophon was a philosopher and poet of the late sixth and early fifth centuries. Although an Ionian by birth, he evidently lived as an exile in Sicily.

1. *(DK 2, W2, lines 11–19)*

. . . Better than the strength
of men or of horses is my *sophia*.[41]
And though it is often foolishly believed to be so, it is not just
  to prefer strength to good *sophia*.
For it is not having a good boxer among the people,   15
  or a good pentathlete or wrestler,
or one who is swift of foot – which has the highest
  honor in men's contests of strength – none
of these could give a city a good constitution (*eunomia*).

2. *(DK 15)*

But if cows and horses and lions had hands
and could draw with their hands and accomplish what men do,
horses would draw images of gods like horses,
and cows like cows, and each would make statues
of the gods like the bodies they have themselves.

---

[41] "My *sophia*": here *sophia* has the specific sense of "poetic skill" along with its general meaning, "wisdom."

3. *(DK 16)*

Ethiopeans make their gods black and snub-nosed,
Thracians make theirs blue-eyed and red-haired.

4. *(DK 11)*

Both Homer and Hesiod have attributed to the gods
everything that calls for blame and reproach among humans:
stealing, adultery, and deceiving one another.

5. *(DK 34)*

And no man has seen with certainty or will ever know
about the gods or any other thing of which I speak;
even if someone happened to speak with highest perfection,
he still would not know, but opinion is built into everything.

6. *(DK 35)*
Let these opinions be taken as likenesses of reality.

Pindar

Pindar (518–c. 440) was an aristocratic Boeotian lyric poet known especially for his odes in honor of victors at festivals such as the one at Olympia. He wrote for rich and powerful patrons throughout the Greek world and was, on the whole, a defender of tradition. The fragment translated here comes from one of the most frequently cited poems of Greek antiquity. It is most notably cited by Herodotus (3.38, fr. 3) and by Plato, Gorgias *484b (Unknown authors, fr. 2), who quotes the first five lines and summarizes part of the remainder (cf.* Laws *690b). About forty lines of the poem have been reconstructed from a recently discovered papyrus and other sources, but the original meaning is increasingly uncertain after line 20. Pindar's point appears to be that, despite the apparent injustice of Heracles' violent treatment of his two victims, the traditional glorification of Heracles' labors makes this behavior just.*

1. *The* Nomos–Basileus *fragment (S 169)*

Custom (*nomos*), king of all,
of mortals and immortals,
takes up and justifies what is most violent
with a supremely high hand. As evidence,
I cite the deeds of Heracles: 5
for he drove the cattle of Geryon
to the Cyclopean courtyard of Eurystheus
without paying, and when they were not for sale.
It was he, too, who stole the horses
of Diomedes after conquering   10

the Kikonian king by the marsh of Bisto,
although Diomedes, the wonderful son
of bronze-armored Enualios,
stood up to Heracles, the great son of Zeus,
not out of greed but because of his valor (*aretē*).   15
For it is better to die defending property
that is being stolen than to live on as a weakling.
Heracles secretly entered the great
house by night and took the road
of physical violence.   20

2. *(S 215)*

Different customary rules (*nomima*) for different people;
  each man praises his own justice (*dikē*).

PART II

TRAGEDY

Aeschylus

Aeschylus, the first of the three great Athenian tragic poets, lived 525–456. Seven of his nearly one hundred tragedies are preserved complete, and we have fragments of several dozen others. His most complex work, the Orestcia trilogy (458), raises many of the social, political, and ethical issues of contemporary Athens, such as the nature of justice, the origins of law and order, and the relations between the sexes. Some modern scholars doubt the authenticity of Prometheus Bound and would date the play after 450, because it shows the apparent influence of sophistic ideas, especially in the passages translated here.

Prometheus Bound

In the excerpts from the Prometheus Bound (1–3), Prometheus addresses the chorus, who are generally sympathetic to him. Cf. Hesiod's treatment of the same myth (Hesiod, 1–2), and Protagoras, 8. "Prometheus" means "Forethought"

1. *Prometheus (228–241)*

As soon as he [Zeus] assumed his father's throne,
he distributed different prerogatives
to the various gods and set up   230
his rule. On wretched mortals
he put no value at all, but wished to obliterate
the entire race and plant another one anew.
No one opposed this plan save I;

43

I dared to rescue mortals   235
from destruction and an end in Hades.
Therefore I am bowed down by these woes,
painful to endure and pitiable to behold.
Just because I pitied mortals, I do not think it right
that I should meet this fate, but thus ruthlessly   240
am I brought into line, a sight that brings disgrace to Zeus.

2. *Prometheus and the Chorus (247–254)*

Chorus: Didn't you do more than that?
Prometheus: I prevented mortals from foreseeing their death.[42]
Chorus: What drug did you find for this disease?
Prometheus: I instilled blind hopes in them.   250
Chorus: This is a great benefit you gave mortals.
Prometheus: What's more, I gave them fire too.
Chorus: So now, though creatures of a day, they have the
                 flame of fire?
Prometheus: Yes, and from it they will learn many crafts (*technai*).

3. *Prometheus (439–471, 476–506)*

What other god than I distributed
rights and privileges to these new gods?   440
But I won't mention that for I would tell you only
things you know. Listen rather to the hardships of mortals,
who once were foolish till I gave them
intelligence and good sense.
I speak not to blame the human race,   445
but to make clear the kindness of my gifts.
At first they looked but looked in vain
and hearing did not understand, but like
the figures in dreams their whole lives
they mixed everything at random. They knew neither   450
mud-brick houses, built to face the sun, nor carpentry,
but lived underground, like scurrying
ants, in the sunless depths of caves.

---

[42] Cf. Plato, *Gorgias* 523d.

They had no reliable sign to mark the winter
or the blossoming spring or the harvest time   455
of summer,[43] but did everything without understanding
until I came and taught them the difficult skill
of interpreting the risings and settings of the stars.
I also discovered numbers for them, the highest skill,
and the combination of letters, which is   460
the memory of all things, hard-working mother of the Muses.
I was first to yoke wild beasts
to be slaves to yokestraps and saddles so that
they could relieve mortals of their greatest burdens;
and to chariots I brought horses, obedient to the reins,   465
the splendor of wealth and luxury;
and it was none other than I who discovered
the sea-wandering, linen-winged conveyors of sailors.
But alas, though I devised such inventions
for mortals, I have no trick by which   470
to escape from this my present misery.

[*The Chorus makes a brief, sympathetic response.*]

When you hear the rest, you will be even more amazed
at the skills (*technai*) and resources that I invented.
The greatest of these was that if people fell sick,
they had no remedy, not food
or drink or ointment, but for lack of drugs   480
they withered away - until, that is, I showed
them the mixing of gentle drugs
that might protect them from every form of disease.
I taught them the many kinds of prophecy,
and was the first to judge from dreams what ought   485
to happen when awake; and I revealed to them the meaning
of voices, hard to interpret, and signs encountered on the road.
I carefully discerned the flight
of crooked-taloned birds, some favorable by nature,
others ill-omened, how each one lives   490

---

[43] The early Greeks thought in terms of three seasons, with summer extending
through the harvest period.

its daily life, which are hostile to each other,
which friendly, and which ones roost together;
and the smoothness of the entrails,[44] and which colors
of bile would be pleasing to the gods,
and the liver's mottled symmetry.   495
By burning the thighbones and the huge backbone
all covered with fat, I set mortals on the path
of this skill (*technē*) that is hard to discern, and I made visible
the fiery signs that formerly were obscure.
All this I did, and then those resources   500
hidden in the earth for mortals –
bronze, iron, gold and silver – who
before me would claim to have discovered these?
No one, I'm quite sure, except a babbling fool.
To summarize, taking everything together, this is the truth: 505
all mortal skills come from Prometheus.[45]

Fragments from lost plays

*Most of these are preserved without any context. They represent views
that were being aired at the time and are a sign of the new learning.*

4. *Bacchae* (TGF 22)

Evil comes swiftly indeed upon mortals,
and error upon him who goes beyond what is right (*themis*).

5. *Danaids* (TGF 44)

Danaids *was the third play of the connected trilogy, whose first play,*
Suppliants, *is preserved. The speaker of these lines is Aphrodite, goddess
of love.*

Holy heaven longs to pierce the ground

---

[44] The innards of a sacrificial animal were frequently examined for their prophetic
significance. Cf. Hesiod's account of the origin of the common Greek practice of
animal sacrifice (fr. 1), where it is explained why mortals burn the bones and fat
for the gods and save the meat for themselves.
[45] There is no mention in this passage of the political skills prominent in Protagoras'
version (Fr. 8).

and love seizes the earth to join in marriage;
the rain, falling from fair-flowing heaven,
impregnates the earth. She brings forth for mortals
food for the herds and Demeter's vital gift,[46]   5
and the fruit of trees; and all that comes from that watery marriage
is accomplished, and of these things I am the cause.

6. *Myrmidons* (TGF *139*)

Great is the fame of the Lydian fable:
The eagle, pierced by the bow's missile, saw the feathery device
and said, "Thus are we taken, not by others but by our own
  feathers."

7. *Niobe* (TGF *154a, lines 9, 15–20*)

When afflicted, a mortal is nothing but a shadow.
. . .
God plants a fault in mortals   15
when he wishes to afflict the house entirely.[47]
But a mortal must still avoid insolent talk,
guarding his god-sent prosperity.
Those who prosper never expect
to slip and lose what they have.   20

8. *Niobe* (TGF *159, line 3*)

Learn not to revere human things too much.

9. *Niobe* (TGF *161*)

Alone among the gods Death does not long for gifts.
You would not get anywhere, even with sacrifices or libations.
He has no altar, no hymns of praise,
and Persuasion stands apart from him alone among divinities.

---

[46] Demeter was goddess of grain.
[47] Lines 15–16 are a famous couplet, quoted by Plato in *Republic* 380a. The following
lines are partially restored by modern scholars.

10. *Palamedes (TGF 181a)*

Palamedes was famous for many inventions. Sophocles also wrote plays about him (19–20). For the sophists he became an intellectual hero, whose contributions to human progress were comparable to Prometheus'; cf. Gorgias' Palamedes *(2) and Alcidamas'* Odysseus *3).*

Then I gave order to the lives of all Greeks
and their allies, who formerly were confused,
and lived like wild beasts. First I discovered
numbers, a clever and most important contrivance.

11. *Palamedes* (TGF *182)*

I assigned commanders to the armies and the companies
of soldiers, and I determined what food should be eaten:
that they should take breakfast, then lunch, then dinner third.

12. *Phrygians* (TGF *266)*

If you wish to help the dead,
or harm them, it makes no difference,
since [once they are dead] they feel no pleasure or pain;
but our indignation (*nemesis*) is all the greater,
and justice (*dikē*) exacts vengeance for the dead man.   5

13. *(*TGF *301)*[48]

A god does not avoid deceit if it is right.

14. *(*TGF *302)*

Sometimes a god respects the right moment to tell a lie.

15. *(*TGF *381)*

When justice (*dikē*) and strength are yoked together,
what team is mightier than this?

[48] The remaining fragments are from unknown plays. Fragments 13 and 14 are quoted in the *Dissoi Logoi* 3.12 (below) .

16. *(*TGF *391)*

Even one who is wiser than wise errs.

17. *(*TGF *394)*

We do not trust a man because of his oaths, but oaths because of the man.

Sophocles

Sophocles lived 496–406. In addition to his poetic activity, he held a minor, hereditary priesthood, and he was elected general, perhaps more than once. His first production was in 468 and we are told that he wrote about 120 plays during his career. He was victorious eighteen times with his plays at the Greater Dionysia (i.e. with seventy-two individual plays).

Antigone

1. Chorus (332–375)

This choral passage, often called the "Ode to Man," follows a long speech by Creon in justification of his decree forbidding the burial of Polyneices on the grounds that he was a traitor to the city. Earlier Antigone had affirmed her intention to bury him. Creon asserts that the primary duty of a king is to uphold law and order in the city. In view of the tragic turn of events, there is undoubtedly irony in the optimistic view of the progress of human civilization expressed in this ode. Antigone was produced about 442, and the ode is one of the earliest surviving expressions of the progressive anthropology developed during the sophistic period. Compare Aeschylus' Prometheus *(frs. 1–3), Protagoras' Myth (fr. 8), Euripides, fr. 4, Critias, fr. 5, and Democritus, fr. 1.*

There are many wonders (*deina*),[49] but nothing
is more wonderful than a human being.

[49] The Greek word has a wide range of meanings: "clever, skillful, dreadful, powerful, wonderful"; here it indicates both admiration and dread of human achievements.

He crosses over the grey sea,
against the stormy wind,   335
passing through swells
breaking all around; and
Earth, greatest of the gods,
immortal and unwearied, he wears away,
as year after year his plows go back and forth,   340
turning the soil with horse-born mules.

The tribe of light-hearted birds
he captures with a cast of his net
and the races of wild beasts,
and the sea-born creatures of the deep,   345
all with his woven coils,
man captures with supreme skill.
With his devices he subdues the wild,
mountain-roaming creature, and
tames the horse with shaggy mane   350
with a yoke around its neck,
and the unwearying mountain bull.

He has taught himself speech
and wind-swift thought
and the dispositions for city life;   355
he has every resource for escaping
the harsh, open-air frosts,
the rains hurled down
by tempests. He never faces
the future without resources.   360
From Death alone
will he devise no escape,
though he has contrived to escape
from overwhelming diseases.

Clever (*sophos*) with the inventiveness of his skill (*technē*)   365
beyond all expectation, he goes forth,
now to evil, now to good.
When he weaves together laws of the land
with oath-bound justice (*dikē*) of the gods,

his city stands high; 370
but anyone who consorts with what is not noble
in his daring, he will have no city at all.
If he does such things,
never let him share my hearth,
or my thoughts. 375

Fragments from lost plays

2. *Locrian Ajax (*TGF *12)*

The golden eye of justice (*dikē*)
watches and requites the wrongdoer.

3. *Locrian Ajax (*TGF *13)*

Man is only breath and shadow.

4. *Locrian Ajax (*TGF *14)*

Tyrants are wise by association with wise men.

5. *Aethiopians (*TGF *28)*

I tell you this as a favor, not to force you:
you should, like wise men, praise justice
but take hold of what is profitable.

6. *Aleadae (*TGF *78)*

It is not easy to resist the just.

7. *Aleadae (*TGF *80)*

A just tongue has great strength.

8. *Aleadae (*TGF *86, line 3)*

Conventional wisdom (*to nomisthen*) is stronger than truth.

9. *Aleadae (*TGF *88)*

Money procures friends for people,
and honors and a seat closest

to the throne of the loftiest tyrant.
No one is born an enemy to money,
and those who naturally hate it deny that they do.   5
Wealth is skilled at entering all places, sacred
and profane, where a poor man,
even if he entered, would not obtain his wish.
It makes even an ugly man, with a bad reputation
for speaking, wise and handsome to the eye.   10
Only the rich man can be happy even when sick,
and can conceal his troubles.

10. *Aletes (P 101)*[50]

A considerate and right-thinking mind
is a better inventor than any intellectual (*sophistēs*).

11. *Aletes (P 106)*

Who would consider prosperity to be
a great thing, or a small thing, or worthless?
For nothing in life ever stays the same.

12. *Aletes (P 107)*

It is terrible that those who are impious and come
from bad families are the ones who fare well,
whereas those who are noble and born
from good families encounter misfortune.
The divinities should not act thus in human affairs,   5
for pious mortals ought to get
a clear reward from the gods;
but those who are unjust ought to receive
the opposite return, as a clear punishment for their wrongs.
In this way no one who was bad (*kakos*) would have good fortune. 10

---

[50] Some scholars doubt frs. 10–12 are by Sophocles; see Bibliographical Note,
§ B.2.

13. *Epigonoi (*TGF *189)*

Woman, who has dared everything and more –
there is not and never will be anything more evil
than woman, as long as any sorrow remains for mortals.

14. *Epigonoi (*TGF *201b)*

When it is not possible to speak freely
and say what is best, when the worse course prevails,
then the city's safety founders on mistakes.

15. *Thyestes (*TGF *247)*

No one is wise unless god honors him.
Looking to the gods you must go where they bid you,
even if it takes you outside of justice (*dikē*);
for where the gods take the lead nothing is shameful.

16. *Creusa (*TGF *352)*

It is not good to speak false words,
but if the truth will bring you terrible destruction,
it is forgivable to say even what is not good.

17. *Creusa (*TGF *354)*

Don't be surprised, lord, that I cling
to wealth. Even mortals who have led
a long life hold fast to gaining wealth;
other things are second to money
for mortals. Some would praise   5
a healthy man, but I think a healthy man
who is poor is no one, but is always sick.

18. *Creusa (*TGF *356)*

It is finest to have justice in one's nature;
it is best to have a healthy life; but it is sweetest
to be able to grasp whatever one longs for each day.

Sophocles

19. *Nauplius* (TGF 432)

Nauplius is speaking about his son Palamedes, who was also the subject of a play by Aeschylus (frs. 10–11, with headnote); cf. Gorgias, Palamedes (fr. 2), esp. section 30, and Alcidamas, Odysseus (fr. 3). There are serious difficulties with the text of this fragment, esp. in line 9.

He devised a wall for the Argive army,
invented weights, numbers, and measures,
the ordering of troops and the signs of heaven.
And he was first to fashion the number ten out of one
and again from ten he discovered fifty   5
and then a thousand. He showed an army how to use the signs
of beacons, and revealed things not previously shown.
He discovered the measures and periods of stars
for sentries, the secure signs for sleep,
and, for the sea-going shepherds of ships,   10
the return of the Great Bear and the cold setting of the dog-star.

20. *Palamedes* (TGF 479)

The setting is Aulis, where the Greek army waited for favorable winds so that they could sail to Troy. The subject is Palamedes.

He did not put an end to their famine (may god approve
my words), but he invented the cleverest of pastimes
for the men, weary of the sea's din:
draughts and dice, a pleasant relief from idleness.

21. *Shepherds* (TGF 505)

The context is shepherds speaking of their sheep; the lines were often used of politicians who court the mob.

Though masters, we are their slaves;
though they are silent we must listen to them.

22. *Polyxena* (TGF 524)

The speaker may be Agamemnon.

No leader of an army can

give in to everyone or satisfy all desires.
Not even Zeus, who is stronger than I in his absolute rule,
can be a friend to all in bringing rain or drought;
but were he brought to account among mortals, he would be fined. 5
How then could I, a mortal born of mortal woman,
be wiser in common sense than Zeus?

23. *Tereus* (TGF *583*)

The speaker is a woman, perhaps Procne. For the sentiment cf. Euripides,
Medea *(fr. 1).*

But now, apart from others, I am nothing; but often
have I observed the nature (*phusis*) of women in this respect,
that we are nothing. As young girls in our father's house,
we live the most pleasant life of all,
for children are always happy in their ignorance.   5
But when we reach the age of understanding,
we are thrust out and traded off,
far from parents and ancestral gods.
Some go to men in other cities, others to barbarians;
some to joyless homes, while others find abuse.   10
And when one single night has put the yoke on her,
she must then accept this fate and think she has done well.

24. *Tereus* (TGF *591*)

One day showed us all to be one tribe of humans,
born from father and mother;
no one is by birth superior to another.
But fate nourishes some of us with misery
and some with prosperity, while others are compelled   5
to bear the yoke of slavery.

25. *Tereus* (TGF *592*)

What delight is there in
many fine things, if an evil-counseling
mind destroys long lasting wealth.

. . .

For wily mischiefs of calamity
alter human life   5
in every season.

26. *Tyndareus (*TGF *646)*

Compare the views of Solon as expressed in Herodotus, fr. 1.

A man with good fortune should not be deemed happy
until his life is completed
and he has finished the running of it.
For in one brief moment of time the greatest wealth
is destroyed by the gift of an evil spirit   5
that changes – so the gods decide.

27. *Tyro (*TGF *665)*

One who errs unintentionally is not bad (*kakos*).

28. *Phaedra (*TGF *682)*

Thus a man could possess no greater evil
than a bad (*kakos*) woman, nor anything better
than a sensible (*sōphrōn*) one.

29. *Phaedra (*TGF *683)*

A city would never be secure
in which justice and moderation (*ta sōphrona*)
are trampled underfoot and a babbling man with
his mischievous goad takes charge of the city.

30. *Phaedra (*TGF *685)*

Children are the anchor of life for a mother.

Unknown plays

31. *(TGF 737)*

I hate the man who investigates hidden matters.

32. *(TGF 811)*

The oaths of a woman I write on water.

33. *(TGF 867)*

Even in disagreement a discussion (*logos*)
brings the two sides firmly together.

34. *(TGF 873)*

Whoever traffics with a tyrant
becomes his slave, even if he came as a free man.

35. *(TGF 932)*

Indeed, a woman may try with oaths to avoid the bitter
pangs of childbirth; but when she is free of the pain,
she is caught in the same nets,
overcome by the desire in her.

36. *(TGF 936)*

Where parents yield to their children,
this is not a city of sensible (*sōphrōn*) men.

37. *(TGF 940)*

If a body is enslaved, still the mind is free.

38. *(TGF 942)*

What mortal house ever prospers,
exalted in luxury, without a good woman?

39. (TGF *943*)

A woman in a house with orphans[51] has a man's spirit.

---

[51] In Greece "orphan" designated a child without a father.

Euripides

Euripides (c. 485 to c. 406) was an Athenian dramatic poet who was heavily influenced by the new learning of the sophists. Although controversial, he had ninety-two plays accepted for production and became after his death the most performed of Greek tragedians. Eighteen or nineteen plays have survived, along with numerous fragments. He is said also to have written the elegy for the Athenian troops lost in Sicily (413).

Euripides' plays represented advanced views about the position of women, and seem also to have been critical of traditional beliefs about the gods and the morality they stood for. His work is important for an understanding of ancient Greek rhetoric and political theory of the fifth century. Here we print only some of the most important passages. (Dates of production, where known, are given in parentheses.)

Medea (431)

1. *On discovering the unfaithfulness of her husband Jason, Medea says:*

230

Of all those who can breathe and have minds,
we women are the most miserable race.
First of all we have to pay too much
to purchase a husband, to take on a tyrant
over our bodies – that's as bad as bad can be.
Then there's the enormous game of chance: will he be bad
or good? Divorce ruins the reputation

235

of a woman; meanwhile she cannot say no to her husband.[52]
And once she's arrived among new ways and new customs
she'd have to be a prophet (since she did not learn this at home)
to know how to make the best of a bedmate. If we come out well   240
from these ordeals and our husbands bear the yoke
of sharing a life without violence, then our lives
are to be envied. Otherwise, we're better dead.
A man, now, when he's annoyed with his family,
goes out and relieves his heartache somewhere else;   245
over to some friend's house, someone his age;
while we are permitted only one soul to turn to.
They say our lives are safe as can be,
because we stay indoors while they go to battle,
the fools! I'd rather take my stand behind a shield   250
three times than bear one child.

2. *When Medea finds that she is under suspicion for her knowledge
of witchcraft, she speaks lines that have been thought to express
Euripides' own anguish at his reputation for his adoption of the new
learning.*

A man whose nature is to think straight will never give
his children too much education or make them clever;   295
for apart from the idleness they will have
they'll incur the bitter envy of the citizens.
If you offer clever new ideas to stupid folk,
they'll think you're useless, stupid by nature;
while those who are supposed to have some fine knowledge   300
will be offended if your fame in the city is greater.
I myself have had a share of this misfortune.

---

[52] Legally, divorce in Athens was a simple matter, requiring only a sworn statement before a magistrate. It could be a financial hardship for the husband, since he would need to return his wife's dowry. It was not a desirable option for respectable women, since a divorced woman would have to return to her father's house and probably remain single and childless – without purpose in the Greek scheme of society. While married, on the other hand, she could not refuse to gratify her husband.

Hippolytus (428)

3. *Hippolytus delivers this diatribe against women after learning of Phaedra's desire for him.*

This makes clear how great an evil a woman is: 627
after begetting her and bringing her up, her father pays
a dowry to move her out, as if to gain relief from an evil;
while a man who takes the maddening creature in   630
is happy to pay for fine ornaments to deck her
foul image, and labors for her gowns;
poor wretch, he wipes out the fortunes of his house.
He has no choice: he keeps up a nasty marriage
by enjoying his in-laws if he's married well;   635
or, if his wife is good while his father-in-law is worthless,
then he lets the good outweigh the bad.
It's easiest if his wife's a nobody, a useless,
simple-minded woman who sits at home.
I hate a clever woman: I don't want one in my house   640
who thinks more thoughts than a woman should.
For Aphrodite brings more evil deeds to birth
in clever women; but one who is incapable
because her mind is small is safe from foolishness.

Suppliant Maidens (*c.* 420)

The action of the play follows the defeat of the seven insurgents at the gates of Thebes and the accession of Creon to power in that city – the same event that precipitated the crisis of the Antigone.

4. *Adrastus, King of Argus, had allied himself with the seven; and now, in his defeat, has come to Theseus for help. He receives the following reply, in which Theseus chides him for not having been content with his lot.*

The passage invites comparison to the "Ode to Man" in Sophocles' Antigone *(fr. 1) and to Aeschylus'* Prometheus, *where progress is also attributed to a god (frs. 1–3).*

I have struggled with others in verbal contests on this   195

point: some have said that there is more
bad in mortal life than there is good;
but I hold the opposite view to that:
there is more good in mortal life than evil.
If this were otherwise, we would not be here on earth.   200
Praise to the god who set us to live apart
from everything chaotic and bestial,
by first of all putting intelligence in us, and then by giving us
a messenger, language, for knowing words,
and then the care of crops, and, to nourish them,   205
raindrops from heaven to feed what comes from earth
and to water her womb. After these he gave us protection
against winter and shelter from god's heat,
and travel by ship, so that we would have
trade with one another for what is missing in the land.   210
And as for what we don't know clearly, what's obscure,
there are prophets to look at fire and the writing pads
of livers, and to tell the future from birds.[53]
Are we not spoiled, then, if this is not enough for us,
since the god gives us such means of livelihood?   215
But our minds keep striving to be stronger
than the god; with haughtiness in our hearts
we think we are wiser than deities.

5. *Later in the speech Theseus delivers this comment on social class; as the
opinion has nothing to do with Theseus' argument, it must have been
of independent interest to Euripides:*

There are three classes of citizens: some are rich
and useless, always with a passion for more;
others, the have-nots, lack means of livelihood   240
(dangerous people, they feed their envy for a larger share
and send off wicked barbs at those who have enough,
deceived by the tongues of evil leaders);
of the three parts, the one in the middle saves the city
and preserves whatever order the city has.   245

[53] These are the three main forms of divination. See also the passages from the
Iphigenia in Tauris and *Helen,* frs. 9–11.

6. *Soon after this speech, a herald arrives from Creon in Thebes, and Theseus engages him in a debate over the merits of tyranny and democracy.*

In earlier Greek, tyrannos *had not carried the connotation of lawlessness, but at this time the word is coming to mean an illegitimate and lawless ruler. This debate lies in the middle of that semantic change: the herald uses the word in the traditional sense, while Theseus speaks in a more modern vein. In mythology he was the legitimate and lawful king of Athens, but here in Euripides' play he speaks for democratic Athens. For more information on Athenian democracy, see Introduction.*

Herald: Who is tyrant of this land? Creon has control of the land
    of Cadmus,
    now that Eteocles is dead at the seven gates,   400
    killed by the hand of his brother Polyneices.
    To whom should I deliver his message?

Theseus: First, you began your speech falsely, stranger,
    asking for a tyrant here. There is no rule
    of one man here: it is a free city.   405
    The people (*dēmos*) are lord here, taking turns
    in annual succession, not giving too much
    to the rich. Even a poor man has a fair share (*ison*).

Herald: You've given me a great advantage in this game:
    the city from which I come   410
    is controlled by one man, rather than a mob;
    there is no one who puffs up my city with speeches
    and turns it this way and that for his private gain,
    no one who gives it immediate gratification and pleasure
    but damages it in the long run, and then hides his mistakes   415
    behind fresh slanders, and so slips away from justice.
    How would the people rightly be able to set the city straight
    when they cannot even straighten out the speechmaking?
    For time is a better teacher than haste,
    but a poor man who works the soil,   420
    even if he's no fool, is still too busy
    to be able to look after public affairs.
    It really plagues the better sort of people
    when a bad man is honored because, by his tongue,
    he has a hold on the people, though he was nothing before.   425

Theseus: You're a clever herald; really, your speech is a work of art.
Since, however, you have turned this into a contest,
listen to me: you began this exchange of speeches.
Nothing means more evil to a city than a tyrant.
First of all, there will be no public laws   430
but one man will have control by owning the law,
himself for himself, and this will not be fair (*ison*).
When the laws are written down, then he who is weak
and he who is rich have equal justice:
the weaker ones may speak as ill of the fortunate   435
as they hear of themselves, and a lesser man
can overcome a great one, if he has justice on his side.
This is freedom, to ask "Who has a good proposal
he wishes to introduce for public discussion?"
And one who responds gains fame, while one who wishes   440
not to is silent. What could be fairer than that in a city?
And besides, when the people govern a country,
they rejoice in the young citizens who are rising to power,
whereas a man who is king thinks them his enemy
and kills the best of them and any he finds   445
to be intelligent, because he fears for his power.
How then could a city continue to be strong
when someone plucks off the young men
as if he were harvesting corn in a spring meadow?
Why should one acquire wealth and livelihood   450
for his children, if the struggle is only to enrich the tyrant further?
Why keep his young daughters virtuously at home,
to be the sweet delights of tyrants, when they please,
and to bring grief to those who prepared them –
I'd rather die than have my daughters wed by violence.   455
So there's my volley in return for yours.

Heracles

7. *Heracles has killed his children in a fit of madness. Theseus attempts to
comfort him by appealing to the example of the gods (cf.* Hippolytus, *451
ff.).*

No mortal is unaffected by changes of fortune,
and no god either, if the poets sing true.   1315

Don't they come together in each other's beds,
which no law permits? Don't they defile with chains
their fathers for the sake of tyrannical power? And yet they dwell
in Olympus as they continue in their course of sin.
So now what do you have to say, if you who are born a mortal   1320
find your fortune especially hard to bear, when the gods do not?

8. *Heracles replies.*

I don't believe the gods enjoy a marriage bed
that is forbidden by *themis* or bind one another with chains.
I have never accepted that, and will never be persuaded,
not even that one was born to lord it over another.
For a god, if he really is a god, needs none of that;   1345
but these stories the poets tell are dreadful.

Iphigenia in Tauris (412?)

9. *Orestes complains of oracles (cf. Helen 744–757):*[54]

Even the gods who are said to be wise   570
are no less deceitful than winged dreams.
There is great confusion in divine and human
matters alike. This is one painful[55] thing –
for a man with his wits about him to believe
an oracle and be destroyed (as those who knew predicted).   575

10. *Iphigenia offers herself in Orestes' place.*

But of course when a man dies it is a grievous loss   1005
to the house, while the loss of a woman is painless.

Helen (412)

11. *The messenger speaks these lines to Menelaus on learning that the Helen for whom they had fought the Trojan war was a mere phantom, a cloud. The speech is not necessary to the play; probably Euripides*

[54] Both *Iphigenia in Tauris* and *Helen* were probably produced not long after the Athenian forces at Syracuse were lost owing to a delay caused by belief in divination; cf. Thucydides 6.18 (passage **6** below).
[55] We translate the ms. reading, though the text is often thought to be corrupt.

meant to remind the Athenians of the danger of relying on divination (cf. 9).

Now I see what prophecy is,
how weak it is and full of lies.   745
There's nothing sound in the sacred flames
or the cries of birds; only a fool
would think that birds give help to mortals.
Calchas[56] never spoke or gave a sign
to the army, as he watched, that they were dying for the sake of
   a cloud,   750
and neither did Helenus; but the city was seized in vain.
You may say, "That's because of the will of the god";
but then why take prophecy at all? To the gods we should
make sacrifices and pray for the best. But let prophecy go;
it was never meant as more than bait for the traps of life.   755
No one got rich wasting his time with sacred flames.
The best prophet is intelligence (*gnōmē*) and good judgment
   (*euboulia*).

Ion (409?)

12. *Ion, a young servant of Apollo, has heard that Apollo seduced a young
   virgin and then abandoned her and the child. Ion is shown reacting
   strongly to the accusation, though it will turn out later to be largely
   false:*

Apollo should have a warning
from me: what's happening to him? Take virgins by violence
and give them up? Secretly beget children
and pay no attention when they die? Don't do that:
since you are powerful, strive for virtue. When anyone who is
   mortal   440
is by nature wicked, he is punished by the gods;
so how could it be just for you to write the laws
for us mortals, and then incur a charge of lawlessness yourselves?
If – it will never happen, but let's suppose –

---

[56] Calchas was the Greek prophet during the Trojan War. Helenus, a Trojan prince
captured by the Greeks, was also a prophet.

you paid us what justice demands for raping women,   445
you and Poseidon and Zeus who rules heaven,
then you'd empty the treasuries of your temples, paying for injustice.
For when you chase pleasures without a thought for the future,
you commit injustice. It will no longer be just to call men bad
if we are only following the "good" examples set by gods;   450
only those who teach such things[57] are rightly called bad.

Orestes (408)

13. *Tyndareus, father of Helen and Clytemnestra, indicts Orestes for his
decision to kill Clytemnestra. Exile, he goes on to say, would have been
the traditional penalty for what Clytemnestra had done.*

If what is good, or not good, were obvious to everyone,
what man would have less understanding than this one?
He paid no attention to justice and did not proceed
according to the common law of the Greeks (*koinos nomos*).   495

14. *Our chief interest in Orestes' reply is in its contrast between law and
justice.*

As for the crimes for which you say I should be stoned,
my answer is that I benefitted all of Greece,   565
for if women grew so bold as this –
to kill their men and seek refuge
with their children, looking for the pity due their breasts –
then it will be nothing for them to betray their husbands
for any grievance that may arise. I did a terrible thing,   570
as you allege, when I set aside this law;
but it was with justice that I slew my mother in hatred...

The Phoenician Women

15. *The two sons of Oedipus, Eteocles and Polyneices, have agreed to share
the rule of Thebes by being king in alternate years. As the elder, Eteocles
took his turn first; but when the year ended he was unwilling to
surrender power to his brother. Here he tells his mother Jocasta why*

---

[57] "Those who teach such things": Ion probably means the poets; cf. Xenophanes,
fr. 4.

he will not give up any power to his brother Polyneices. Her advice to
share power, he implies, is wise counsel, but not for him.

If the same thing were by nature good and wise at once for all
there'd be nothing in doubt for humans to fight over;   500
but as things are, nothing is even (*homoion*) or fair (*ison*) among
     mortals,
except in name. But this name is not the actual thing.

16. *Jocasta replies.*

Why do you follow the worst of deities, my son –
ambition? Don't do it; she is an unjust god.
Many happy homes and cities have had her in –
and out – to the destruction of those who experience her.
You're mad to follow her. You'd do better, child, to honor   535
Fairness,[58] which always holds friends together
with friends, binds city to city and allies to allies.
Fairness is by nature the norm (*nomimon*[59]) for human beings
but if one side has too much, the loser always
goes to war, and that brings on the days of hate.   540
For it is fairness that gave us weights and measures,
and counted out numbers in their order.
And in fairness the blind eye of night
and the light of the sun proceed in their yearly cycle:
neither is conquered, so neither bears a grudge.   545
If the sun and night serve mortal needs,
will you not allow fairness in your house,
and give Polyneices his share? Where then is justice?
Why do you value tyrannical power, that unjust happiness,
excessively, and think it a great thing?   550
Is admiration of value to you? It would be empty then.
Do you want to have many things in your house
at the cost of many pains? What is "more"? Merely a word.
Since enough suffices, at least for the wise,

---

[58] "Fairness": *isotēs*, which could be translated "equality," but means a fair, rather
than an exactly equal, division.
[59] Here we follow the ms. reading. Some editors prefer the conjecture *monimon*,
which gives the meaning: "fairness naturally brings stability to humans."

we mortals do not acquire wealth of our own –   555
we merely take care of the gods' possessions,
which they take back again whenever they have need.
Wealth does not last: it is ours for a day.

Fragments from lost plays

17. *Alexander (N 53)*

Our speech is a waste of words
if we praise high birth in humans.
For long ago when we first came to be
the earth that gave birth to mortals decided
to rear us all to have the same appearance.   5
We are nothing special:
the well-born and ill-born are one race,
but time and *nomos* brought about this haughtiness.
To be intelligent is to be well-born, but good sense
is a gift of the god, not of wealth.   10

18. *Antigone (N 172)*

To rule without law, to be a tyrant, is neither reasonable (*eikos*)
nor right. Even the wish is foolishness
when a man wants to have sole power over his equals.

19. *Antiope (N 189)*

For any issue you could set up a contest (*agōn*)
of double speeches (*dissoi logoi*), if you want to be a clever speaker.

20. *Diktus (N 334)*

There is one common law (*nomos*) for humans and gods
and for all animals, a view I plainly maintain:
that parents love their children.
In all other matters we follow separate laws.

21. *Melanippe (N 508)*

Do you think injustices spring up on wings
to the gods? That someone writes them down
on Zeus's tablets? That Zeus looks at this
and gives justice to mortals? All of heaven
would not be large enough for Zeus to write   5
the sins of men; he could not take note
and punish everyone. But justice
is right here near us, if you care to look.

22. *Melanippe* [60]

The reproaches men throw at women are groundless,
their insults like the twang of an empty bowstring.
Women are better than men, and I'll prove it.

[The next five lines are fragmentary.]

They manage their households and keep the imported goods   5
safe inside their houses. And a house without a woman
is a mess and does not prosper.
In religion (which I consider of the first importance)
we have the largest role, for it is women
who explain the intention of Apollo in his oracles;   10
and at the holy site of Dodona
by the sacred oak the female race conveys
the intentions of Zeus to those who come from Greece to ask. [61]
The holy rituals due the fates and nameless goddesses
are not righteous if they are set up for men to do,   15
but they all flourish among women.
That's how just it is for women to have a role in
religion. How then could it be right
for the race of women to be insulted? Won't there be
an end to men's groundless reproaches – these men   20

---

[60] We use the text of D. L. Page (see Bibliographical Note, § B. 2).
[61] The oracles at Delphi and Dodona were the most important in Greece. Women
delivered the messages at both sites, though, in fact, interpretation was left to
male prophets.

who are too ready to think all women should be blamed alike
if they find one who is bad? My speech will make this distinction:
nothing is worse than a bad woman;
but nothing at all is better by nature
than a good woman. Their natures are different. . .   25

23. *Peliades (N 608)*

The most amazing thing in human life
is tyranny – you won't find anything more miserable.
You have to ruin and kill your friends,
for you will live in the greatest fear if you do not.

Other tragic fragments

The following fragments are attributed to minor tragedians, or are anonymous tragic fragments plausibly assigned to the period. Authors who are not native Athenians probably wrote their tragedies for production in Athens.

1. *Thespis*[62] *(TGF 1 F 3)*

You see that Zeus is first among the gods in this respect,
that he does not lie or boast or laugh foolishly.
Only he does not know pleasure.

2. *Aristarchus of Tegea,*[63] Tantalus *(TGF 14 F 1b)*

About these matters [the gods] it's all the same to speak well or
    badly,
to inquire or to remain ignorant.
For the wise (*sophoi*) know no more about them than the ignorant,
and if one man speaks about them better than another,
his superiority is only in his ability to speak.

3. *Ion of Chios,*[64] Alcmene *(TGF 19 F 5a)*

All things are born ignorant at first
and are taught by experience.

---

[62] Reportedly the first victor in the competition of tragedies in Athens (535).
[63] Second half of the fifth century.
[64] Ion came to Athens around 460, remained active for several decades, and is the main figure in Plato's *Ion*.

4. *Ion of Chios,* Alcmene *(TGF 19 F 55)*

The maxim "know thyself" is not much to say,
but only Zeus among the gods knows how to do it.

5. *Iophon,*[65] Bacchae *(TGF 22 F 2)*

Being a woman I know this,
that the more one seeks to know matters divine,
the less one knows.

6. *Agathon*[66] *(TGF 39 F 5)*

This thing only is beyond the power of god:
to make it so that what has been done never happened.

7. *Agathon*[67] *(TGF 39 F 9)*

One might say that this too is likely (*eikos*):
that things that are not likely often happen to mortals.

8. *Antiphon*[68] *(TGF 55 F 4)*

We conquer by art (*technē*) things that defeat us by nature (*phusis*).

Unknown authorship

9.[69] *(TGF F 26)*

For you will see this other law for mortals
if you discriminate well. Nothing is proper or shameful
in every way, but the occasion (*kairos*) takes the same things
and makes them shameful or changes them into something proper.

---

[65] Son of the tragedian Sophocles, he lived in the last third of the fifth century.
[66] A late fifth-century tragedian, Agathon is one of the main characters of Plato's
Symposium. The fragment is quoted in Aristotle's *Nicomachean Ethics* 6.2.
[67] Quoted in Aristotle's *Rhetoric* 2.24.
[68] Not the same as the sophist/orator, this Antiphon was a tragic poet during the
rule of Dionysius, tyrant of Syracuse *c.* 400–367.
[69] This fragment is quoted in the *Dissoi Logoi* 2.19.

10.[70] *(TGF F 304)*

You are a slave by nature and have no share of reason.

11. *(TGF F 326)*

By nature slaves have no share of the laws.

---

[70] This and the next fragment are undated and may belong to a later period.

PART III

HISTORY AND FOLKLORE

Herodotus

Herodotus was born in Halicarnassus in Asia Minor about 485, while the city was ruled through tyrants by the Persian empire. His life spanned the period between the Persian and the Peloponnesian Wars. At an early age he moved to Samos for fear of the tyrant Lygdamis. Herodotus spent many years traveling through Greece and other lands, and settled in Thurii in southern Italy when the colony was established there in 443. He evidently composed his History *during the third quarter of the fifth century. Part of it was presented orally in Athens and elsewhere, and the final version was written around 430 425. Its observations on politics and related themes represent intellectual movements of his lifetime.*

1. On happiness (1.30.2–34.1)

The Athenian wise man Solon visited the magnificent court of Croesus, King of the Lydians in Sardis. After showing off his treasures, Croesus asked:

"Athenian visitor, we have heard much about you and your travels in search of wisdom, and about how you have traveled widely as an observer and for the love of knowledge. So now I am longing to ask you: of all those you have seen, who is the happiest?" He asked this in the hope that he would be the happiest of human beings, but Solon was no flatterer and he told the truth:

"Tellus the Athenian, O King."

Astonished by this answer, Croesus asked severely, "Why do you judge Tellus the happiest?"

77

He answered, "Tellus belonged to a city that was well-off; he had sons who were fine and good, and saw children born to all of them, and they all survived him. Besides that, he was well-off his whole life by our standards, and he came to a glorious end. During a battle between the Athenians and their neighbors in Eleusis, he fought in support of the Athenians, turned the enemy around, and died nobly; the Athenians buried him where he fell at public expense and gave him great honor."

[31] As Solon was leading Croesus on, telling him many happy facts about Tellus, Croesus asked who was the second happiest person he had seen, thinking that surely he would be given second prize.

But Solon said: "Cleobis and Biton. For these men of Argos had a sufficient livelihood; they had great physical strength besides, and enjoyed equal success in athletic contests. Most importantly, this tale is told about them: during a festival of the Argives for Hera it was absolutely necessary that their mother be driven to the temple in an oxcart, but the oxen did not come in from the field in time. So under pressure of time the two young men harnessed themselves to the yoke to pull the cart. Their mother got in the cart and they transported her a distance of forty-five stades to the temple [more than five miles]. After they had done this in full view of the crowd, they ended their lives in the best possible way, and the god showed in their case that it is better for a human being to die than to live. While the Argive men came up to congratulate them on their strength, the women praised their mother for giving birth to such fine boys. Delighted by what they had done and by the high praise, she stood in front of the statue and prayed for her sons Cleobis and Biton; because they had given her great honor, she asked the goddess to grant them the best fate that can come to a human being. After she had prayed, and after they had made the sacrifices and enjoyed the feast, the young men went to sleep in the temple and never rose again; that was how they ended their lives. The Argives made statues of them and set them up in Delphi, because they held them to be the best of men."

[32] So Solon gave them the second prize for happiness, but Croesus was annoyed: "Athenian visitor," he said, "has our own happiness dwindled to nothing? Is that why you think we are not worth as much as these private citizens?"

Solon answered: "Croesus, when you ask me about human affairs I know that every god is liable to be envious and likes to cause pain. Over many years a man sees and suffers many things that he would wish otherwise. I put a human life at seventy years, and those seventy years have 25,200 days not counting the months that are added so that the seasons will come around when they should. If you want to add these months – one month every second year – you must increase the total by thirty-five months over the seventy years, and the days in those months add up to 1,050. This yields a total of 26,250 days, and none of these days will bring you anything at all like any other. So in this way, Croesus, a human life is all chance.

"I can see that you are very rich and king over many people, but I will not answer your question until I learn that you have ended your life well. A very rich man is no happier than one who lives from day to day unless he meets the good fortune of ending his life while everything is still well for him. Many very rich men are unhappy, and many of those with moderate means enjoy good fortune. A very rich man, if he is unhappy, is better off than a fortunate one in only two ways, while a fortunate man is better off than a rich unhappy man in many ways. A rich man is better able to satisfy his desires and to bear up if a great disaster (*atē*) falls upon him; but the other is better off in all the following ways: though not as able as the first to bear the weight of desire or disaster, his good fortune wards off these things; he is healthy and fit and untouched by troubles, and he has good looks and good sons. If besides all this he should end his life well, then this is the man you are asking about, the one who deserves to be called happy. But until he dies, hold back and do not call him happy yet, but only fortunate.

"As things are, no human being can possibly have all these things together, just as no country provides everything it needs, but a country has some things and lacks others. The best country, however, is the one that has the most. So it is with a human life: no one is self-sufficient; everyone has some things and lacks others. But if anyone has most of these things to the end and also ends his life beautifully, then in my opinion, O king, using the word 'happy' for him is justified. In every such matter, you must look to see how it comes out in the end. For the god gives many people a foretaste of happiness and then destroys them root and branch."[71]

[71] This advice was much discussed by later thinkers; see, e.g., Aristotle, *Nicomachean Ethics* I.10.

[33] These words were not very pleasing to Croesus, who sent Solon away without taking his speech seriously. For Croesus thought Solon was very naive to dismiss the good things he had at hand, and to tell him to watch everything to see how it would end. [34] But after Solon had left, great *nemesis* from the god came upon Croesus, apparently because he had thought himself the happiest of men.

2. Early government and justice (1.96–100)

Deioces was the legendary first king of the Medes, a tribe in what is now Iran. He may have been the historical figure who appears in Assyrian records as a local chief. In any event, this tale of his rise to power probably reflects fifth-century Greek ideas about the origins of social order. Herodotus' account begins towards the end of the old Assyrian Empire, in the seventh century.

The various nations on the continent [of Asia] were now independent, but they once more became subject to tyranny in the following way. There was a wise man (*sophos*) among the Medes by the name of Deioces, son of Phraortes, who longed to be a tyrant. The Medes were living in scattered villages, and Deioces proceeded as follows: he was already prominent in his own village, but he now made it a point to practice justice (*dikaiosunē*) even more zealously. He did this during a period of considerable lawlessness throughout the country, for he understood the inevitable conflict between right and wrong. When the Medes from his own village observed his qualities, they regularly chose him to be their judge. Ever mindful of his goal of ruling, Deioces acted with fairness and justice, thereby winning considerable praise from his fellow villagers. As a result, people in other villages began to hear that Deioces was the only man who would judge cases fairly (*kata to orthon*); and since at that time they were being subjected to many unjust judgments, as soon as they heard this, they too gladly began to come to Deioces to have their cases heard. In the end they would turn to no one else.

[97] When the number of such litigants grew larger, as people learned of the fairness and objectivity of his settlements, Deioces

realized that the entire process was now in his hands. He declared himself unwilling any longer to sit where he formerly sat giving judgments and said he would no longer settle cases; for it did him no good to neglect his own affairs in order to spend all day settling his neighbors' disputes. With this there arose throughout the villages considerably more pillaging and lawlessness than there had been before, and so the Medes then held a meeting to discuss the situation. (I think most of the talking was done by Deioces' friends.) "We are unable to live in this country in its present condition, so let us appoint one of us king. Then the country will be well governed and we can return to our work and not be driven from our homes by lawlessness." With these arguments they were persuaded to establish kingship. [98] Then they had to decide whom to appoint as king, and since Deioces was praised by everyone, they agreed that he should be their king. He ordered them to build him a palace worthy of a king and to protect him with a force of guards.

[*Herodotus then tells how Deioces has the Medes build him the fortified city of Ecbatana.*]

[99] When all this had been built, Deioces was the first to establish royal protocol: no one was allowed into the presence of the king, but all business was conducted through messengers. The king was not to be seen by anyone, nor was it allowed for anyone to laugh or spit in his presence. In this way he exalted his own person, in order that his colleagues, who were brought up with him and were as good as he in birth and character, would not see him, be irritated, and begin plotting against him. If they did not see him, he hoped, they would think him different from themselves. [100] Once he had established this protocol and solidified his power, he became a severe guardian of justice. People had to put their cases in writing and have them sent in to him; then he made his decisions and sent them back. In addition to this procedure for legal disputes, he established others: if he heard of anyone assaulting someone, he would send for him and impose on him a punishment appropriate to the crime, and he had spies and observers throughout the extent of his kingdom.

3. Nomos *and ethics. Cambyses, king of Persia 530–522, conquered Egypt and there violated tombs and mocked the religious rituals that were sacred (3.38).*

I have no doubt that Cambyses was totally insane. Otherwise he would never have ventured to ridicule rites that are sacred and established by custom (*nomos*). If you should ask all people to select the best from among all the various conventional practices, each group would choose their own, even after examining them all; for they would consider their own practices to be by far the best. So it makes no sense for anyone but a madman to ridicule such things. Everyone thinks this way about customs, as I can prove by many weighty arguments. Take, for example, the following:

During his reign, Darius called in some Greeks who were in Persia, and asked them how much money would make them willing to eat the dead bodies of their fathers; and they said they would not do this for anything. After that, Darius called in some people from India called Callatians, who do eat their parents. (The Greeks were there, and understood what they said through an interpreter.) Then Darius asked the Callatians what sum of money they would take to burn their fathers on a pyre after their death;[72] the Callatians gave a great shriek and told him not to speak sacrilege. So we see that these things are set by custom; and Pindar, in my opinion, was right when he called custom "king of all."[73]

4. *The debate on constitutions (3.80–82)*

After deposing a government of priests, who had themselves deposed King Cambyses, a group of Persian aristocrats meet to discuss the form their new government should take. Although the conversation is supposed to have taken place in Persia in the late sixth century, the ideas are Greek and from the mid-fifth century and the discussions of democracy refer to several elements (selection by lot, the examination of magistrates) that were characteristically Athenian (see Introduction). Cf. the similar anachronistic discussions of democracy in Euripides'. Suppliant Maidens (fr. 6).

[72] This was the Greek custom.
[73] Pindar, fr. 1.

After the shouting was over, five days later, those who had rebelled against the priests met to discuss the whole business. Some Greeks don't believe that these speeches were made at that meeting, but they certainly were.

Otanes asked them to turn over the affairs of state to all the Persians, on the basis of this argument:

"I no longer agree to making one of us the single ruler,[74] for rule by one man is neither pleasant nor good. You know how far Cambyses' arrogance (*hubris*) carried him, and you felt your share of the arrogance of the Priests. How could this ever be an orderly system, since it allows a ruler to do whatever he wants without any public examination?[75] Once he arrives at that position of power, even the best of men will find himself falling away from the former pattern of his thoughts: he will acquire arrogance from the many goods he enjoys, and envy of course is fundamental to human nature. These two – arrogance and envy – will lead to every sort of wickedness; for a man who is full of arrogance will commit many atrocities, and envy will lead him to commit many others. Of course, a tyrant ought not to be envious, since he has every good thing; but he naturally treats his fellow citizens as if the opposite were true: he will envy the best of them their life itself, simply for their survival; and he will take delight in the most wicked of his citizens. Besides, he will be very good indeed at listening to slander. He will be totally inconsistent: if you are moderate in your admiration for him, he will be angry that you do not always flatter him; but if you always flatter, he will be angry because you are a toady. The worst remains to be told, however: he disrupts our ancestral laws and customs, he takes women by force, and he kills men without trial.

"In favor of rule by the majority (*to plēthos*), I will make two points: first, it has the finest of all names: *isonomia* – equality in law – and, second, it does none of those things that single rulers do. Positions of power are given by lot, and are held subject to a

---

[74] The Greek is *monarchos* but we have not translated it "monarch" because this in English is usually taken to mean "hereditary monarch," which would have been *basileus* (see Glossary). The general form of government in question includes all types of rule by one man, monarchy, tyranny, dictatorship, etc.

[75] A reference to the *euthunai* (see Glossary), which, along with the selection of officials by lot and public decision-making, was one of the hallmarks of Athenian democracy.

public examination. All issues are brought to the public [for deliberation]. Therefore I propose we give up rule by one man and lift up the majority to power; for all things belong to the many."

[81] After Otanes made that proposal, Megabyxos asked them to turn things over to an oligarchy, on the basis of this argument:

"Allow me to second everything Otanes has said in favor of putting an end to tyranny. But when he told us to give power to the majority, his proposal was far from the best. For nothing is stupider or more arrogant than a useless mob. To escape the arrogance of a tyrant and then fall into the undisciplined arrogance of the people (*dēmos*) – that would be completely intolerable. When a tyrant takes action, at least he knows what it is that he does, but the people have no knowledge of anything. How could they, when they have not been taught, and do not know what is fine or appropriate, when they rush into things mindlessly, as if they were falling into a river in spate? Leave democracy to those who plan evil against Persia, but let us select a group of the best men and give them power. We ourselves will be included, and it is reasonable to expect that the best policy should come from the best men."

When Megabyxos had made his proposal, the third man, Darius, argued his case as follows:

[82] "I think that what Megabyxos said about the majority is quite right, but what he said about oligarchy is not. Of the three forms of government before us, each of them – democracy, oligarchy, and monarchy – is best in theory; but I claim that the last is far superior. For nothing could turn out to be better than one man, if he is the best. Because his judgment will be as good as his character, he will be a blameless guardian of the people, and he, more than anyone, will be able to keep secret his plans against those who are troublemakers.

"In an oligarchy, with many people striving for excellence in public affairs, fierce personal feuds tend to develop. Each man wants to be supreme, and wants his proposals to win out, and so they work up to great feuds with each other, from which a division into factions (*stasis*) can develop. From factions comes bloodshed; and the way out of bloodshed is the rule of one. This makes it quite clear how much the rule of one is best.

"If the people rule, it is impossible to prevent wrongdoing from taking place, but in a democracy wrongdoing does not lead to public feuds among the wrongdoers; instead, they form strong friendships and huddle together in order to control public affairs. This sort of thing continues until someone stands forth on behalf of the people and puts a stop to the wrongdoers. This wins him the admiration of the people; and such admiration, of course, makes him sole ruler. So this also shows that the rule of one man is dominant.

"To put all of this in one word: where did our liberty come from? Who gave it to us? Was it the people? An oligarchy? Or the rule of one man?[76] I propose, therefore, that since we were set free by one man we preserve that form of government, and, moreover, that we not give up our ancestral laws, since they are in good condition, and nothing else would be an improvement."

[After the debate, the Persians vote for the third and then choose Darius as their first king.]

---

[76] Cyrus the Great liberated the Persians from the overlordship of the Medes and founded the Achaemenid dynasty in 549.

Thucydides

Of the life of Thucydides we know little beyond what he tells us. We believe he was born around 460–455, and we know that he was an elected general in 424. During that year he was in charge of forces that were unable to save Amphipolis from the Spartans. Democratic Athens frequently brought criminal charges against unsuccessful generals, so Thucydides went into a twenty-year exile during which he visited the Peloponnesus (including Sparta) and probably also traveled to Syracuse. Most of the time he probably spent in Thrace, where his family had longstanding connections. He returned to Athens after the war but apparently did not live to finish the History.

His education must have included some study with the sophists who were beginning to be popular in Athens during his youth. His style of writing, however, is uniquely his own, and he must be counted as one of the most original prose stylists of the Greek or any language.

The first phase of the Peloponnesian War began in 431 and lasted ten years. Although the Athenians met some reverses, they were victorious on the whole. Their greatest success in this period was the capture in 425 of a band of 120 Spartan citizen soldiers on a small island called Sphacteria, near Pylos. So much did the Spartans value their citizens that they were willing to sue for peace on virtually any terms to get their men back. Athens, however, was under the aggressive influence of Cleon and refused to make peace, so that this period of the war continued until after Cleon's death. Although favorable to Athenian interests, the Peace of Nicias that ensued (421–414) was an uneasy affair, as it did not resolve the fundamental problems between Athens and Sparta, and the fighting never really stopped. In 415, Alcibiades revived an old plan

*to expand Athenian influence in the western Mediterranean by sending
an expedition to make conquests in Sicily. Then, in 413, Syracuse defeated
the Athenian expedition with the help of the Spartan general Gylippus,
utterly destroying the Athenian and allied armies and navies. In 412,
when news of this disaster got about, many Athenian allies rebelled, and
in 411 an oligarchic party (the Four Hundred) seized power in Athens,
while a large Athenian force on Samos remained stubbornly democratic.
Thucydides' account breaks off abruptly after his description of the chaotic
maneuvering of various parties in Athens and on Samos.*

The history of the war was picked up by Xenophon in his Hellenica.
*Its elements are quickly told: democracy was soon restored in Athens, and
Athens made a valiant effort to restore enough of the empire to stay
afloat. The Athenians still had good hopes of defense until the destruction
of their fleet at Aegospotami in 405. After this, Athens was besieged by
Sparta and forced to surrender unconditionally in 404. The victorious
Spartans tore down the long walls between Athens and Piraeus that had
secured Athenian access to the sea, thus effectively disabling Athens from
waging further war. Meanwhile, the Spartans installed an oligarchical
regime favorable to themselves, the group known later as the "Thirty
Tyrants." These are the authorities Socrates refused to serve, as he tells
us in the* Apology *of Plato. Their rule lasted less than a year, and in
403 democracy was restored in Athens.*

1. Aims and methods

1a. Thucydides' preface (1.1)

Thucydides,[77] an Athenian, wrote up the war of the Peloponnesians
and the Athenians as they fought against each other. He began to
write as soon as the war was afoot, with the expectation that it
would turn out to be a great one and that, more than all earlier
wars, this one would deserve to be recorded. He made this predic-
tion because both sides were at their peak in every sort of preparation for war, and also because he saw the rest of the Greek
world taking one side or the other, some right away, others planning
to do so.

This was certainly the greatest upheaval there had ever been
among the Greeks. It also reached many foreigners – indeed, one

---

[77] Thucydides usually refers to himself in the third person.

might say that it affected most people everywhere. Because of the great passage of time it is impossible to discover clearly what happened long ago or even just before these events; still, I have looked into the evidence as far as can be done, and I am confident that nothing great happened in or out of war before this.

1b. *Thucydides' methods (1.20.3–22)*

The search for truth strains the patience of most people, who would rather believe the first things that come to hand. [21] But if the evidence cited leads a reader to think that things were mostly as I have described them, he would not go wrong, as he would if he believed what the poets have sung about them, which they have much embellished, or what the prose-writers have strung together, which aims more to delight the ear than to be true. Their accounts cannot be tested, you see, and many are not credible, as they have achieved the status of myth over time. But the reader should believe that I have investigated these matters adequately, considering their antiquity, using the best evidence available. . .

[22] What particular people said in their speeches (*logoi*), either just before or during the war, was hard to recall exactly, whether they were speeches I heard myself or those that were reported to me at second hand. I have made each speaker say what I thought the situation demanded, keeping as near as possible to the general sense of what was actually said.

And as for the real action (*erga*) of the war, I did not think it right to set down either what I heard from people I happened to meet or what I merely believed to be true. Even for events at which I was present myself, I tracked down detailed information from other sources as far as I could. It was hard work to find out what happened, because those who were present at each event gave different reports, depending on which side they favored and how well they remembered.

This history may not be the most delightful to hear, since there is no mythology in it. But those who want to look into the truth of what was done in the past – which, given the human condition, will recur in the future, either in the same fashion or nearly so – those readers will find this *History* valuable enough, as this was composed to be a lasting possession and not to be heard for a prize at the moment of a contest.

2. On the political background of the war

2a. Thucydides' explanation for the war (1.23.4–6)

All these hardships came upon them during this war, which began when the Athenians and Peloponnesians broke the Thirty Years' Peace that had been agreed between them after the conquest of Euboca. I will first write down an account of the disputes that explain their breaking the Peace, so that no one will ever wonder from what ground so great a war could arise among the Greeks. I believe, however, that the truest reason for the quarrel, though least evident in what was said at the time, was the growth of Athenian power, which put fear into the Spartans and so compelled them into war, while the explanations both sides gave in public for breaking the Peace and starting the war are as follows.[78]

2b. The Corinthian view of Athens on the eve of the war, addressed to the Spartans (from the debate at Sparta) (1.70)

We don't think you have thought through what sort of people these Athenians are: your struggle will be with people totally different from yourselves. They love innovation, and are quick to invent a plan and then to carry it out in action, while you are good only for keeping things as they are, and you never invent anything or even go as far as necessary in action. Moreover, they are bold beyond their power, take thoughtless risks, and still hope for the best in danger; whereas your actions always fall short of your power, you distrust even what you know in your minds to be certain, and you never think you will be delivered from danger. Above all, they never hesitate; you are always delaying; they are never at home, and you are the worst homebodies, because they

---

[78] The immediate causes that were alleged were three Athenian actions: its siege of Potidaea, its decision to help defend the island of Corcyra against Corinth, and its decree restricting trade with Megara. All three places were Dorian, and were linked to the Peloponnesian allies of the Spartans in other ways as well.

count on getting something by going abroad, while you fear you will lose what you have if you go out.

When they overcome their enemies, they advance the farthest; and when overcome by them, they fall back the least. And as for their bodies, they devote them utterly to the service of the city as if they were not their own, while they keep total possession of their minds when they do anything for its sake. Unless they accomplish what they have once set their minds on, they count themselves deprived of their own property. And if they do get what they went for, they think lightly of it compared to what their next action will bring, but if they happen to fail in any attempt, they turn to other hopes and make up the loss that way. You see, they alone get what they hope for as soon as they think of it, through the speed with which they execute their plans.

At this they toil, filling all the days of their lives with hard work and danger. What they have, they have no leisure to enjoy, because they are continually getting more. They do not consider any day a holiday unless they have done something that needed to be done; and they think that an idle rest is as much trouble as hard work. Thus, in a word, it is true to say that they are born never to allow themselves or anyone else a rest.

2c. *The Athenians defend their imperial policies (from the debate at Sparta) (1.75.4–77)*

No one should be blamed for looking after his own interests to fend off such great dangers. [76] You Spartans, for example, use your position of leadership in the Peloponnesus to arrange affairs in the cities there to your own advantage. If you had stayed on as leaders of the alliance against the Persians, you would have been as much hated by all as we are now, and we are sure that your leadership would have been no less painful to the allies than ours has been. You too would have been compelled to rule with a strong hand or else put yourselves in danger. We have not done anything in this that should cause surprise, and we have not deviated from normal human behavior: we simply accepted an empire that was offered us and then refused to surrender it. If we have been overcome by three of the strongest motives – ambition, fear, and our own advantage – we have not been the first to do this. It has always been established that the weaker are held down by the stronger.[79] Besides, we took this upon ourselves because we thought we were worthy of it, and you thought so too, until now that you are reckoning up your own advantage and appealing to justice – which no one has ever preferred to force, if he had a chance to achieve something by that and gain an advantage.

When people follow their natural human inclination to rule over others, they deserve to be praised if they use more justice than they have to, in view of their power. And we think that if anyone else had our position, you would really see how moderate we have been; yet our very fairness has brought contempt on us instead of the praise we deserve.

[77] Although we have been at a disadvantage in lawsuits arising from treaties with our allies and have allowed them trial in our own city by impartial laws, we have nevertheless been given a reputation for litigiousness.[80] No one notices that others, who have empires in other places, and are less moderate toward their subject states than we, are never upbraided for it. Those who have the power to use force, you see, have no need at all to go to law. And yet because these men have been used to dealing with us on equal terms, if they lose anything at all which they think they should not have lost, either by sentence of our courts or by the power of our government, they are not thankful for the large amount that they retain. Instead, they complain more about their slight loss than they would if we had put law to one side and openly seized their goods at the start. For in that event, not even they could deny that the weaker must give way to the stronger. People are apparently more passionate over injustice than violence, because then they feel that someone who is their equal has taken an unfair advantage, while they accept violence from someone stronger as a matter of necessity. At least, when they suffered worse things under the rule of the Persians, they accepted them; but now they find our empire

---

[79] See the Melian dialogue 5.105 (fr. 5b) and Democritus, fr. 2: "By nature it is fitting for the stronger to rule."

[80] The text is ambiguous on a crucial point, and allows the following translation as well as the one we have given: "For because we found ourselves at a disadvantage in lawsuits against our allies, in cases controlled by inter-state agreements, and so transferred such cases to Athens where the laws are equal for all, we are supposed to be too fond of dragging people into court" – Hornblower.

hard to bear. And that was to be expected: the present is always the worst to those who are subject to the rule of others.

As for you [Spartans], if you should defeat us and reign yourselves, you would soon find a change from the love they bear you now out of fear of us, at least if you are planning the sort of behavior you showed when you were their leaders for that short time against the Persians.[81] The customs in your country are not compatible with those of others; and to make matters worse, when any one of you travels abroad, he neither follows your customs nor those of the rest of Greece.

2d. *Why most Greeks supported the Spartans (2.8)*

Neither side made small plans, and both put their whole strength into the war. This was only to be expected, for in the beginning of an enterprise everyone is most eager. Besides, there were many young men in the Peloponnesus at that time, and many in Athens, who for want of experience undertook the war quite willingly. And the rest of Greece watched in suspense as its two principal cities came into conflict. Many prophecies were told, and many sung by the priests of the oracles, both in the cities about to make war and in others. There was also an earthquake in Delos a little before this, where the earth had never been shaken before in the memory of the Greeks. This was said to be a sign of what was going to happen afterwards, and people believed that. And if anything else of this sort happened by chance, people started looking for an explanation.

Men's sympathies for the most part went with the Spartans, especially because they gave out that they would recover the Greeks' liberty. Everyone, private citizens and cities alike, endeavored in word and deed to assist them as much as they could; and everyone thought that the affair would be held back if they were not part of it. That is how angry most people were against the Athenians, some out of the desire to be set free from their empire, and others for fear of falling under it.

---

[81] "The sort of behavior you showed": see 1.94–95, 3.93 and 5.52.

3. Pericles

3a. *The funeral oration (2.35–46)*

During the first winter of the war (431/o) Athens held a public funeral for the soldiers and sailors who had lost their lives in various small actions. Pericles, who had been for some time the most effective leader in Athens, was asked to deliver the funeral oration. The most famous speech that has come down to us from antiquity, it shows how some Athenians thought of their political and cultural institutions. Thucydides reconstructs it as follows.

Most of those who have spoken before me on this occasion have praised the man who added this oration to our customs because it gives honor to those who have died in the wars; yet I would have thought it sufficient that those who have shown their mettle in action should also receive their honor in an action, as now you see they have, in this burial performed for them at public expense, so that the virtue of many does not depend on whether one person is believed to have spoken well or poorly. It is a hard matter to speak in due measure when there is no firm consensus about the truth. A hearer who is favorable and knows what was done will perhaps think that a eulogy falls short of what he wants to hear and knows to be true; while an ignorant one will find some of the praise to be exaggerated, especially if he hears of anything beyond his own talent – because that would make him envious. Hearing another man praised is bearable only so long as the hearer thinks he could himself have done what he hears. But if a speaker goes beyond that, the hearer soon becomes envious and ceases to believe. Since our ancestors have thought it good, however, I too should follow the custom and endeavor to answer to the desires and opinions of every one of you, as far as I can.

[36] I will begin with our ancestors, since it is both just and fitting that they be given the honor of remembrance at such a time. Because they have always lived in this land, they have so far always handed it down in liberty through their valor to successive generations up to now. They deserve praise; but our fathers deserve even more, for with great toil they acquired our present empire in addition to what they had received, and they delivered it in turn

to the present generation. We ourselves who are here now in the prime of life have expanded most parts of the empire; and we have furnished the city with everything it needs to be self-sufficient both in peace and in war. The acts of war by which all this was attained, the valiant deeds of arms that we and our fathers performed against foreign or Greek invaders – these I will pass over, to avoid making a long speech on a subject with which you are well acquainted. But the practices that brought us to this point, the form of government and the way of life that have made our city great – these I shall disclose before I turn to praise these men. I think these subjects are quite suitable for the occasion, and the whole gathering of citizens and guests will profit by hearing them discussed.

[37] We have a form of government that does not try to imitate the laws of our neighboring states.[82] We are more an example to others, than they to us. In name, it is called a democracy, because it is managed not for a few people, but for the majority. Still, although we have equality at law for everyone here in private disputes, we do not let our system of rotating public offices undermine our judgment of a candidate's virtue;[83] and no one is held back by poverty or because his reputation is not well known, as long as he can do good service to the city. We are free and generous not only in our public activities as citizens, but also in our daily lives: there is no suspicion in our dealings with one another, and we are not offended by our neighbor for following his own pleasure. We do not cast on anyone the censorious looks that – though they are no punishment – are nevertheless painful. We live together without taking offense on private matters; and as for public affairs, we respect the law greatly and fear to violate it, since we are obedient to those in office at any time, and also to the laws – especially to those laws that were made to help people

---

[82] The contrast is with Sparta, which is said to have borrowed its form of government from cities in Crete. On the constitutions of Athens and Sparta, see Introduction.

[83] "We do not let our system of rotating public offices undermine our judgment of a candidate's virtue": the meaning of this sentence is in doubt. Pericles is evidently defending Athens against the charge that the best men are not given the most power in democracies. He is probably referring to the use of the lottery and the related system of the rotation of offices, which ensured the participation of a wide variety of citizens in democracy. Individual merit was undoubtedly a factor in the advance screening of candidates for selection by such means; but Thucydides may also be referring to the relevance of individual merit to the election of generals.

who have suffered an injustice, and to the unwritten laws that bring shame on their transgressors by the agreement of all.

[38] Moreover, we have provided many ways to give our minds recreation from labor: we have instituted regular contests and sacrifices throughout the year, while the attractive furnishings of our private homes give us daily delight and expel sadness. The greatness of our city has caused all things from all parts of the earth to be imported here, so that we enjoy the products of other nations with no less familiarity than we do our own.

[39] Then, too, we differ from our enemies in preparing for war: we leave our city open to all; and we have never expelled strangers in order to prevent them from learning or seeing things that, if they were not hidden, might give an advantage to the enemy. We do not rely on secret preparation and deceit so much as on our own courage in action. And as for education, our enemies train to be men from early youth by rigorous exercise, while we live a more relaxed life and still take on dangers as great as they do.

The evidence for this is that the Spartans do not invade our country by themselves, but with the aid of all their allies; when we invade our neighbors, however, we usually overcome them by ourselves without difficulty, even though we are fighting on hostile ground against people who are defending their own homes. Besides, no enemy has yet faced our whole force at once, because at the same time we are busy with our navy and sending men by land to many different places. But when our enemies run into part of our forces and get the better of them, they boast that they have beaten our whole force; and when they are defeated, they claim they were beaten by all of us. We are willing to go into danger with easy minds and natural courage rather than through rigorous training and laws, and that gives us an advantage: we'll never weaken ourselves in advance by preparing for future troubles, but we'll turn out to be no less daring in action than those who are always training hard. In this, as in other things, our city is worthy of admiration.

[40] We are lovers of nobility with restraint, and lovers of wisdom without any softening of character.[84] We use wealth as an

---

[84] "We are lovers of nobility with restraint, and lovers of wisdom without any softening of character": *philokaloumen te gar met' euteleias kai philosophoumen aneu*

opportunity for action, rather than for boastful speeches. And as for poverty, we think there is no shame in confessing it; what is shameful is doing nothing to escape it. Moreover, the very men who take care of public affairs look after their own at the same time; and even those who are devoted to their own businesses know enough about the city's affairs. For we alone think that a man who does not take part in public affairs is good for nothing, while others only say he is "minding his own business." We are the ones who develop policy, or at least decide what is to be done;[85] for we believe that what spoils action (*ergon*) is not speeches (*logoi*), but going into action without first being instructed through speeches. In this too we excel over others: ours is the bravery of people who think through what they will take in hand, and discuss it thoroughly; with other men, ignorance makes them brave and thinking makes them cowards. But the people who most deserve to be judged tough-minded are those who know exactly what terrors or pleasures lie ahead, and are not turned away from danger by that knowledge. Again we are opposite to most men in matters of virtue (*aretē*): we win our friends by doing them favors, rather than by accepting favors from them. A person who does a good turn is a more faithful friend: his goodwill towards the recipient preserves his feeling that he should do more; but the friendship of a person who has to return a good deed is dull and flat, because he knows he will be merely paying a debt – rather than doing a favor – when he shows his virtue in return. So that we alone do good to others not after calculating the profit, but fearlessly and in the confidence of our freedom.

[41] In sum, I say that our city as a whole is a lesson for Greece, and that each of us presents himself as a self-sufficient individual, disposed to the widest possible diversity of actions, with every grace

malakias. We have translated *kalon* here as "nobility," meaning nobility of character, but the reader should be warned that it can mean beauty as well. *Met' euteleias* could also mean "without excessive expenditure," but this seems inappropriate. If Pericles means that Athens is not extravagant, his claim is preposterous in view of his magnificent building program. "Lovers of wisdom" translates *philosophoumen*, which is cognate to our "philosophize" but has a much wider meaning. For the charge that such studies make people soft, see especially Aristophanes' *Clouds* and Plato's *Gorgias* 486 with *Republic* 410e.

[85] Although not all Athenians were involved in developing policy, all were involved in the making of decisions in the Assembly. Pericles holds that it is up to the leaders of Athens to develop policy and then to instruct the people to carry it out.

and great versatility. This is not merely a boast in words for the occasion, but the truth in fact, as the power of this city, which we have obtained by having this character, makes evident.

For Athens is the only power now that is greater than its fame when it comes to the test. Only in the case of Athens can enemies never be upset over the quality of those who defeat them when they invade; only in our empire can subject states never complain that their rulers are unworthy. We are proving our power with strong evidence, and we are not without witnesses: we shall be the admiration of people now and in the future. We do not need Homer, or anyone else, to praise our power with words that bring delight for a moment, when the truth will refute his assumptions about what was done. For we have compelled all seas and all lands to be open to us by our daring; and we have set up eternal monuments on all sides, of our setbacks as well as of our accomplishments.[86]

Such is the city for which these men fought valiantly and died, in the firm belief that it should never be destroyed, and for which every man of you who is left should be willing to endure distress.

[42] That is why I have spoken at such length concerning the city in general, to show you that the stakes are not the same, between us and the enemy – for their city is not like ours in any way – and, at the same time, to bring evidence to back up the eulogy of the men for whom I speak. The greatest part of their praise has already been delivered, for it was their virtues, and the virtues of men like them, that made what I praised in the city so beautiful. Not many Greeks have done deeds that are obviously equal to their own reputations, but these men have. The present end these men have met is, I think, either the first indication, or the final confirmation, of a life of virtue. And even those who were inferior in other ways deserve to have their faults overshadowed by their courageous deaths in war for the sake of their country. Their good actions have wiped out the memory of any wrong they have done, and they have produced more public good than private harm. None of them became a coward because he set a higher value on enjoying the wealth that he had; none of them put off

---

[86] "Of our setbacks as well as of our accomplishments": this could also mean: "of the evil we have done [to our enemies], and of the good we have done [to our friends]."

the terrible day of his death in hopes that he might overcome his poverty and attain riches. Their longing to punish their enemies was stronger than this; and because they believed this to be the most honorable sort of danger, they chose to punish their enemies at this risk, and to let everything else go. The uncertainty of success they entrusted to hope; but for that which was before their eyes they decided to rely on themselves in action. They believed that this choice entailed resistance and suffering, rather than surrender and safety; they ran away from the word of shame, and stood up in action at risk of their lives. And so, in the one brief moment allotted them, at the peak of their fame and not in fear, they departed.

[43] Such were these men, worthy of their country. And you who remain may pray for a safer fortune, but you must resolve to be no less daring in your intentions against the enemy. Do not weigh the good they have done on the basis of one speech. Any long-winded orator could tell you how much good lies in resisting our enemies; but you already know this. Look instead at the power our city shows in action every day, and so become lovers of Athens. When the power of the city seems great to you, consider then that this was purchased by valiant men who knew their duty and kept their honor in battle, by men who were resolved to contribute the most noble gift to their city: even if they should fail in their attempt, at least they would leave their fine character (*aretē*) to the city. For in giving their lives for the common good, each man won praise for himself that will never grow old; and the monument that awaits them is the most splendid – not where they are buried, but where their glory is laid up to be remembered forever, whenever the time comes for speech or action. For to famous men, all the earth is a monument, and their virtues are attested not only by inscriptions on stone at home; but an unwritten record of the mind lives on for each of them, even in foreign lands, better than any gravestone.

Try to be like these men, therefore: realize that happiness lies in liberty, and liberty in valor, and do not hold back from the dangers of war. Miserable men, who have no hope of prosperity, do not have a just reason to be generous with their lives; no, it is rather those who face the danger of a complete reversal of fortune for whom defeat would make the biggest difference: they are the ones who should risk their lives. Any man of intelligence will hold that death, when it comes unperceived to a man at full strength and with hope for his country, is not so bitter as miserable defeat for a man grown soft.

[44] That is why I offer you who are here as parents of these men consolation rather than a lament. You know your lives teem with all sorts of calamities, and that it is good fortune for anyone to draw a glorious end for his lot, as these men have done. While your lot was grief, theirs was a life that was happy as long as it lasted. I know it is a hard matter to dissuade you from sorrow, when you will often be reminded by the good fortune of others of the joys you once had; for sorrow is not for the want of a good never tasted, but for the loss of a good we are accustomed to having. Yet those of you who are of an age to have children may bear this loss in the hope of having more. On a personal level new children will help some of you forget those who are no more; while the city will gain doubly by this, in population and in security. It is not possible for people to give fair and just advice to the state, if they are not exposing their own children to the same danger when they advance a risky policy. As for you who are past having children, you are to think of the greater part of your life as pure profit, while the part that remains is short and its burden lightened by the glory of these men. For the love of honor is the one thing that never grows old, and useless old age takes delight not in gathering wealth (as some say),[87] but in being honored.

[45] As for you who are the children or the brothers of these men, I see that you will have considerable competition. Everyone is used to praising the dead, so that even extreme virtue will scarcely win you a reputation equal to theirs, but it will fall a little short. That is because people envy the living as competing with them, but they honor those who are not in their way, and their good will towards the dead is free of rivalry.

And now, since I must say something about feminine virtue, I shall express it in this brief admonition to you who are now widows: your glory is great if you do not fall beneath the natural condition of your sex, and if you have as little fame among men as is possible, whether for virtue or by way of reproach.

[46] Thus I have delivered, according to custom, what was appropriate in a speech, while those men who are buried here have

---

[87] E.g. Simonides (Plutarch, *Moralia* 786b).

already been honored by their own actions. It remains to maintain their children at the expense of the city until they grow up. This benefit is the city's victory garland for them and for those they leave behind after such contests as these, because the city that gives the greatest rewards for virtue has the finest citizens.

So now, when everyone has mourned for his own, you may go.

3b. *From Pericles' last speech (2.60.2–4, 63)*

After the second Spartan invasion of Attica, the spirits of the citizens began to flag and they turned in anger against Pericles, who was responsible for the decision to let the Spartans lay waste to Attica. Thucydides reconstructs Pericles' attempt to restore confidence with a speech from which the following paragraphs on duty to one's country and the necessity of empire stand out.

I believe that if the city is sound as a whole, it does more good to its private citizens than if it benefits them as individuals while faltering as a collective unit. It does not matter whether a man prospers as an individual: if his country is destroyed, he is lost along with it; but if he meets with misfortune, he is far safer in a fortunate city than he would be otherwise. Since, therefore, a city is able to sustain its private citizens in whatever befalls them, while no one individual is strong enough to carry his city, are we not all obliged to defend it? . . .

[63] You have reason (*eikos*) besides to support the dignity our city derives from its empire, in which you all take pride; you should not decline the trouble, unless you cease to pursue the honor, of empire. And do not think that the only thing we are fighting for is our freedom from being subjugated: you are in danger of losing the empire, and if you do, the anger of the people you have ruled will raise other dangers. You are in no position to walk away from your empire, though some people might propose to do so from fear of the current situation, and act the part of virtue because they do not want to be involved in public affairs. You see, your empire is really like a tyranny – though it may have been thought unjust to seize, it is now unsafe to surrender.[88] People who would

---

[88] For the thought that the empire was founded on injustice, and was therefore like a tyranny, see 1.122, 2.8, 3.37 (fr. 5a). This was, of course, the basic Spartan charge against Athens. For the idea that justice cannot be served safely, see 5.107

persuade the city to do such a thing would quickly destroy it, and if they set up their own government they would destroy that too. Those who stay out of public affairs survive only with the help of other people who take action; and they are no use to a city that rules an empire, though in a subject state they may serve safely enough.

3c. Thucydides' judgment of Pericles (2.65.5–13)

Thucydides tells us that this speech did restore public confidence in the war, but not in Pericles. Other sources tell us Pericles was removed from public office, his accounts were examined, and he was tried for the misappropriation of public funds. He was found guilty and made to pay a fine.[89] In the following year, however, Pericles was re-elected to high office, and Thucydides gives us the following assessment of the man, his manner of politics, and his strategy for the war. Thucydides' assessment of the next generation of Athenian leaders, such as Cleon, is highly critical.

As long as he was at the head of the city in time of peace, he governed it with moderation and guarded it securely; and it was greatest under him. After the war was afoot, it was obvious that he also foresaw what the city could do in this. He lived two years and six months after the war began. And after his death his foresight about the war was even better recognized, for he told them that if they would be quiet and take care of their navy, and not seek to expand the empire during this war or endanger the city itself, they should then have the upper hand. But they did the opposite on all points, and in other things that seemed not to concern the war they managed the state for their private ambition and private gain, to the detriment of themselves and their allies. Whatever succeeded brought honor and profit mostly to private individuals, while whatever went wrong damaged the city in the war.

The reason for Pericles' success was this: he was powerful because of his prestige and his intelligence, and also because he

---

(fr. **5b**). For Alcibiades' view that an empire must grow in order to survive, see 6.18 (fr. **6**).

[89] Pericles' fine was said to have been fifty talents, a very large sum (see Glossary).

was known to be highly incorruptible. He therefore controlled the people without inhibition, and was not so much led by them, as he led them. He would not humor the people in his speeches so as to get power by improper means, but because of their esteem for him he could risk their anger by opposing them. Therefore, whenever he saw them insolently bold out of season, he would put them into fear with his speeches; and again, when they were afraid without reason, he would raise up their spirits and give them courage. Athens was in name a democracy,[90] but in fact was a government by its first man. But because those who came after were more equal among themselves, with everyone aiming to be the chief, they gave up taking care of the commonwealth in order to please the people.

Since Athens was a great imperial city, these mistakes led to many others, such as the voyage against Sicily, which was due not so much to mistaking the power of those they attacked, as it was to poor decisions on the part of the senders, who failed to support the people they sent out. They weakened the strength of the army through private quarrels about popular leadership, and they troubled the state at home with discord for the first time. After their debacle in Sicily, when they lost most of their navy along with the rest of the expedition, and the city was divided by civil strife, they still held out eight years against their original enemies, who were now allied with the Sicilians, against most of their own rebellious allies besides, and also eventually against Cyrus, the son of the king of Persia, who took part with, and sent money to, the Peloponnesians to maintain their fleet. And they never gave in until they had brought about their own downfall through private quarrels.

So Pericles had more than enough reasons to predict that the city might easily outlast the Peloponnesians in this war.

4. *Human nature in extreme circumstances*

4a. *The plague (2.52–53)*

During the second year of the war, in 430, when refugees from the countryside were crowded into Athens for safety from Spartan raiding

---

[90] See 2.37 in fr. 3a above.

parties, a terrible plague struck Athens. Thucydides plunges into a vivid account of the plague right after reporting Pericles' funeral oration. The juxtaposition of these two passages is a striking instance of Thucydides' organization of material: the funeral oration gives us a bright picture of a wonderfully civilized city; the story of the plague shows how easily civilization slips away when times are hard. The plague persisted in Athens for four years.

The present affliction was aggravated by the crowding of country folk into the city, which was especially unpleasant for those who came in. They had no houses, and because they were living in shelters that were stifling in the summer, their mortality was out of control. Dead and dying lay tumbling on top of one another in the streets, and at every water fountain lay men half-dead with thirst. The temples also, where they pitched their tents, were all full of the bodies of those who died in them, for people grew careless of holy and profane things alike, since they were oppressed by the violence of the calamity and did not know what to do. And the laws they had followed before concerning funerals were all disrupted now, everyone burying their dead wherever they could. Many were forced, by a shortage of necessary materials after so many deaths, to take disgraceful measures for the funerals of their relatives: when one person had made a funeral pyre, another would get before him, throw on his dead, and give it fire; others would come to a pyre that was already burning, throw on the bodies they carried, and go their way again.

[53] The great lawlessness that grew everywhere in the city began with this disease, for, as the rich suddenly died and men previously worth nothing took over their estates, people saw before their eyes such quick reversals that they dared to do freely things they would have hidden before – things they never would have admitted they did for pleasure. And so, because they thought their lives and their property were equally ephemeral, they justified seeking quick satisfaction in easy pleasures. As for doing what had been considered noble, no one was eager to take any further pains for this, because they thought it uncertain whether they should die or not before they achieved it. But the pleasure of the moment, and whatever contributed to that, were set up as standards of nobility and usefulness. No one was held back in awe, either by

fear of the gods or by the laws of men: not by the gods, because men concluded it was all the same whether they worshipped or not, seeing that they all perished alike; and not by the laws, because no one expected to live till he was tried and punished for his crimes. But they thought that a far greater sentence hung over their heads now, and that before this fell they had a reason to get some pleasure in life.

4b. *Civil war in Corcyra (3.81.2–84)*

Corcyra, an island off the western coast of Greece, was torn by civil war in 427. Each side called in allies from abroad.

When the people of Corcyra heard that the Athenian ships were approaching and the Peloponnesians were leaving, they brought in the Messenian soldiers[91] who had been outside into the city, and ordered the ships they had manned to come around into the Hyllaic port. While they were going around, the Corcyrean democrats killed all the opposing faction they could lay hands on; and as for the ones they had persuaded to man the ships, they killed them all as they disembarked. And they came to the temple of Hera and persuaded fifty of the oligarchic sympathizers who had taken sanctuary there to submit themselves to a trial; then they condemned them all to death. When they saw what was being done, most of the suppliants – all those who were not induced to stand trial by law – killed one another right there in the temple; some hanged themselves on trees, and everyone made away with himself by what means he could. For the seven days that the Athenian admiral Eurymedon stayed there with his sixty ships, the Corcyreans went on killing as many of their own people as they took to be their enemies. They accused them of subverting the democracy, but some of the victims were killed on account of private hatred, and some by their debtors for the money they had lent them. Every form of death was seen at this time; and (as tends to happen in such cases) there was nothing people would not do, and more:

---

[91] The Messenians here were former Helots (serfs) of the Spartans who had been resettled by Athens in Naupactus near Corcyra after the failure of their revolt against Sparta in 464. They had been brought to Corcyra by the Athenians to support the democrats there.

fathers killed their sons; men were dragged out of the temples and then killed hard by; and some who were walled up in the temple of Dionysus died inside it.

[82] So cruel was the course of this civil war (*stasis*), and it seemed all the more so because it was among the first of these. Afterwards, virtually all Greece was in upheaval, and quarrels arose everywhere between the democratic leaders, who sought to bring in the Athenians, and the oligarchs, who wanted to bring in the Spartans. In time of peace they could have had no pretext and would not have been so eager to call them in, but because it was war, and allies were to be had for either party to hurt their enemies and strengthen themselves at the same time, invitations to intervene came readily from those who wanted a new government. Civil war brought many hardships to the cities, such as happen and will always happen as long as human nature is the same, although they may be more or less violent or take different forms, depending on the circumstances in each case. In peace and prosperity, cities and private individuals alike are better minded because they are not plunged into the necessity of doing anything against their will; but war is a violent teacher: it gives most people impulses that are as bad as their situation when it takes away the easy supply of what they need for daily life.

So civil war ran through cities; those it struck later heard what the first cities had done and far exceeded them in inventing artful means for attack and bizarre forms of revenge. And they reversed the usual ways of using words to evaluate actions.[92] Ill-considered boldness was counted as loyal manliness; prudent hesitation was held to be cowardice in disguise, and moderation merely the cloak of an unmanly nature. A mind that could grasp the good of the whole was considered wholly lazy. Sudden fury was accepted as part of manly valor, while plotting for one's own security was thought a reasonable excuse for delaying action. A man who started a quarrel was always to be trusted, while one who opposed him was under suspicion. A man who made a plot was intelligent if it

---

[92] "And they reversed the usual ways of using words to evaluate actions": they applied terms of moral judgment in novel ways without changing their meanings, so as to commend what used to be thought evil and condemn what used to be thought good. Compare Plato's *Republic* 560d. See Nussbaum, *Fragility of goodness* (Bibliographical Note, §A.2), pp. 404–405, with p. 508, n. 24.

happened to succeed, while one who could smell out a plot was deemed even more clever. But anyone who took precautions so as not to need to do either one had been frightened by the other side (they would say) into subverting his own political party. In brief, a man was praised if he could commit some evil action before anyone else did, or if he could cheer on another person who had never meant to do such a thing.

Family ties were not so close as those of the political parties, because their members would readily dare to do anything on the slightest pretext. These parties were not formed under existing laws for the good, but for avarice in violation of established law. And the oaths they swore to each other had their authority not so much by divine law, as by their being partners in breaking the law. If their opponents made good proposals when they were the stronger party, they did not receive these in a generous spirit, but with an eye to prevent their taking effect.

To take revenge was of higher value than never to have received injury. And as for oaths of reconciliation[93] (when there were any!), these were offered for the moment when both sides were at an impasse, and were in force only while neither side had help from abroad; but on the first opportunity, when one person saw the other unguarded and dared to act, he found his revenge sweeter because he had broken trust than if he had acted openly: he had taken the safer course, and he gave himself the prize for intelligence if he had triumphed by fraud. Evildoers are called skillful sooner than simpletons are called good, and people are ashamed to be called simpletons but take pride in being thought skillful.

The cause of all this was the desire to rule out of avarice and ambition, and the zeal for winning that proceeds from those two. Those who led their parties in the cities promoted their policies under decent-sounding names: "equality for ordinary citizens" on one side, and "moderate aristocracy" on the other. And though they pretended to serve the public in their speeches, they actually treated it as the prize for their competition; and striving by whatever means to win, both sides ventured on most horrible outrages and exacted even greater revenge, without any regard for justice or the

---

[93] "Oaths of reconciliation": oaths sworn between opposing parties, in contrast to the oaths party members swore to each other, which are treated in the preceding paragraph.

public good. Each party was limited only by its own appetite at the time, and stood ready to satisfy its ambition of the moment either by voting for an unjust verdict or seizing control by force. So neither side thought much of piety,[94] but they praised those who could pass a horrible measure under the cover of a fine speech. The citizens who remained in the middle were destroyed by both parties, partly because they would not side with them, and partly for envy that they might escape in this way.

[83] Thus was every kind of wickedness afoot throughout all Greece by the occasion of civil wars. Simplicity, which is the chief part of a generous spirit,[95] was laughed down and disappeared. Citizens were sharply divided into opposing camps, and, without trust, their thoughts were in battle array. No speech was so powerful, no oath so terrible, as to overcome this mutual hostility. The more they reckoned up their chances, the less hope they had for a firm peace, and so they were all looking to avoid harm from each other, and were unable to rely on trust. For the most part, those with the weakest minds had the greatest success, since a sense of their own inferiority and the subtlety of their opponents put them into great fear that they would be overcome in debate or by schemes due to their enemies' intelligence. They therefore went immediately to work against them in action, while their more intelligent opponents, scornful and confident that they could foresee any attack, thought they had no need to take by force what might be gotten by wit. They were therefore unprotected, and so more easily killed.

Section 84 is believed by some scholars to be a work of imitation. We include it because it is thoroughly Thucydidean in thought and style, and of considerable interest in its own right.

Most of these atrocities were committed first in Corcyra, including all the acts of revenge people take, when they have the opportunity, against rulers who have shown more arrogance than good sense,

---

[94] "Piety": *eusebeia*. This evidently includes all of the virtues in which the Greek gods were supposed to take an interest.

[95] "Simplicity, which is the chief cause of a generous spirit": literally, "simplicity, of which a generous spirit most takes part." This probably means that simplicity is what best explains generosity. See Nussbaum (above, n. 92).

and all the actions some people choose unjustly to escape longstanding poverty. Most of these acted from a passionate desire for their neighbors' possessions, but there were also those who attacked the wealthy not for their own gain, but out of zeal for equality, and they were the most carried away by their undisciplined anger to commit savage and pitiless attacks. Now that life had been thrown into confusion in the city, human nature – which is accustomed to violate justice and the laws – came to dominate law altogether, and showed itself with delight to be the slave of anger, the master of justice, and the enemy of anyone superior. Without the destructive force of envy people would not value revenge over piety, or profits over justice. When they want revenge on others, people are determined first to destroy without a trace the laws that commonly govern such matters, though it is only because of these that someone in trouble can hope to be saved, and anyone might be in danger someday and stand in need of such laws.

5. *Justice and power*

5a. *The Mytilenean debate (3.37–50)*

In 427 the citizens of Mytilene on the island of Lesbos rebelled. Since Mytilene had been a privileged ally the Athenians were especially angry. After their successful siege of the city, they therefore decreed that all Mytilenean men of military age be put to death and the rest enslaved. The day after this decree, many Athenians had second thoughts and an assembly was convened to reconsider the issue. Here is the debate as Thucydides reconstructs it:

[Cleon.[96]]

For my part, I have often seen that a democracy is not capable of ruling an empire, and I see it most clearly now, in your change of heart concerning the Mytileneans. Because you are not afraid of conspiracies among yourselves in your daily life, you imagine you can be the same with your allies, and so it does not occur to

---

[96] It was Cleon who had persuaded the Assembly to pass the original motion for killing the Mytileneans. Thucydides takes Cleon to be typical of the new generation of leaders who took over in Athens after the death of Pericles.

you that when you let them persuade you to make a mistake, or you relent out of compassion, your softness puts you in danger and does not win you the affection of your allies; and you do not see that your empire is a tyranny,[97] and that you have unwilling subjects who are continually plotting against you. They obey you not because of any good turns you might do them to your own detriment, and not because of any good will they might have, but only because you exceed them in strength. But it will be the worst mischief of all if none of our decisions stand firm, and if we never realize that a city with inferior laws is better if they are never relaxed than a city with good laws that have no force, that people are more use if they are sensible without education than if they are clever without self-control, and that the more common sort of people generally govern a city better than those who are more intelligent. For those intellectuals love to appear wiser than the laws and to win a victory in every public debate – as if there were no more important ways for them to show their wisdom! And that sort of thing usually leads to disaster for their city. But the other sort of people, who mistrust their own wits, are content to admit they know less than the laws and that they cannot criticize a speech as powerfully as a fine orator can; and so, as impartial judges rather than contestants, they govern a city for the most part very well. We should do the same, therefore, and not be carried away by cleverness and contests of wit, or give to you, the people, advice that runs against our own judgment.

[38] As for me, I have the same opinion I had before, and I am amazed at these men who have brought this matter of the Mytileneans into question again, thus causing a delay that works more to the advantage of those who have committed injustice. After a delay, you see, the victim comes at the wrongdoer with his anger dulled; but the punishment he gives right after an injury is the biggest and most appropriate. I am also amazed that there is anyone to oppose me, anyone who will try to prove that the injustice the Mytileneans have committed is good for us and that what goes wrong for us is really damaging to our allies. Clearly, he must have great trust in his eloquence if he is trying to make you believe that you did not decree what you decreed. Either that, or he has

---

[97] See Pericles' last speech, 2.63 (fr. 3b).

been bribed to try to lead you astray with a fine-sounding and elaborate speech.

Now the city gives prizes to others in contests of eloquence like this one, but the risks it must carry itself. You are to blame for conducting these speaking contests so badly. The habits you've formed! You look on at discussions, and treat real actions as a story! You judge the feasibility of projects for the future on the quality of the speeches delivered in their favor; and as for judging what was done in the past, you think that seeing an action with your own eyes is less reliable than hearing someone criticize it in a fine speech. You are excellent men – at least for being deceived by novelties of oratory and for never wanting to follow advice that is tried and proven. You bow down like slaves to anything unusual, but look with suspicion on anything ordinary. Each of you wishes chiefly to be an effective speaker, but, if not, then you enter into competition with those who are. You don't want to be thought slow in following their meaning, so you applaud a sharp point before it is even made; and you are as eager to anticipate what will be said, as you are slow to foresee its consequences. You seek to hear about almost anything outside the experience of our daily lives, and yet you do not adequately understand what is right before your eyes. To speak plainly, you are so overcome with the delight of the ear that you are more like an audience for the sophists than an assembly deliberating for the good of the city.

[39] To put you out of these habits, I tell you that the Mytileneans have done us a far greater injustice than any other single city. For my part, I can forgive those cities that rebelled because they could not bear being ruled by us, or because they were compelled to do so by the enemy. But these people were islanders, their city was walled, and they had no fear of our enemies except by sea, where they were adequately protected by their fleet of triremes. Besides, they were governed by their own laws and were held by us in the highest honor. That they should have done this! What is it but a conspiracy or a betrayal? It is not a rebellion, for a rebellion can come only from people who have been violently oppressed, whereas these people have joined our bitterest enemies to destroy us! This is far worse than if they had made war on us to increase their own power.

They'd learned nothing from the example of their neighbors' calamities – everyone who has rebelled against us so far has been put down – and their prosperity did not make them at all cautious before rushing into danger. They were bold in the face of the future and they had hopes above their power to achieve, though below what they desired. And so they started this war, resolved to put strength before justice, for as soon as they thought they could win, they attacked us, who had done them no injustice.

It is usual for cities to turn insolent when they have suddenly come to great and unexpected prosperity. In general, good fortune is more secure in human hands when it comes in reasonable measure, than when it arrives unexpectedly; and, generally, it is easier to keep misfortune away than to preserve great happiness. Long ago we should have given the Mytileneans no more privileges than our other allies, and then they would not have come to this degree of insolence, for, generally, it is human nature to look with contempt on those who serve your interests, and to admire those who never give in to you.

They should be punished right now, therefore, as they deserve for their injustice. And do not put all the blame on the oligarchs and absolve the common people, for they all alike took up arms against you. The democrats could have come over to our side and would long since have recovered their city, but they thought it safer to join in the oligarchs' rebellion.

Now consider your allies. If you inflict the same punishment on those who rebel under compulsion by the enemy, as on those who rebel of their own accord, don't you think anyone would seize the slightest pretext to rebel, when if they succeed they will win their liberty, but if they fail they will suffer nothing that can't be mended? And then we would have to risk our lives and our money against one city after another. If we succeed we recover only a ruined city, and so lose its future revenue, on which our strength is based. But if we fail, we add these as new enemies to those we had before, and the time we need to spend fighting our old enemies we must use up fighting our own allies.

[40] We must not, therefore, give our allies any hope that pardon may be secured by bribery or by persuading us that "it is only human to err." For these people conspired against us in full

knowledge and did us an injury of their own will, while only involuntary wrongs may be pardoned. Therefore I contend then and now that you ought not to alter your former decision, and you ought not to make the mistake of giving in to the three things that are most damaging to an empire: pity, delight in speeches, and a sense of fairness (*epieikeia*). It may be right to show pity to those who are like-minded, but not to those who will never have pity on us and who must necessarily be our enemies for ever after. As for the orators who delight you with their speeches – let them play for their prizes on matters of less weight, and not on a subject that will make the city pay a heavy price for a light pleasure, while the speakers themselves will be well rewarded for speaking well. And as for fairness, we should show that only towards people who will be our friends in the future, and not towards those who will still be our enemies if we let them live, as they are now.

In sum I say only this: if you follow my advice, you will do justice to the Mytileneans and promote your own interests at the same time. But if you see the matter differently, you will not win their favor; instead, you will be condemning yourselves: if they were right to rebel, you ought not to have been their rulers. But then suppose your empire is not justified: if you resolve to hold it anyway, then you must give these people an unreasonable punishment for the benefit of the empire, or else stop having an empire so that you can give charity without taking any risks.

If you keep in mind what it would have been reasonable for them to do to you if they had prevailed, then you – the intended victims – cannot turn out to be less responsive to perceived wrong than those who hatched the plot, and you *must* think they deserve the same punishment they'd have given you – especially since they were the first to commit an injustice. Those who wrong someone without any excuse are the ones who press him the hardest, even to the death, when they see how dangerous an enemy he will be if he survives; for (they will think) if one side is wronged without cause, and escapes, it will be more harsh than if the two sides had hated each other equally in the beginning.

Therefore, do not be traitors to yourselves. Recall as vividly as you can what they did to you, and how it was more important than anything else for you to defeat them then. Pay them back now, and do not be softened at the sight of their present condition, or forget how terrible a danger hung over us at that time. Give these people the punishment they deserve, and set up a clear example for our other allies, to show that the penalty for rebellion is death. Once they know this, you will less often have occasion to neglect your enemies and fight against your own allies.

[41] So spoke Cleon. After him, Diodotus, the son of Eucrates, who in the earlier assembly had strongly opposed putting the Mytileneans to death, came forward this time also, and spoke as follows.

[Diodotus[98]]

[42] I find no fault with those who have brought the Mytilenean business forward for another debate, and I have no praise for those who object to our having frequent discussions on matters of great importance. In my opinion, nothing is more contrary to good judgment (*euboulia*) than these two – haste and anger. Of these, the one is usually thoughtless, while the other is ill-informed and narrow-minded. And anyone who contends that discussion is not instructive for action either is stupid or is defending some private interest of his own. He is stupid if he thinks there is anything other than words that we can use to consider what lies hidden from sight in the future. And he has a private interest if he wants to persuade you to do something awful, but knows that a good speech will not carry a bad cause, and so tries to browbeat his opponents and audience with some good slander instead: the most difficult opponents are those who also accuse one of putting on a show of oratory for a bribe. If the accusation were merely of ignorance, a speaker could lose his case and still go home with a reputation more for stupidity than injustice; but once corruption is imputed to him, then he will be under suspicion even if he wins, and if he loses he will be thought both stupid and unjust. Such accusations do not do the city any good, since it loses good advisers from fear of them. The city would do best if this kind of citizen had the least ability as speakers, for they would then persuade the

---

[98] Of Diodotus we know only what we learn from Thucydides' representation of him in this debate.

city to fewer errors. A good citizen should not go about terrifying those who speak against him, but should try to look better in a fair debate. A sensible city should neither add to, nor reduce, the honor in which it holds its best advisers, nor should it punish or even dishonor those whose advice it does not take. This would make it less attractive for a successful speaker to seek greater popularity by speaking against his better judgment, or for an unsuccessful one to strive in this way to gratify the people and gain a majority.

[43] But we do the opposite of that here; and besides, if anyone is suspected of corruption, but gives the best advice anyway, we are so resentful of the profit we think he is making (though this is uncertain), that we give up benefits the city would certainly have received. It has become the rule also to treat good advice honestly given as being no less under suspicion than bad, so that a man who has something rather good to say must tell lies in order to be believed, just as a man who gives terrible advice must win over the people by deception. Because of these suspicions, ours is the only city that no one can possibly benefit openly, without deception, since if anyone does good openly to the city, his reward will be the suspicion that he had something secretly to gain from this.

But on the most important matters, such as these, we orators must decide to show more foresight than is found in you shortsighted citizens, especially since we stand accountable for the advice we give, but you listeners are not accountable to anyone, because if you were subject to the same penalties as the advisers you follow, you would make more sensible decisions. As it is, whenever you fail, you give in to your momentary anger and punish the man who persuaded you for his one error of judgment, instead of yourselves for the many mistakes in which you had a part.

[44] For my part, I did not come forward to speak about Mytilene with any purpose to contradict or to accuse. Our dispute, if we are sensible, will concern not their injustice to us, but our judgment as to what is best for us (*euboulia*). Even if I proved them guilty of terrible injustice, I still would not advise the death penalty for this, unless that was to our advantage. Even if they deserved to be pardoned, I would not have you pardon them if it did not turn out to be good for the city. In my opinion, what we are discussing concerns the future more than the present. And as for this point

that Cleon insists on – that the death penalty will be to our advantage in the future, by keeping the others from rebelling – I maintain exactly the opposite view, and I too am looking at our future well-being. I urge you not to reject the usefulness of my advice in favor of the apparent attractions of his. In view of your present anger against the Mytileneans, you may agree that his argument is more in accord with justice. But we are not at law with them, and so have no need to speak of justice. We are in council instead, and must decide how the Mytileneans can be put to the best use for us.

[45] The death penalty has been ordained for many offenses in various cities, and these are minor offenses compared to this one; yet people still risk their lives when they are buoyed up by hope, and no one has ever gone into a dangerous conspiracy convinced that he would not succeed. What city would ever attempt a rebellion on the supposition that its resources, whether from home or from its alliance with other states, are too weak for this? They all have it by nature to do wrong, both men and cities, and there is no law that will prevent it. People have gone through all possible penalties, adding to them in the hope that fewer crimes will then be done to them by evildoers. It stands to reason that there were milder punishments in the old days, even for the most heinous crimes; but as the laws continued to be violated, in time most cities arrived at the death penalty. And still the laws are violated.

Either some greater terror than death must be found, therefore, or else punishment will not deter crime. Poverty compels the poor to be daring, while the powerful are led by pride and arrogance into taking more than their share. Each human condition is dominated by some great and incurable passion that impels people to danger. Hope and passionate desire (*erōs*), however, dominate every situation: with desire as the leader and hope as the companion, desire thinking out a plan, and hope promising a wealth of good fortune, these two cause the greatest mischief, and because they are invisible they are more dangerous than the evils we see. Besides these, fortune (*tuchē*) plays no less a part in leading men on, since she can present herself unexpectedly and excite them to take a risk, even with inadequate resources. This happens especially to cities, because of the serious issues at stake – their own freedom and their empire over others – and because an individual who is acting with everyone else has an unreasonably high estimate of his own ability. In a word, it is an impossible thing – you would have to be simple-minded to believe that people can be deterred, by force of law or by anything else that is frightening, from doing what human nature is earnestly bent on doing.

[46] We should not, therefore, make a bad decision, relying on capital punishment to protect us, or set such hopeless conditions that our rebels have no opportunity to repent and atone for their crime as quickly as possible. Consider this: if a city in rebellion knew it could not hold out, as things are it would come to terms while it could still pay our expenses and make its remaining contributions; but if we take Cleon's way, wouldn't any city prepare better for a rebellion than they do now, and hold out in a siege to the very last, since it would mean the same whether they gave in late or early? And what is this if not harmful to us – to have the expense of a siege because they will not come to terms, and then, when we have taken a city, to find it ruined and to lose its revenue for the future?[99] You see, our strength against our enemies depends on that revenue.

We should not, then, be strict judges in punishing offenders, and so harm ourselves; instead, we should look for a way to impose moderate penalties to ensure that we will in the future be able to make use of cities that can make substantial payments to us. We should not plan to keep them in check by the rigor of laws, but by watching their actions closely. We are doing the opposite now, if we think we should punish cruelly a city that used to be free, was held in our empire by force, rebelled from us for a good reason – to restore its autonomy – and now has been defeated. What we ought to do in the case of a city of free men is not to impose extreme penalties after they rebel, but to be extremely watchful before they rebel, and to take care that the idea of rebellion never crosses their minds. And once we have overcome them, we should lay the fault upon as few of them as we can.

[47] Consider also how great a mistake you will be making on this score if you follow Cleon's advice: as things are, the democrats in all the cities are your friends, and either they do not join the

---

[99] See 3.39 (this fragment, above) where Cleon makes the point to which this responds.

oligarchs in rebellion or, if they are forced to, they remain hostile to the rebels, so that when you go to war with them, you have their common people on your side; but if you destroy the democrats of Mytilene, who had no part in the rebellion, and who delivered the city into your hands of their own will as soon as they were armed, then you will, first, commit an injustice by killing those who have done you good service, and, second, accomplish exactly what oligarchs everywhere want the most: when they have made a city rebel, they will immediately have the democrats on their side, because you will have shown them in advance that those who are not guilty of injustice suffer the same penalty as those who are. And even if they were guilty, however, we should pretend that they were not, so that the only party still allied with us will not become our enemy. And in order to keep our empire intact, I think it much more advantageous for us to put up with an injustice willingly, than for us justly to destroy people we ought not to destroy. And as for Cleon's idea that justice and our own advantage come to the same in the case of punishment – these two cannot be found to coincide in the present case.

[48] Now I want you to accept my proposal because you see that it is the best course, and not because you are swayed more by pity or a sense of fairness. I would not have you influenced by those factors any more than Cleon would. But take my advice and judge the leaders of the rebellion at your leisure, while you let the rest enjoy their city. That will be good for the future, and it will strike fear into your enemies today. Those who plan well against their enemies, you see, are more formidable than those who attack with active force and foolishness combined.

[49] So spoke Diodotus. After these two quite opposite opinions were delivered, the Athenians were at odds with each other, and the show of hands was almost equal on both sides. But the opinion of Diodotus prevailed.

On this they immediately sent out another ship in haste, so they would not find the city already destroyed by coming in after the first ship (which had left a day and a night earlier). The Mytilenean ambassadors provided wine and barley cakes for the second ship and promised them great rewards if they overtook the first. And so they rowed in such haste that they ate their barley cakes steeped in wine and oil while they rowed, and took turns rowing while others slept.[100] They were lucky in that there was no wind against them. And since the first ship was not sailing in any haste on its perverse mission, while the second one hurried on in the manner described, the first ship did arrive first, but only by the time it took Paches to read the decree. He was about to execute the sentence when the second ship came in and prevented the destruction of the city. That was how close Mytilene came to destruction.

[50] As for the other men Paches had sent away as being most to blame for the rebellion, the Athenians did kill them as Cleon had advised, just over a thousand of them. They also razed the walls of Mytilene and confiscated their ships. Afterwards, they stopped collecting payments directly from Lesbos. Instead, they divided the land (all but that of Methymna[101]) into three thousand allotments, of which they consecrated three hundred to the gods, the rest going to Athenians who were chosen by lot and sent out as allotment holders. The people of Lesbos were required to pay them two silver *minas*[102] annually for each lot, and worked the land themselves. The Athenians also took over the communities that Mytilene had controlled on the mainland and made them subject to Athens. So ended the business on Lesbos.

5b. *The Melian dialogue (5.84.3–114)*

The Athenians attacked the island of Melos in 416 and demanded its surrender, although the Melians had tried to remain neutral.

Now the Athenian generals, Cleomedes and Tisias, set up camp in Melian territory with these forces. Before doing any harm to the Melian land, they first sent ambassadors to negotiate. The Melians refused to bring these ambassadors before the common people, but ordered them to deliver their message to a few officials and leading citizens. The Athenians spoke as follows:

[85] **Athenians:** Since we may not speak before the common people, for fear that they would be led astray if they heard our

---

[100] The normal practice was for sailors to eat and sleep on land.

[101] Methymna, a city on the north coast of Lesbos, had not joined the rebellion.

[102] As two *minas* was roughly a hoplite's annual pay, this may have been intended to support a hoplite garrison.

persuasive and unanswerable arguments all at once in a continuous speech – we know that is what you had in mind in bringing us to the few leading citizens – you who are sitting here should make your situation still more secure: answer every particular point, not in a single speech, but interrupting us immediately whenever we say anything that seems wrong to you. And first, tell us whether you like this proposal.

[86] To this the Melian Council replied:

Melians: We would not find fault with the fairness of a leisurely debate, but these acts of war – happening right now, not in the future – do not seem to be consistent with that. We see that you have come to be judges of this proceeding, so we expect the result to be this: if we make the better case for justice and do not surrender because of that, we will have war, but if you win the argument, we will have servitude.

[87] **Athenians:** Well, then, if you came to this meeting to reason on the basis of suspicions about the future, or for any other purpose than to work out how to save your city on the basis of what you see here today – we should stop now. But if that is your purpose, let's speak to it.

[88] **Melians:** People in our situation can be expected to turn their words and thoughts to many things, and should be pardoned for that. Since, however, this meeting is to consider only the point of our survival, let's have our discussion on the terms you have proposed, if that is your decision.

[89] **Athenians:** For our part, we will not make a long speech no one would believe, full of fine moral arguments – that our empire is justified because we defeated the Persians, or that we are coming against you for an injustice you have done to us. And we don't want you to think you can persuade us by saying that you did not fight on the side of the Spartans in the war, though you were their colony, or that you have done us no injustice. Instead, let's work out what we can do on the basis of what both sides truly accept: we both know that decisions about justice are made in human discussions only when both sides are under equal compulsion; but when one side is stronger, it gets as much as it can, and the weak must accept that.

[90] **Melians:** Well, then, since you put your interest in place of justice, our view must be that it is in your interest not to subvert this rule that is good for all: that a plea of justice and fairness should do some good for a man who has fallen into danger, if he can win over his judges, even if he is not perfectly persuasive. And this rule concerns you no less than us: if you ever stumble, you might receive a terrible punishment and be an example to others.

[91] **Athenians:** We are not downhearted at the prospect of our empire's coming to an end, though it may happen. Those who rule over others (such as the Spartans, who are not our present concern) are not as cruel to those they conquer as are a subject people who attack their rulers and overcome them. But let us be the ones to worry about that danger. We will merely declare that we are here for the benefit of our empire, and we will speak for the survival of your city: we would like to rule over you without trouble, and preserve you for our mutual advantage.

[92] **Melians:** But how could it be as much to our advantage to serve, as it is yours to rule?

[93] **Athenians:** Because if you obey, you will save yourselves from a very cruel fate; and we will reap a profit from you if we don't destroy you.

[94] **Melians:** So you would not accept a peaceful solution? We could be friends rather than enemies, and fight with neither side.

[95] **Athenians:** No. Your enmity does not hurt us as much as your friendship would. That would be a sign of our weakness to those who are ruled by us; but your hatred would prove our power.

[96] **Melians:** Why? Do your subjects reason so unfairly that they put us, who never had anything to do with you, in the same category as themselves, when most of them were your colonies, or else rebels whom you defeated?

[97] **Athenians:** Why not? They think we have as good a justification for controlling you as we do for them; they say the independent cities survive because they are powerful, and that we do not attack them because we are afraid. So when you have been trampled down by us, you will add not only to our empire, but to our security, by not staying independent. And this is especially true because you are islanders who are weaker than the others, and we are masters of the sea.

[98] **Melians:** But don't you think there is safety in our proposal of neutrality? Here again, since you have driven us away from a

plea for justice, and are telling us to surrender to whatever is in your interest, we must show you what would be good for us, and try to persuade you that your interests coincide with ours. Won't this turn the people who are now neutral into your enemies? Once they've seen this, they will expect you to attack them eventually also. And what would this accomplish, but to make the enemies you already have still greater, and to make others your enemies against their will, when they would not have been so?

[99] **Athenians:** We do not think the free mainlanders will be terrible enemies to us; it will be long before they so much as keep guard against us. But islanders worry us – those outside the empire like you, and those under the empire who resent the force that keeps them that way – these may indeed act recklessly and bring themselves and us into foreseeable danger.

[100] **Melians:** Yes, but if you would face such extreme danger to retain your empire, and if your subjects would do so to get free of you, then wouldn't it be great weakness and cowardice on our part, since we are still free, not to go to every extreme rather than be your subjects?

[101] **Athenians:** No, not if you think sensibly. Your contest with us is not an equal match of courage against courage; no honor is lost if you submit. This is a conference about your survival and about not resisting those who are far stronger than you.

[102] **Melians:** But we know that in war the odds sometimes are more even than the difference in numbers between the two sides, and that if we yield, all our hope is lost immediately; but if we hold out, we can still hope to stand tall.

[103] **Athenians:** Hope! It *is* a comfort in danger, and though it may be harmful to people who have many other advantages, it will not destroy them. But people who put everything they have at risk will learn what hope is when it fails them, for hope is prodigal by nature; and once they have learned this, it is too late to take precautions for the future. Do not let this happen to you, since you are weak and have only this one throw of the dice. And do not be like the ordinary people who could use human means to save themselves but turn to blind hopes when they are forced to give up their sensible ones – to divination, oracles, and other such things that destroy men by giving them hope.[103]

---

[103] The application of this warning to the Sicilian expedition (which follows immediately in Thucydides' account) is striking. In Sicily the Athenian armada was

[104] **Melians:** You can be sure we think it hard to contend against your power and good fortune, unless we might do so on equal terms. Nevertheless, we trust that our good fortune will be no less than yours. The gods are on our side, because we stand innocent against men who are unjust. And as for power, what we lack will be supplied by the alliance we will make with the Spartans, who must defend us as a matter of honor, if only because we are related to them. So our confidence is not as totally unreasonable as you might think.

[105] **Athenians:** Well, the favor of the gods should be as much on our side as yours. Neither our principles nor our actions are contrary to what men believe about the gods, or would want for themselves. Nature always compels gods (we believe) and men (we are certain) to rule over anyone they can control. We did not make this law, and we were not the first to follow it; but we will take it as we found it and leave it to posterity forever, because we know that you would do the same if you had our power, and so would anyone else. So as far as the favor of the gods is concerned, we have no reason to fear that we will do worse than you.

As for your opinion about the Spartans – your trust that they will help you in order to preserve their own honor – we admire your blessed innocence, but we don't envy you your foolishness. Granted, the Spartans do show a high degree of virtue towards each other according to their local customs; but one could say many things about their treatment of other people. We'll make this as brief and as clear as possible: of all the people we know, they are the ones who make it most obvious that they hold whatever pleases them to be honorable, and whatever profits them to be just. So your plan will not support your hope for survival, and it now seems reckless.

[106] **Melians:** But on that point we most firmly trust the Spartans to pursue their own advantage – *not* to betray their colonists, the Melians, for in doing so they would benefit their enemies by losing the confidence of their friends among the Greeks.

[107] **Athenians:** Don't you realize that advantage lies with safety, and that the pursuit of justice and honor brings danger? Which the Spartans are usually least willing to face?

destroyed because their general, Nicias, had too much faith in divination; see Euripides, frs. 9 and 11.

[108] **Melians:** But we believe they will take a dangerous mission in hand for our sake. They will think it safer to do so for us than for anyone else, since we are close enough to the Peloponnesus for action, and we will be more faithful to them than others because our kinship gives us common views.

[109] **Athenians:** But the good will of those who call for help does not offer any security to those who might fight for them. They will be safe only if they have superior power in action. The Spartans are more aware of this than anyone else; at least they have no confidence in their own forces, and therefore take many allies along with them when they attack a neighbor. So while we are masters of the sea, you cannot reasonably expect them to cross over to an island.

[110] **Melians:** Yes, but they may have others to send. The Sea of Crete is wide; it is harder for its masters to seize ships there, than it is for people who want to escape to slip through. And if the Spartans failed in this, they would turn their arms against your own land or the lands of your allies that have still not been invaded by Brasidas [a Spartan general]. And then you will be troubled about your own land, and that of your allies, and no longer about a country that does not concern you.

[111] **Athenians:** With your experience of what might happen, you are surely not unaware that Athens has never given up a single siege through fear of anyone else.[104] We are struck by the fact that though you said you would confer about your survival, in all this discussion you have never mentioned a single thing that people could rely on and expect to survive. Your strongest points are mere hopes for the future, and your actual resources are too small for your survival in view of the forces arrayed against you. Your planning will be utterly irrational, unless (after letting us withdraw from the meeting) you decide on a more sensible policy. Do not be distracted by a sense of honor; this destroys people all too often, when dishonor and death stand before their eyes. Many have been so overcome by the power of this seductive word, "honor," that even when they foresee the dangers to which it carries them,

---

[104] This was quite true at the time, and is borne out by the histories of Mytilene and Potidaea, both of which were taken after long sieges while Spartan forces were harassing Attica. The point foreshadows the siege of Syracuse, however, which the Athenians will be forced to abandon.

they are drawn by a mere word into an action that is an irreparable disaster; and so, intentionally, they fall into a dishonor that is more shameful than mere misfortune, since it is due to their own foolishness.

You must guard against this if you are to deliberate wisely, and you must not think it unseemly for you to submit to a city of such great power, which offers such reasonable conditions – to be our allies, and to enjoy your own property under tribute to us. You are being given a choice between war and survival: do not make the wrong decision out of a passion for victory. Remember what is usually the best course: do not give way to equals, but have the right attitude towards your superiors and use moderation towards your inferiors. So think about this when we withdraw from the meeting, and keep this often in your mind: you are considering what to do for your country – your only country – and this one discussion will determine whether it meets success or failure.

[112] So the Athenians withdrew from the conference, and the Melians, left to themselves, decided on much the same position as they had taken in the debate. Then the Melians answered as follows:

Melians: Athenians, our resolution is no different from what it was before: we will not, in a short time, give up the liberty in which our city has remained for the seven hundred years since its foundation. We will trust in the fortune of the gods, which has preserved it up to now, and in the help of men – the Spartans – and we will do our best to maintain our liberty. We offer this, however: we will be your friends; we will be enemies to neither side; and you will depart from our land, after making whatever treaty we both think fit.

[113] That was the answer of the Melians. As they broke off the conference, the Athenians said:

Athenians: It seems to us, on the basis of this discussion, that you are the only men who think you know the future more clearly than what is before your eyes, and who, through wishful thinking, see doubtful events as if they had already come to pass. You have staked everything on your trust in hope, good fortune, and the Spartans; and you will be ruined in everything.

[114] Then the Athenian ambassadors went back to their camp. When the generals saw that the Melians would not submit, they turned immediately to war and surrounded the Melian city with a wall, after dividing up the work with their allies. After that, the Athenians left a contingent of Athenian and allied troops there to guard the city by land and sea, and went home with the greater part of their army. The rest stayed behind to besiege the place.

Thucydides goes on to describe the siege of Melos, which led eventually to the capture of the city. After taking Melos, the Athenians killed all adult males there and enslaved the women and children.

6. The expedition against Syracuse: From the debate at Athens (6.18)

That same winter, immediately after the destruction of Melos, Athens decided to attempt the conquest of the Greeks on Sicily, an enormous undertaking and a very dangerous one, as the Athenians were not well informed about the relative strengths of their allies and their enemies in Sicily. Athens had long wanted to establish bases on Sicily, and evidently hoped also to establish sources of grain and timber in the western Mediterranean. Athenians in favor of continuing the war thought that control over substantial parts of Sicily would increase Athenian power to the point at which the Peloponnesians would not be able to resist them. They wished, however, to make it appear that their expedition was merely a response to a call for aid from their allies.

Leontini, a Greek city in Sicily, had been an ally of Athens. In 422 its democracy was overthrown by an army from Syracuse and its people sent into exile, while its aristocrats took up residence in Syracuse. At the time, Athens had been unable to forge an alliance that would enable it to rescue the people of Leontini; but anti-Syracusan sentiment was strong in Athens, and many Athenians were eager for a chance to cut Syracuse down to size.

Conveniently, in 416, the Sicilian city of Egesta sought help from Athens. They had engaged in a war with their neighbor Selinus, which was being helped by Syracuse. A delegation from Egesta came to Athens asking for help; meanwhile, Athenian ambassadors who had been to Egesta to evaluate the situation there returned with glowing reports.

After a seasoned general named Nicias advised caution, Alcibiades made a speech which concludes as follows. This is the brilliant young man who makes an appearance in Plato's Symposium.

What reasonable case could we make for holding back? What excuse could we make to our allies in Sicily for denying them assistance? We ought to defend them, if only because we have sworn to do so, without objecting that they have not aided us in return. We did not take them into our alliance so that they would come to our assistance, but so that they would trouble our enemies there and so prevent them from coming against us here.

This is how we got our empire – as did everyone else who rules – by eagerly coming to the support of anyone who calls on us, whether Greek or foreign. If we all sat still, or waited to decide which race of people we should help, then we would be adding little to our own empire, and therefore putting it at greater risk.[105] In dealing with a stronger power, one should not only defend oneself when it attacks; one should take advance action to preempt an attack. We cannot control the size of empire we want as we would a budget: in our situation we are compelled to plan new conquests as well as not to let our old subjects go free, because if we do not rule others we run the risk of being ruled by them ourselves.[106] You should not weigh peace in the same balance as others do unless you plan to change your way of life to match theirs.

Let us conclude, then, that sailing to Sicily will increase our power at home, and let us make the voyage, so that we may cast down the pride of the Peloponnesians and show them the contempt we have for the current peace by sailing against Sicily. And along with this we will either become masters of all of Greece by the addition of those cities, as we expect, or we will at least ruin Syracuse, to the benefit of ourselves and our allies. As for our safety, our ships will protect us whether we are successful and stay, or whether we leave; since we will be masters of the sea against all the Sicilians put together

Don't give in to Nicias' arguments for his do-nothing policy. Don't let him distract you from this expedition by starting a quarrel between the young men and their elders. Follow the usual procedure instead, as our ancestors did when they brought us to our present height by consulting young and old together. Try to advance the

---

[105] This is a reply to Nicias, who had opposed helping the Egestans because they were not Greek (6.9).
[106] Cf 2.62 and 63 (fr. 3b).

cause of our city by the same means now. And don't think that either youth or age has any power without the other: remember that the greatest strength comes from a mixture of the simplest people with the middle sort and those who make the most exact judgments, all together. Keep this in mind, also: that a city is like anything else: if it rests, it will wear itself out by itself. All human skills decay, but the waging of war continually adds to a city's experience and puts it in the habit of resisting the enemy in action, rather than making speeches. On the whole, I find that if a city which is used to being active grows idle, it will quickly be destroyed by this change; and the safest way for a people to live is to conduct civic affairs according to their current laws and customs for better or for worse, with the least possible change.[107]

7. Democracy vs. oligarchy

7a. From the debate at Syracuse (6.39)

The Syracusan democratic leader Athenagoras made light of the threat from Athens. First, he argued that the idea that Athens would send an expedition was simply not reasonable (not eikos*). Second (he said), the whole story appears to be a fabrication put forward to frighten the democrats into turning to the oligarchs for safety. Athenagoras closed by promising to guard against a takeover by the oligarchs, and then gave these remarks in defense of democracy:*[108]

Some will say that democracy is neither intelligent nor fair (*ison*) and that the wealthy are best able to rule. But I answer first that the *dēmos* is the name for the whole people,[109] while *oligarchy* names only a part. Second, though the rich are indeed the best guardians of the city's money, the best councilors are the intelligent, and the

---

[107] Cf 3.37 (fr. 5a).

[108] Since Athenagoras' advice is all bad, there is a bite to Thucydides' decision to join it to this defense of democracy, a form of government Thucydides tends to distrust.

[109] In fact, *dēmos* has a number of meanings: although it can refer to the entire citizen body, it more often designates the poor or common people, and may mean simply a political group that claims to represent their interest. Athenagoras is using what is called a persuasive definition. His contemporaries would not have been moved; to most of them democracy meant mob rule, not rule in the interest of the whole people. See Glossary.

best judges of what they hear are the many. Now in a democracy all three groups enjoy a fair share, both the groups and their members. But while an oligarchy allows the many their share of dangers; it takes more than its share of the profits – not only that, it runs off with everything.

7b. *Alcibiades on democracy (6.89.3–6, 6.92.2–4)*

Alcibiades fled to Sparta rather than face charges of impiety that were brought by his enemies in Athens after he left for Sicily. In order to win the confidence of the Spartans, Alcibiades explained in this speech why he was willing to help them now after years of service to the Athenian democracy:

If anyone thought worse of me for siding with the people, he should realize that he is not right to be offended. We[110] have always been in disagreement with tyrants, you see. Whatever is opposed to an autocrat is identified with the people (*dēmos*) and because of this we have continued as leaders of the majority party. Besides, in a city governed by democracy, we were generally compelled to conform to prevailing conditions; we have tried, nevertheless, to be more moderate in politics than the headstrong temper that now prevails. There have been others in the past – there still are some – who have incited the mob to worse things. These are the ones who have driven me out. But as for us, we were leaders of the city as a whole, and we thought it right to join in preserving the city in the same form in which it turned out to be greatest and most free – the form in which we had received it. We did this even though anyone with any sense knows well enough what democracy is – I as well as anyone (that's why I could lambaste it if I wanted, although there is nothing new to say about a form of government that everyone agrees is foolish). Besides, we thought it was not safe to change our government when you were bearing down on us as enemies.

[92.2] Now in my judgment no one should think worse of me because I, who was once thought a lover of my own city, am now of my own power going against it with its greatest enemies; and I

---

[110] Alcibiades' noble family, including Pericles.

do not think you should distrust my word as coming from the zeal of a fugitive. For though I am fleeing from the malice of those who drove me out, I shall not, if you take my advice, flee from helping you. Those who have merely harmed their enemies, as you have, are not so much enemies as are those who have compelled their friends to become enemies.[111] I do love my city, but as a place where I could safely engage in public life, not as the site of injustice to me. I do not think the city I am going against is my own; it is much more a matter of my recovering a city that is not mine. A true lover of his city is not the man who refuses to invade the city he has lost through injustice, but the man who desires so much to be in it that he will attempt to recover it by any means he can.

7c. *From the debate on Samos (8.48.5–6, 8.64.5)*

In 411, agitation for oligarchy developed on two fronts among the Athenians – in the city and in the large fleet that Athens had posted on the island of Samos, in the eastern Aegean. Some Athenians had argued that oligarchy in Athens would be well received in the empire. The counterargument was given by a general named Phrynichus:

As for the allied cities to whom the conspirators promise oligarchies, because they will be rid of democracy in Athens, Phrynichus said he knew full well that this would neither make those who had already rebelled more likely to return, nor would it strengthen the loyalty of those who remained. For they would not want to be subject to an empire, whether democracy or oligarchy, if they could have their liberty with either form of government. And even those who are called "good and noble men" would, he thought, give them no less trouble than the democracy has done, since those men had devised evil projects into which they had led the people, and then they had themselves made the largest profit from them. Besides, under an oligarchy, allies would be put to death violently without trial; whereas democracy offers a refuge to ordinary people and is a moderating influence on the oligarchs.

---

[111] That is, in harming the democrats (the true enemy) the Spartans have not played the part of an enemy to Athens; the democrats, on the other hand, in making Alcibiades their enemy, have made themselves enemies to Athens.

[The event proved that Phrynichus was right. Those allies that did turn to oligarchy turned at the same time to freedom from the Athenian empire. The oligarchy established at this time on Thasos, for example, left the empire within two months.]

[64.5] At Thasos the outcome was contrary to what was expected by the Athenians who had installed the oligarchy; and so, in my opinion, it was in many of the other parts of their empire. For as soon as the cities adopted "sensible policies" (*sōphrosunē*) and felt free from fear in their actions, they moved straightway to freedom from the superficial "good government" (*eunomia*) given them by the Athenians, for which they had no respect.

7d. The "Four Hundred" (8.68.4 and 8.89.3)

The cause of oligarchy gained momentum and in June, 411, a new government was established in Athens, known as the "Four Hundred," promising to extend power to a wider group of Five Thousand (a promise they probably never intended to make good). One of the most important of the oligarchic reforms was the elimination of all forms of state pay for public service (except for military service). Such payments had enabled the poor to take part in government, and indeed may have enticed them to do so. The Four Hundred managed to intimidate the people of Athens, so that in the beginning the oligarchy met little resistance. Thucydides was struck by their success:

It was no marvel that this business succeeded, since it was managed by many intelligent men;[112] but it was a great undertaking, for the Athenian people took it hard, to lose their freedom almost a hundred years after the expulsion of the tyrants. During this time they had not been subject to anyone, and for half of it had grown accustomed to being the rulers of others.

[The oligarchy in Athens did not fare well, partly because the oligarchs were not getting along with each other:]

---

[112] The man who planned the coup was Antiphon, who was also well known as a sophist. Thucydides expresses great respect for Antiphon's intelligence. After the restoration of democracy, Antiphon was put on trial for his life. Part of the speech he made in his own defense (much admired by Thucydides) has survived in a papyrus (fr. 1).

[89.3] Most of the Four Hundred fell into the private ambition that is fatal to an oligarchy grown out of a democracy. For at once each of them claimed not merely to be equal to the others, but to be the top man by far. In a democracy, on the other hand, if a man is defeated in an election he bears it better, because he does not think he has been beaten by his equals.[113]

7e. *The "Five Thousand" (8.97)*

In the fleet at Samos, democracy eventually prevailed; and the sailors soon brought pressure to restore the democracy at home. Meanwhile, there was a panic in Athens over the loss of the nearby island of Euboea. The Four Hundred oligarchs were ousted and a new form of government introduced:

The Athenians ... immediately called an assembly on the Pnyx, where they had been accustomed to assemble in former times.[114] There they deposed the Four Hundred and voted to entrust affairs of state to the Five Thousand – or the number that could afford a hoplite's equipment[115] – and to give no one a salary for holding any public office, on pain of a curse. There were also frequent assemblies after this, in which they elected law-makers and voted in other measures towards a constitution. And now for the first time, at least in my life, the Athenians seemed to have ordered their constitution well: it consisted now of a moderate blending, in the interests of the few and the many. And this was the first thing, after so many misfortunes had occurred, that made the city raise its head again.

We do not know as much as we would like about the Five Thousand, or about why Thucydides thought so well of this form of government. The career of the Five Thousand was short, and may have been only a ploy of the oligarchs to win over the hoplite class to their side. In any

---

[113] This is a troublesome paradox. The idea seems to be that in democracy a good man who is defeated can be consoled by the belief that the people who beat him were his inferiors, as would be true in class terms when an aristocrat is defeated by a common man.

[114] The Pnyx is a hill near the Acropolis and, as the regular meeting place of the Assembly, had symbolic importance for the democracy.

[115] hoplite: see Glossary.

case, Thucydides' History *breaks off shortly after this passage, and we are left to make out the story of the rest of the war from other sources.*

The Old Oligarch

The "Old Oligarch" is the name commonly given by modern scholars to the author of this anonymous treatise on the government of Athens, which was preserved among the writings of the Athenian historian and thinker, Xenophon (born c. 430). Technically it is called pseudo-Xenophon's Constitution of the Athenians. *The date of the treatise is uncertain, but the consensus is that it was written after 446 (because of events mentioned in 3.11) but probably before 424 (because of an event not mentioned in 2.5).*

The author may be an Athenian in exile, for he speaks of Athenians as "they" (1.1 etc.) but also as "we" (1.12 etc.). He disapproves of their democratic constitution but admires the skill with which they have implemented this system. His style is very uneven, and the purpose of the treatise has long puzzled scholars. In our view the treatise belongs to the fifth-century debate about the relative merits of different constitutions[116] and may have been an exercise that, like the Dissoi Logoi, *required the assessment of both pros and cons.*

I

[1] My subject is the constitution (*politeia*) of the Athenians. I do not approve their choice of this type of constitution, for in making their choice they preferred the well-being of the inferior class (*ponēroi*) at the expense of the better class (*chrēstoi*).[117] For this

---

[116] Cf. Herodotus 3.80–82 (fr. 4) and Euripides, *Suppliants* 399–456 (fr. 6).

[117] *Chrēstos* ("useful, good") and *ponēros* ("worthless, evil") clearly have social connotations of upper and lower class throughout this treatise.

reason, then, I do not approve of it. But since they think these policies best, I will show how they successfully preserve their constitution and manage their other affairs in ways that seem mistaken to the rest of the Greeks.

[2] My first point is this: It is just (*dikaios*) for the poor and the common people (*dēmos*) there to have more than the well-born and wealthy because it is the common people who man the ships and confer power on the city – helmsmen, signalmen, captains, look-out men, and shipwrights – these are the ones who confer power on the city much more than the hoplites,[118] the well-born and the better class. Since this is the case, it seems just to allow everyone access to the political offices, whether assigned by lot or election, and to allow any citizen to speak if he wishes. [3] Second, the people do not ask that the offices that bring safety to the people if managed well, and danger to all if managed poorly, be open to everyone: they don't think they should be given access by lot to positions of general or cavalry commander. For the people know that it is more beneficial for them not to hold these offices, but to let the most capable men hold them. They themselves seek to hold only the offices that carry a salary and bring personal gain.

[4] Now it surprises some that everywhere they distribute more to the inferior class, the poor, and the common people than to the better class, but it is clear that in precisely this way they preserve democracy. For when the poor, the common people, and the worst citizens are well off and their kind is many, they increase the power of the democracy, but when the wealthy and the better class are well off, the common people are making their opposition stronger. [5] Everywhere on earth the best element is opposed to democracy. For in the best citizens there is the least injustice and lack of restraint and the greatest concern for good things, but in the common people there is the greatest ignorance, unruliness, and wickedness. For poverty drives them more to shameful acts, and some men go without culture and education for lack of money.

[6] Someone might say that they should not allow everyone equal opportunity to speak and to deliberate, but only the most skillful and the best men. Yet here too in allowing even the lower class to speak they show excellent judgment. For if the better class alone

---

[118] Hoplites: see Glossary.

spoke and deliberated, the results would be good for those like themselves but not good for those belonging to the common class. But as it is, any inferior man who wishes rises up and speaks and tries to obtain what is good for himself and those like himself. [7] Someone might ask how a man of this sort would know what is good for himself and the common people, but they know that the ignorance, baseness, and good will of this man is more advantageous than the excellence (*aretē*), wisdom, and ill will of a better man. [8] A city would not be the best as a result of such practices, but in this way democracy would be most effectively preserved. For the common people do not want to be slaves in a city with good government (*eunomoumenēs*),[119] but to be free and hold power. Bad government (*kakonomia*) is of little concern to them. And what you regard as a government of bad laws is, in fact, the source of the common people's strength and freedom. [9] If you seek good government (*eunomia*), you will first see the most skillful men establishing the laws. Then the better class will restrain the inferior class, and the better class will make decisions about the city's affairs and not allow madmen to deliberate or speak or form an assembly. Through these good practices, however, the common people would very quickly fall into slavery. [10] In Athens, on the other hand, the slaves and the *metics*[120] show the greatest lack of restraint. There, one is not permitted to strike them, and a slave will not step aside for you. I will explain why this is their custom. If it were lawful for a free man to strike a slave or a *metic* or a freedman, one would often strike an Athenian, thinking he was a slave! For the common people there dress no better than the slaves and *metics*, nor is their physical appearance any better. [11] And if anyone is also surprised that they allow slaves there to live luxuriously and some of them magnificently, clearly they do this too by design. For where there is a naval power, it is necessary to be slaves to one's slaves in order to pay for their services, and eventually to set them free.[121] And where there are wealthy slaves,

---

[119] *Eunomoumenēs*, the participle form for *eunomia*, means, literally, "having good laws." *Eunomia* was widely considered a special virtue of Spartan government. In some contexts it is a code-word for oligarchy.

[120] *metics*: see Glossary.

[121] Slaves were often hired out by their masters, and some were allowed to keep part of the wages they earned in this way. The sense of this sentence (whose text is very uncertain) seems to be that the need for a large number of rowers

it is no longer advantageous for my slave to be afraid of you. In Sparta, my slave is afraid of you, and if your slave fears me, he will risk giving up even his own money so that he can avoid any risk of bodily harm. [12] So, for this reason we gave slaves the same freedom to speak (*isēgoria*) as free men and *metics* the same freedom to speak as citizens, because the city needs *metics* for many businesses and for the fleet. And so, for this reason, it was reasonable for us to give the *metics* equal freedom to speak.

[13] Those who practice athletics there and pursue music and poetry[122] have been ruined by the common people who do not consider this a fine activity, knowing that they cannot engage in these pursuits. In the sponsorship of choruses, athletic contests, and triremes,[123] they know that the wealthy provide the choruses, and that the wealthy provide the athletic contests and the triremes, while the common people are provided with triremes and athletic contests. Nonetheless, the common people think they deserve to be paid for singing and running and dancing and sailing in ships, so that they can have their pay while the rich get poorer! Likewise in the law courts justice is of no more concern to them than their own advantage.

[14] As for their allies – they appear to sail out and lay false charges against the better people (in those cities), whom they hate, for they know that a ruler is necessarily hated by the ruled and that, if the wealthy and powerful class is strong in these cities, the rule of the people of Athens will last a very short time. So, for these reasons, they deprive the better class of their rights, confiscate their property, force them into exile, and execute them; but they cause the lower class to flourish. The better class at Athens, on the other hand, tries to save the better class in the allied cities; for they know that it is always to their advantage to support the better citizens in these cities. [15] Someone might say that this is the strength of the Athenians, that the allies are able to pay revenue. But the common class believe it a greater good for each individual

to man the fleet might force the Athenians to use slaves and either to promise them freedom because they lacked the money to pay for their services, or to pay them enough so that they could eventually purchase their freedom.

122 Athletics and music were pursuits of the leisure class at Athens. At Sparta all citizens underwent athletic training. Cf. Pericles in Thucydides 2.39.1 (fr. 3a).

123 For the Athenian system of sponsorship, known as *leitourgia*, see Antiphon's *First Tetralogy* (fr. 2b.12), with n. 226.

Athenian to have the property of the allies, and for the allies to have only enough to live on and work, while being unable to plot trouble.

[16] One might think that the common people in Athens also show poor judgment in compelling the allies to sail to Athens for legal trials.[124] In response, they enumerate the benefits this practice brings to the people. First, from the court fees they can pay for jurors throughout the year. Then, while sitting at home without sailing out in their ships they manage the allied cities and they protect those litigants who belong to the common people while destroying their opponents in the law courts. If the allies each held trials in their own city, in their anger at the Athenians they would destroy those of their own citizens who were most friendly to the Athenian people. [17] Besides these benefits the Athenian common people gain others from the allies' having their trials at Athens. First, revenue from the one-percent tax in the Piraeus[125] is increased. Then, anyone with a room to rent does better, as does anyone with a wagon or a slave for hire. Furthermore, messengers prosper from the visits of the allies. [18] In addition, if the allies did not come for their trials, they would court the favor of only those Athenians who sail out of the city – the generals, the trireme-captains, and envoys. But as it is now, every single one of the allies is forced to flatter the Athenian people, since they know they must come to Athens to settle their legal affairs before no other court than the people, as required by law at Athens. In the courts he is also forced to plead with and grasp the hand of anyone who enters.[126] Consequently, the allies have become more and more slaves of the common people at Athens.

[19] Because of their property and public posts abroad, moreover, Athenians and their servants have, without realizing it, learned how to row. For a man who often travels by sea must take up an oar and his servant must too, and they must learn the terms used in sailing. [20] They also become good pilots through their experience of sea-travel and through practice. Some practiced steering on passenger boats, others on merchant vessels, and some went on

---

[124] See Thucydides 1.77 (fr. 2c).

[125] The port of Athens.

[126] On the flattery accorded jurors in Athens as they arrive at the court, see Aristophanes, *Wasps* 550–558.

from there to triremes. The majority are able to sail as soon as they go on board, since they have been practicing throughout their entire lives.

2

[1] The Athenian hoplite force seems to be in the worst condition, but they [the Athenian people] have designed it to be this way. They reason that although their hoplites are weaker and smaller in number than their enemies, even on land they are stronger than their allies, who pay tribute, and they believe their hoplites suffice if they are stronger than their allies.

[2] An additional factor has arisen for them by chance: those who are ruled by land can combine forces from small cities and fight together but those who are ruled by sea are mostly islanders, who cannot bring their cities together into a single force. The sea separates their cities from each other, and their rulers are masters of the sea. And even if they can secretly come together into a single group on one island, they will die of starvation. [3] As for the cities on the mainland that are ruled by Athens, the large ones are ruled by fear, and the small ones completely by need. For no city at all is free from the need to import or export, but a city cannot engage in trade unless it submits to the power that rules the sea. [4] Moreover, those who rule the sea can do what is only sometimes possible for those who rule the land: lay waste the land of stronger cities. For they can sail to any place along the coast where the enemy is either absent or present in small numbers; and then, if the enemy forces approach, they can board their ships and sail off. In this way they are less vulnerable than if they had an infantry force helping them. [5] Then too, those who rule by sea can sail on voyages that take them as far from their own city as they like; whereas those who rule by land cannot march out on a journey that takes them many days from their city.[127] Marches are slow, and it is impossible to carry provisions for a long journey while traveling on foot. Also, a force that travels on foot must

---

[127] In 424 the Spartan Brasidas led a long expedition overland to northern Greece. This event would obviously invalidate this statement; thus the work probably antedates 424.

either pass through friendly territory or win its way by fighting; whereas a force that travels by ship can land wherever it is superior, ⟨and where it is weaker it need not land in⟩[128] this territory, but can sail along until it comes to friendly territory or to a weaker country. [6] Moreover, the powers strongest on the land suffer greatly when Zeus-sent diseases blight their crops, while the powers strongest on the sea suffer little from these. For the whole earth is not blighted at the same time; and so crops can come to those who rule the sea from lands that are healthy.

[7] I will also mention, if I may, some less important consequences of their rule of the sea. First, by consorting with various other peoples, they have discovered the ways of luxury. Whatever delicacy is to be found in Sicily, in Italy, in Cyprus, in Egypt, in Lydia, around the Black Sea, in the Peloponnese, or anywhere else – all these have been collected in one place through their rule of the sea. [8] Moreover, since they hear all the different dialects, they have picked up certain expressions from each for their own use. And, whereas Greeks normally adhere each to their own dialect, lifestyle, and dress, the Athenians adopt a mixture of elements taken from everyone, Greek and barbarian. [9] As to sacrifices, shrines, festivals, and sacred precincts, the people realized that poor men could not individually afford to sacrifice and feast lavishly, or own shrines, or live in a large, beautiful city, but they found a way to achieve these things. The city sacrifices many victims at public expense, but it is the people who divide up the victims and enjoy the feast. [10] And as to gymnasia, baths and dressing rooms, a few of the rich individuals have these for their private use; but the common people themselves have built for their own use many palaestras, dressing rooms, and bathhouses. And the masses benefit more from these facilities than the elite few and the fortunate.

[11] They alone among Greeks and barbarians are able to possess wealth. For if a city is rich in timber for ship-building, where will it dispose of this without the consent of the ruler of the sea? And what if a city is rich in iron, or copper, or flax for sails? Where will it dispose of these without the consent of the ruler of the sea?

---

[128] The words in angle brackets are not in the surviving text but are necessary to complete the sense.

But these very materials have provided me with ships – wood, iron, copper, flax, and wax – each from a different place. [12] Besides this, they prohibit others from exporting goods to any enemies of ours, threatening to deprive them of the use of the sea. And so without doing anything I possess all these materials from the land because of the sea, whereas no other city has more than one of them. No single city has both wood and flax: for where flax is abundant, there is level ground, bare of trees. Nor does the same city produce both copper and iron, and no one city has two or three other materials; rather, one city has one and another city another.

[13] And furthermore, along every mainland there is a peninsula, or an offshore island, or a strait, so that those who rule the sea can set up a blockade and inflict damage on the inhabitants of the mainland. [14] They do, however, have one disadvantage. If the Athenians were masters of the sea and lived on an island, they could harm others, if they wished, without suffering a thing, as long as they ruled the sea: their own land would not be ravaged or invaded by their enemies. But as it is now, the farmers and the rich Athenians curry favor with the enemy, whereas the common people, well aware that the enemy will not burn or cut down their crops, live without fear and make no overtures to them. [15] Besides this, if they lived on an island, they would avoid another fear: a few men could never betray the city by opening the gates and letting the enemy burst in. For how could this happen if they lived on an island? Nor, again, would anyone start civil strife (*stasis*) against the people if they lived on an island. But now, if civil strife should arise, they would fight in the hope that the enemy could be brought in by land, whereas, if they lived on an island, even these fears would be put to rest. [16] Since they have never had the good fortune to live on an island, they now do as follows: trusting in their rule of the sea, they transfer their possessions to islands, and allow the crops of Attica to be cut down for they know that if they are greatly concerned for these, they will be deprived of other greater goods.

[17] Furthermore, as for alliances and oaths, cities governed by oligarchy must abide by these. If they violate their agreements, or if you are wronged by one of them, the names of those who swore to the agreement are known, since they are so few. But whatever

agreements the people make, they can lay the blame for these on the one man who proposed the measure or called for a vote, while the rest can deny that they were there, or claim they did not approve, when you remind them that it was agreed to in a full Assembly. And if they change their minds on these matters, they have contrived countless excuses for not doing what they don't want to do. Then too, if the plans of the people turn out badly, they charge that a few men were working against them and ruined their plans. But if they turn out well, they give themselves credit for this.

[18] But then again, they do not tolerate any satire or censure of the people as a whole, so that they will not hear themselves being maligned, but they encourage anyone who wishes to satirize an individual; for they are well aware that the person satirized is usually wealthy, or well born, or powerful, rather than from the people or the masses. Only a few of the poor or the common people are satirized, and these only if they are meddlesome or have sought to raise themselves above the people. They don't mind seeing such people satirized also.

[19] So I say that the common people at Athens recognize which citizens are better and which are inferior. With full knowledge of this, they favor those who are useful to them and serve their interests, even if they are inferior; and they tend to be hostile toward good men. For they do not believe that the excellence (*aretē*) of these men by nature favors the good of the people but rather their harm. And yet in contrast to this, some are truly on the people's side, but they are not democratic by nature. [20] I can understand democracy for the common people. It is understandable when anyone pursues his own well-being. But if someone who is not from the common people has chosen, nonetheless, to live in a democratic instead of an oligarchic city, he is prepared to commit injustice and has recognized that a bad man is better able to go unnoticed in a democratic city than in an oligarchic one.

3

[1] And so, my view of the constitution of the Athenians is that I do not endorse its character, but since they thought it best to have

a democracy, I think they preserve the democracy well by the means I have described.

Still, I notice that some people also criticize the Athenians because sometimes a man there cannot transact his business with the Council or the Assembly, even if he sits waiting all year.[129] The only reason this happens at Athens is the size of their agenda: they cannot send everyone on his way with his business fully transacted. [2] Indeed, how could they? First, they need to celebrate more festivals than any other Greek city and on these occasions they are less able to conduct any of the city's business. Then, they have to decide more civil and criminal cases[130] and conduct more examinations[131] into the conduct of their officials than all other people combined. And the Council has to make many decisions about the war, about raising revenues and making laws, about local city matters that arise constantly, and about matters concerning the allies. It must also see to the receipt of tribute and the supervision of dockyards and shrines. Is it any wonder then that they are unable to transact business with everyone when so many other matters concern them? [3] Some say: "If a man approaches the Council or the Assembly with money in his hands, he transacts his business." And I would agree with them that much is accomplished in Athens with money, and even more would get done if more people brought money. I am quite certain, however, that the city lacks the resources to accomplish everyone's business, no matter how much gold and silver one might offer it!

[4] Then, they also have to settle disputes when someone is lax in the upkeep of his ship,[132] or builds something on public property,[133] as well as disputes each year about chorus sponsors for the Dionysia, the Thargelia, the Panathenaea, the Promethia, and the

---

[129] All terms of offices in Athens were one year.

[130] The Greek terms *dikē* and *graphē* correspond in some procedural details to our civil and criminal cases, but many offenses that we treat as crimes (theft, homicide, etc.) were normally treated as *dikai*, or private suits. The *graphē* was the newer procedure used in public crimes and some private matters.

[131] At the end of a term in office, each official's conduct was officially examined, primarily for financial mismanagement.

[132] A trierarch was responsible for the upkeep of a ship for a year. A trierarch might claim the ship was handed over to him in disrepair and ask the previous trierarch to pay for the damage; these disputes are referred to in the next sentence.

[133] This may refer to houses jutting out into a public street.

Hephaestia.[134] Also, four hundred trireme sponsors are appointed annually, and each year they have to settle whatever disputes any of these men might bring. And in addition to these matters, they have to approve the appointments of public officials, and settle their disputes, approve the claims of orphans, and appoint prison guards. These are their annual duties. [5] But periodically they have to decide cases of desertion and any other unforeseeable crimes, such as sudden acts of insolence or impiety. I am passing over a great many more matters, but I have indicated the most important, aside from the assessments of tribute, which usually occur every four years. [6] Well, should we think that they need not decide all these matters? Then let someone say which matters need not be decided there. But if we must admit that they have to decide all of them, then they will be forced to do this all year, since even now, when they are settling disputes all year, they are unable to stop the wrongdoers because of the size of the population.

[7] Well, then, someone will say that they must judge cases but that fewer men should do the judging. In that case, however, unless only a few courts are operating, there will necessarily be only a few jurors in each court, and as a result it will be easier for men to prepare themselves for a few jurors and bribe them to pass judgments with much less justice. [8] Besides this, we should keep in mind that the Athenians also have to celebrate festivals, during which they cannot have trials. And they celebrate twice as many festivals as other people, but I'll assume the same number as those in the city with the fewest. Under these circumstances, therefore, I maintain that matters at Athens cannot be otherwise than they are now unless one can add or subtract something bit by bit, but one cannot change much without taking something from the democracy. [9] One can find many ways to make their constitution better, but it is not easy to find sufficient means to improve the government while it remains a democracy – except, as I just mentioned, for piecemeal additions or subtractions.

---

[134] All these Athenian festivals featured choral performances. Rich men took turns paying the expenses of these choruses (see below n. 226 on liturgies). If your turn came up and you thought that another man who had not had his turn was richer than you, you could challenge him to an *antidosis*, or "exchange of property." He could then choose either to pay for the chorus or to exchange his property with you. A trial might be required to settle disputes arising out of these challenges.

[10] I think the Athenians also make the wrong decision when they side with the worst citizens in cities that are engaged in civil strife, but they do this by design. For if they sided with the best citizens, they would side with those who do not share their views, since in no city is the best element well disposed to the people, but rather the worst element is everywhere well disposed to the people. Indeed, like is well disposed to like. For these reasons the Athenians side with those elements akin to themselves.[135] [11] Each time they have undertaken to side with the better citizens, the result has not been in their interest[136] but rather within a short time the people in Boeotia were enslaved; moreover when they sided with the best men in Miletus, within a short time these men revolted and cut down the people; and when they sided with the Spartans against the Messenians, within a short time the Spartans subdued the Messenians and began waging war against Athens.

[12] Someone might reply: Has no one in Athens been unjustly deprived of his rights? I admit that there are some men who have been unjustly deprived of their rights – but only a few. But those who intend to attack the democracy at Athens need more than a few, since it is surely true that men who have been justly deprived of their rights do not form plots, but those who have been unjustly deprived. [13] How could anyone think that the many have been unjustly deprived of their rights at Athens, where the people are the ones who hold the offices? People become disenfranchised at Athens for such things as not governing justly, or not saying or doing what is just. One who reflects on these facts should not think that disenfranchisement is a danger to Athens.

---

[135] This analysis is well supported by Thucydides' report of civil strife on Corcyra (3.81–84; fr. 4b).
[136] The following examples refer to events that occurred around the middle of the fifth century B.C. (c. 460–446).

Aesop

The fables that have come down to us under Aesop's name represent an accumulation of popular wisdom on moral and political issues. We have translated here the fables of political interest that seem to derive from the sixth and fifth centuries.

1. *The fox and the hedgehog (Perry 427; Aristotle,* Rhetoric *2.20)*

Aesop spoke in Samos in defense of a demagogue who was on trial for his life. "A fox," he said, "was swept into a gully while trying to cross a river. She was unable to get out, and suffered for a long time, especially from the large number of dog-ticks she had on her. A hedgehog who was passing by took pity on her and asked if he could take off the dog-ticks. But the fox would not let him do so. When the hedgehog asked why, the fox said, 'These ticks have already had their fill of me, and they are taking only a little blood; but if you take these away, others will come and in their hunger will drink up the rest of my blood.'

"Now in your case, men of Samos, this man is no longer doing you any harm, because he is rich. But if you kill him, others will come who are poor, and they will steal your common property and squander it."

2. *Lions and hares (Perry 450; Aristotle,* Politics *3.13.2)*

When the hares were making public speeches and arguing that they should all have equal shares, the lions said: "Your speeches, O Hares, lack claws and teeth such as we have."

3. *The wolf and the lamb (Perry 155; cf. Perry 16 for the same story with a cat and a rooster)*

Watching a lamb drink from a river, a wolf wanted a reasonable excuse (*aitia*) to dine upon him. So he stood upstream and accused the lamb of muddying the water and not letting him drink. The lamb answered that he drank only with the tip of his lips, and that in any case he could not disturb the water upstream while standing below.

Since this excuse failed, the wolf said, "But last year you slandered my father." When the lamb answered that he had not even been born at that time, the wolf said to him, "Even though you have a good supply of answers, shall I not eat you up?"

The story shows that even a just defense has no strength against those whose purpose is to do injustice.

4. *General Wolf and the ass (Perry 348)*[137]

The very people who seem to make laws justly do not really abide by the laws they make and enforce:

A wolf who had been made general over the other wolves established laws for all, so that whatever any of them caught while hunting he would bring to the whole pack and give an equal share to everyone, so that the rest would not eat each other out of hunger. But an ass came forward, shaking his mane, and said, "That was a fine plan from the mind of a wolf. But how is it that you put yesterday's kill back in your den? Bring it to the whole pack, and divide it into shares." Thus exposed, the wolf repealed the law.

5. *The frogs ask for a king (Perry 44)*

The frogs were unhappy with the anarchy in which they lived, so they sent representatives to Zeus asking him to provide them with a king. He saw how simple they were and set up a piece of wood in their pond. At first the frogs were frightened by the noise Zeus

---

[137] This fable seems to apply well to the sort of circumstance Solon writes of, in which some aristocrats supported the cancellation of debts and the equalization of land ownership.

had made, and they hid themselves in the depths of the pond; but later, since the wood did not move, they came up and were so contemptuous of it that they climbed up on it and sat there. Feeling that they did not deserve such a king they went to Zeus a second time and insisted that he give them a different ruler, as the first one was too lazy. This made Zeus angry, and he sent them a water-snake who caught them and ate them up.

6. *The wild boar, the horse, and the huntsman (Perry 269)*

A wild boar and a horse used to graze in the same meadow; but the boar was destroying the grass and muddying the water, so the horse, wanting to protect himself, fled to a huntsman to be his ally. The huntsman said he could not come to help him unless he submitted to the bridle and let the hunter ride on his back, and the horse submitted to all this. So the huntsman rode on the horse and overcame the boar; and then he led the horse to his stall and tied him there.

In the same way, many people subjugate themselves to others through irrational anger, in their desire to ward off their enemies.[138]

7. *The North Wind and the Sun (Perry 46)*

The North Wind and the Sun were quarreling over who had the greater power, and decided to give the victory to whichever of them could strip the clothes off a man who was traveling by. The North Wind went first and blew violently, and blew still harder when the man pulled his clothes around him. But the man was still more distressed by the cold and put on an outer garment, until the North Wind got tired and gave the Sun his turn. The Sun first shone moderately, and, when the man removed his outer cloak, he increased the heat until the man was unable to bear it, took off his clothes, and went for a swim in a river that was flowing by.

The story shows that persuasion is often more effective than violence.

---

[138] The moral would seem to apply to cities in *stasis* that call in outside help. See Thucydides 3.81–84 (fr. **4b**) with Aristotle, *Rhetoric* 2.20, and Critias, fr. 26, sections 25–29.

8. *Belly and feet (Perry 130)*

Belly and feet were quarreling over who had the greater power. When the feet kept saying that they were so far superior in strength that they carried the belly, the latter answered, "But, you fools, if I do not take nourishment, you would not be able to carry anything."

So too in an army the masses are nothing unless the generals plan very well.

9. *The birdcatcher and the lark (Perry 193)*

A birdcatcher was setting a snare for birds. A lark saw him and asked what he was doing. He answered that he was founding a city, and then he went a short way off. The lark was persuaded by his arguments. He came up, ate the bait, and fell into the noose unaware. When the birdcatcher ran up and seized him, the lark said, "You fool! If this is the sort of city you are founding, you will not find many people to live in it."

The story shows that settlements and cities are most likely to be abandoned when their leaders are harsh.

10. *The lion and the dolphin (Perry 145)*

A lion was walking along on the seashore and saw a dolphin watching him. He invited him into an alliance, saying that it was most fitting for them to be friends and allies, for one of them was king of the sea animals, and the other of those on land. The dolphin gladly assented, and not long afterwards the lion had a fight with a wild bull and called on the dolphin to come to his support. But even if he had wished to do so, the dolphin was unable to come out of the sea, and the lion accused him of being a traitor. But the dolphin answered, "Don't blame me, but my nature, which made me a sea animal and so keeps me from walking on the land."

When sealing an alliance, we too must pick such allies as can be with us in danger.

11. *The dog and the sheep (Perry 356a; Xenophon,* Memorabilia *2.7.13)*[139]

They say that when animals could talk, a sheep said to her master: "What you are doing is amazing: although we give you wool and lambs and milk, you give us nothing but what we take from the land; while you share whatever food you have with your dog, who provides you with nothing of the sort." On hearing this the dog said, "Yes, by Zeus! For I am the one who protects you, so that you are not stolen by men or carried off by wolves; if I did not guard you, you could not graze for fear of being destroyed."

12. *The two roads (Perry 383* = Life of Aesop *94)*[140]

The Samians asked Aesop for advice as to whether to take tribute to the King of Persia. Instead, he told this story:

Chance shows us two roads in life; one is the road of freedom, which has a rough beginning that is hard to walk, but an ending that is smooth and even; the other is the road of servitude, which has a level beginning, but an ending that is hard and dangerous.

13. *The farmer's quarreling sons (Perry 53)*

A farmer's sons used to quarrel [to engage in *stasis*], and though he tried many times, he could not persuade them to change by means of arguments (*logoi*); so he realized that he would have to do this through action, and he asked them to bring him a bundle of sticks. When they had done as they were told, he first gave them the sticks all together and ordered them to break the bundle. When they could not do this, no matter how much force they used, he then untied the bundle and gave sticks to them one at a time. These they broke easily, and he said, "So it is with you, my sons. If you are like-minded, you will be unconquerable by your enemies; but if you quarrel, you will be easily taken."

The story shows that like-mindedness (*homonoia*) is as strong as *stasis* is easy to overcome.

---

[139] The tale is told by Socrates in a manner that implies that it is already well known. Cf. the fable in Babrius 128 (see Bibliographical Note, § B.3).
[140] Cf. Prodicus' fable in the *Choice of Heracles* (fr. 4).

PART IV

PHILOSOPHY AND SCIENCE

Heraclitus

Heraclitus of Ephesus lived during the reign of Darius (521–487) and wrote around the beginning of the fifth century. Ephesus was at that time under Persian control. Its rich neighbor, Miletus, was destroyed in 494 after the failure of the Ionian revolt, and Ephesus thereafter was unrivaled among Greek cities in Asia Minor. The fragmentary quotations of Heraclitus that have come down to us are rife with puzzles and ambiguities. We have included the fragments that can be read as carrying a political meaning.

1. *(DK 1)*

Although this is the true *logos*, people are always stupid about it, before they have heard it and after they have heard it for the first time. For although everything happens in accordance with this *logos*, people seem like those of no experience when they experience words and deeds such as the ones I am expounding when I mark off each thing by its nature and say how it is. And other people are not aware of what they do while awake, just as they forget what they did while asleep.

2. *(DK 113)*

Understanding is shared by all.

3. *(DK 2)*[141]

Although the *logos* is shared, most people live as if they had a private understanding.

---

[141] Excluding the preceding clause, "Therefore one needs to follow what is shared," as does Kahn, *The art and thought of Heraclitus* (Bibliographical Note, § B.4).

4. *(DK 116)*

All human beings share in knowing themselves and thinking soundly.

5. *(DK 112)*

Thinking soundly (*sōphronein*) is the greatest virtue, and wisdom is saying what is true and acting with understanding according to nature.

6. *(DK 114)*

Those who speak with intelligence should strongly defend what is shared by all,[142] as a city does its law, only much more strongly. For all human laws are nourished by one divine law; it controls as much as it wants, it is sufficient for all things, and it prevails.

7. *(DK 44)*

The people (*dēmos*) must fight for the law as they would for the city walls.

8. *(DK 33)*

And it is law to obey the counsel of one man.

9. *(DK 49)*

For me, one man is ten thousand, if he be the best.

10. *(DK 121)*

All the adult Ephesians deserve to be hanged and leave their city to the boys, for they drove out their most valuable man, Hermodorus, and said: "Let there not be one man among us who is best; and if there is, let him be elsewhere and with others."

---

[142] Heraclitus puns on "with intelligence" (*xun noōi*) and "shared by all" (*xunōi*).

11. *(DK 29)*

The best men choose one thing over all else: everlasting fame among mortals. But most men stuff themselves like cattle.

12. *(DK 104)*

What intelligence or understanding do they have? They believe the popular poets and treat the crowd as their teachers, not knowing that "the many are bad, and few are good."[143]

13. *(DK 52)*

A lifetime is a child at play, making moves at checkers; kingship belongs to a child.

14. *(DK 102)*

Heraclitus says that to god all things are beautiful and good and just, but human beings have taken some things to be unjust and others just.

15. *(DK 61)*

The sea is the most pure and the most foul water: for fish it is drinkable and it is their salvation; for human beings it is undrinkable and it is their destruction.

16. *(DK 110–111)*

It is not better for human beings to have everything they want. Disease makes health pleasant and good, famine does this for plenty, and weariness for rest.

17. *(DK 23)*

They would not have known the name of Justice if it were not for these things [injustices].

---

[143] A saying attributed to Bias of Priene, one of the "Seven Wise Men" (see n. 39 above).

18. *(DK 58)*

Doctors who cut and burn their patients complain that they do not receive the fee they deserve for doing this.

19. *(DK 11)*

Every animal on earth is driven to pasture by blows.

20. *(DK 53)*

War is father of all and king of all; some he has revealed as god, others as humans; some he has made slaves, others free.

21. *(Aristotle,* Eudemian Ethics *1235a25)*

Heraclitus took issue with the poet who said "I wish conflict would perish from among gods and human beings" [*Iliad* 18.107]; for there would be no attunement if there were no high or low notes, and no animals without male and female, and these are opposites.

22. *(DK 80)*

One must know that war is common, that justice is conflict (*eris*), and that all things must happen in accordance with conflict and need.

23. *(DK 94)*

The Sun will not overstep his measured limits. If he did, the Furies, those allies of Justice, will find him out.

24. *(DK 28)*

Justice will catch up with those who make up lies and bear false witness.

25. *(DK 43)*

One must put out *hubris* faster than a blazing fire.

26. *(DK 5)*

Those who are polluted with blood and try to purify themselves with blood do so in vain, as if one who had stepped into mud tried to clean himself off with mud. Anyone who saw him doing this would think he was crazy.

27. *(DK 78)*

Human character (*ēthos*) does not hold to its purposes, but the divine does. Besides, they pray to these images as one might chat with a house, because they do not know what the gods and heroes are really like.

28. *(DK 64)*

The thunderbolt governs all things.

Democritus

Democritus came from Abdera, a city in Thrace. He lived c. 460–380, a generation later than two other philosophers from Abdera, Protagoras (below, p. 173) and Leucippus. Democritus and Leucippus are known as the inventors of atomism, the theory that all matter consists of atoms and void. In addition to fragments on physics, more than a hundred ethical/political fragments are attributed to Democritus. Although their authenticity has been doubted, a majority of scholars accept them as authentic. We present here only those fragments that deal with the themes of this volume.

1. (DK 5)

This is an excerpt from the History *of Diodorus Siculus (1.8) who wrote in the first century. It does not mention Democritus, but is based on the work of a fifth-century thinker, and this is likely to have been Democritus (see Cole, Bibliographical Note, § B.4).*

The generations of humans born in the beginning led an unruly and bestial life. They foraged individually for food and consumed the most pleasing of the plants and whatever fruit fell from the trees. When attacked by wild beasts, they helped each other, learning that this was mutually advantageous, and when they were thus brought together by fear, little by little they learned each other's ways. The sounds of their voices were confused and unintelligible at first, but gradually they articulated words, and by establishing signs (*symbola*) for each existing thing, they taught each other the meanings of each of them. But since communities of this sort emerged throughout the inhabited world, people did not all have the same language, since each community assigned expressions to things by chance. This is why there are all different kinds of languages today; moreover, from these original communities come all the different nations. The first human beings lived lives full of hardship, since none of the things we use in our lives had yet been discovered: they had no clothing, knew nothing of housing or fire, and were entirely ignorant of cultivation. Since they did not know about the harvesting of wild food, they did not store up any produce for times of need. As a result, many of them died during the winters because of the cold and the lack of food; but from this they gradually learned by experience how to take refuge in caves in the winter and how to store up those fruits that could be kept. And when they had come to know fire and the other useful things, gradually they also learned crafts (*technai*) and the other things that can benefit the life of the community; for as a general rule, in all things need itself was people's teacher, providing the appropriate instruction in each area for a creature that was both well endowed by nature and had helpers for everything, namely hands and language and a shrewd mind.

2. *(DK 267)*

By nature ruling belongs to the stronger.

3. *(DK 252)*

One must attach the greatest importance of all to seeing that the affairs of the *polis* are well managed. Do not be competitive beyond what is proper, and do not acquire power for yourself contrary to the common good; for a well managed *polis* is the most prosperous. Everything depends on this: if the city is secure, everything is secure, but if it is destroyed, then all is destroyed.

4. *(DK 250)*

With concord (*homonoia*) cities are able to accomplish the greatest deeds in war, but not otherwise.

5. *(DK 249)*

Factional strife (*stasis*) among kinsmen is bad for both sides, for it destroys the victors and the vanquished alike.

6. *(DK 157)*

Learn the political craft (*politikē technē*), since it is the greatest, and pursue its labors, which lead to great and glorious things.

7. *(DK 263)*

He who worthily discharges the highest offices has the greatest share of justice and *aretē*.

8. *(DK 251)*

Poverty under a democracy is preferable to so-called prosperity under a dictator (*dunastēs*) to the same extent as freedom is preferable to slavery.

9. *(DK 283)*

Poverty, wealth: these are names for need and sufficiency. Someone in need is not wealthy; someone without need is not poor.

10. *(DK 287)*

The poverty of a community is harder to bear than that of an individual, since there is no hope of assistance.

11. *(DK 291)*

A sensible person (*sōphrōn*) bears poverty well.

12. *(DK 255)*

When those who are in power venture to provide funds for the poor and to assist and be kind to them, the result is compassion, an end to isolation, the formation of friendships, mutual defense, concord among the citizens, and other benefits too numerous to list.

13. *(DK 253)*

It is not advantageous for good men to neglect their own affairs and attend to other matters, for their private affairs suffer. But if someone neglects public affairs, he is criticized even if he does not steal or commit any crime. Indeed even if one does not neglect public affairs or do wrong, there is a risk of being criticized and even suffering harm. To err is inevitable, but it is not easy for people to forgive.

14. *(DK 265)*

People remember mistakes more than things done well; and that is just. A man who repays a loan does not deserve praise, but someone who does not repay it does deserve criticism and punishment; the same goes for a magistrate, for he was not elected to make mistakes but to do things well.

15. *(DK 266)*

In the current state of affairs there is no way that magistrates can avoid wrongdoing, even if they are very good *(agathos)*. For it is likely that the wrongdoing of others will be attributed to them.[144] These things must somehow be arranged in such a way that if someone who does no wrong vigorously investigates wrongdoers, he will not come under their sway; but an ordinance or something else will protect those who act justly.

16. *(DK 254)*

When bad men *(kakoi)* gain office, the more unworthy they are the more they become thoughtless and full of folly and recklessness.

---

[144] The text of this sentence is corrupt; our translation offers only a guess at the original meaning.

17. *(DK 49)*

It is hard to be ruled by an inferior.

8. *(DK 47)*

It is proper to yield to a law or a ruler or someone wiser than yourself.

19. *(DK 111)*

To be ruled by a woman would be the ultimate insult (*hubris*) to a man.

20. *(DK 110)*

Do not let a woman practice argument (*logos*); for that is frightful.

21. *(DK 181)*

It is clearly better to promote *aretē* by means of exhortation and persuasion than by law and compulsion. For someone who is deterred from injustice by law will probably do wrong in secret, but someone who is led to do his duty by persuasion will probably not do anything improper either secretly or openly. Thus the person who acts correctly out of understanding and knowledge becomes both courageous and straight-thinking.

22. *(DK 245)*

The laws would not prevent each of us from living as he wishes, if people did not do each other harm; for ill-will causes the beginning of discord (*stasis*).

23. *(DK 248)*

The law wants to improve people's lives; and it can do so when they themselves wish to do well, for to those who obey it it reveals their own particular *aretē*.

24. *(DK 41)*

Refrain from wrongdoing, not from fear but from duty.

25. *(DK 259)*

I think one should do the same thing among humans as I have written concerning foxes and snakes who are hostile: kill an enemy in accordance with traditional laws in every society whose law does not prohibit this. But local religious rules, treaties and oaths prevent this.

26. *(DK 260)*

Anyone who kills a highwayman or a pirate with his own hand, or by ordering another, or by voting [to convict him], would suffer no penalty.

27. *(DK 261)*

One should punish wrongdoers as best one can and not pass over them, for to do so is right *(dikaios)* and good *(agathos)*, but not to do so is wrong and bad.

28. *(DK 262)*

Those whose deeds deserve exile or imprisonment or a fine should be convicted, not acquitted; if anyone unlawfully acquits someone, deciding the case for his own profit or pleasure, he does wrong and this will necessarily weigh heavily on his heart.

29. *(DK 264)*

You should not feel more shame in front of others than by yourself, nor should you do wrong more readily when no one will see you than when everyone will. Rather, have the most respect for yourself and lay down this law for your soul: do not do anything improper.

30. *(DK 184)*

Continuous association with bad men increases one's inclination to wickedness.

31. *(DK 3)*

Whoever wishes to be content in life should not engage in many activities, either public or private, nor do anything beyond his ability and nature. Rather he should protect himself so that when fortune strikes and leads him on to seeming prosperity, he can put it aside and not grasp for more than he can manage. For a moderate amount is more secure than a large amount.

32. *(DK 242)*

More people are good *(agathos)* from practice than by nature.

33. *(DK 33)*

Nature and teaching are closely related; for teaching reforms a person, and by reforming, remakes his nature.

34. *(DK 278)*

The possession of children seems to be a necessity for humans, supported by nature and long-established custom. This is clearly the case for other creatures too; for they all have offspring by nature, and not for the sake of any resulting benefits. When they are born, the parents work hard and rear each child as best they can, and are full of fear when it is little, and grieve if something happens to it. For such is the nature of all living creatures; but human beings have become accustomed to think that there should also be some profit from a child.

35. *(DK 277)*

Whoever feels a need to have children does better, I think, to get them from friends [by adoption]. The child will then be just the sort he wishes, since he can select the kind he wants: a child who seems suitable and especially one who is naturally obedient. There is this big difference: in this case he can take the kind of child he wants from among many, as he pleases; but if he has the child himself, he runs many risks, for he must necessarily make do with whatever child is born.

36. *(DK 279)*

You should distribute as much of your property as can be divided to your children, but at the same time watch them carefully so that they do not do something disastrous when they have control of it. For they will become both more thrifty and more eager for possessions, and will compete with each other. For although expenses are not so painful when shared as when paid by one person, profits also are much less gratifying.

37. *(DK 280)*

It is possible to educate your children without spending much of your money, and thus to erect a protective wall around their persons and their property.

Medical writers from the Hippocratic corpus

The Hippocratic corpus is a collection of medical writings by different authors representing different schools of thought. We do not know for certain when specific works in the corpus were written, but we believe that some of them come from the later fifth century and so belong to our period. The texts translated below belong to the group which is considered early. It is unlikely that any of the preserved texts was written by Hippocrates himself.

Airs, Waters, Places

1. *This work is an essay on the effects of environment on human culture. The following excerpts introduce political considerations (16):*

These, then, are the features of physical nature (*phusis*) and appearance that distinguish the peoples of Asia.[145] As for the lack of courage and spirit in these people, the fact that Asians, by comparison with Europeans, are less aggressive in battle and more docile in character is primarily explained by the climate: their seasons do not produce sharp fluctuations between hot and cold, but are nearly the same. For they do not receive the sudden shocks to the mind or the strong changes in their bodies that would be likely to give them harsher tempers and more passionate spirits than those who are always in the same condition. It is change in all circumstances that stirs up the human mind and makes it restless.

---

[145] By "Asia" the author refers mainly to what we call Asia Minor (modern Turkey); but he may also have Persia in mind.

These, in my opinion, are the reasons for the weakness of the Asian race; but this is also due to their political institutions (*nomoi*), for most of Asia is ruled by kings, and wherever people are not their own masters and do not rule themselves, but are under tyranny, they have no reason to train for war, but every reason not to appear warlike. For the risks are not the same for them:[146] under tyrants, warlike men are likely to be compelled to go to war for the sake of their masters, to endure hardship, and to die far from their children, their wives, and all others who are dear to them. And whatever noble and brave deeds they do serve only to strengthen and advance their tyrants, while the men themselves reap only danger and death. In addition to these factors, the spirits of such men are necessarily softened by idleness and the lack of military exercise.[147] Thus even if a man is born brave and courageous by nature, his mind is turned away from war by the political institutions. Good evidence for this comes from all the people in Asia who are not ruled by tyrants, both Greeks and foreigners: being autonomous, they endure hardship for their own sake, and they are the most warlike of all. For they take risks on their own behalf and carry off the prizes for bravery themselves, just as they bear the penalties for cowardice.

2. (23.6–8)

The climate, then, makes those who dwell in Europe more warlike, but this is due also to their political institutions (*nomoi*), since unlike the Asians they are not ruled by kings. For whenever people are ruled by kings they are necessarily extremely cowardly, as I said earlier. For their souls are enslaved, and they are unwilling to volunteer for unreasonable risks in order to advance another man's power. But Europeans rule themselves; they choose to take risks for their own sake rather than for others; and they eagerly and voluntarily go into danger, since they themselves bear off the rewards of victory. Thus, in no small way, political institutions build courage.

---

[146] The point is that soldiering is more dangerous, and offers a lower chance of paying off, for people who are not free than for people who are.
[147] The text and translation of this sentence are uncertain.

On the Nature of Humans

3. *(1)*

The treatise On the Nature of Humans *is the work of an unknown author of the fifth century. He refutes those who assert that all existence is a unity by noting that those who say this do not agree among themselves about what this unity is, some saying air, some fire, etc. For support he refers to debating contests, using the same metaphor from wrestling that Protagoras used when he entitled his main treatise* Kataballontes *(sc.* Logoi*) or "The Downthrowing [Arguments]."*

Someone would understand this best, if he were present when they were debating (*antilegein*). For when the same speakers debate in front of the same audience, the same man never wins the debate three times in a row, but sometimes one wins, sometimes another, and sometimes whoever happens to have the most fluent tongue in addressing a crowd. And yet someone who says he has correct knowledge of the facts should, in all justice (*dikaion*), always make his own argument (*logos*) prevail, if indeed he knows what is the case and demonstrates it correctly. But I think that out of ignorance such people overthrow (*kataballein*) themselves by the wording of their arguments.

Antisthenes

Antisthenes (c. 455–360) was an Athenian, a pupil of Socrates and the founder of the Cynic school of philosophy. Numerous surviving fragments, most of them witty ripostes, echo his cynical views, but we have no complete work or even substantial fragment except for this pair of speeches. They are in the tradition of Gorgias' Helen *and* Palamedes, *and Antiphon's* Tetralogies, *and are probably early works of Antisthenes. The character of Odysseus prefigures several of the qualities valued by the Cynics.*

The contest for the armor of Achilles was a well-known episode of the Trojan War. After the death of Achilles at Troy, the Greeks decided to give his armor to the next best warrior. The choice was between Ajax, clearly the strongest and most powerful fighter, and Odysseus, who was not as mighty but was more intelligent and resourceful. When the vote came out for Odysseus, Ajax felt (with some justification) that he had been cheated of what was rightly his, and feeling disgraced he committed suicide. In a famous scene in the Odyssey *(11.543–567) Odysseus sees the ghost of Ajax in Hades and makes a friendly overture toward him, but Ajax turns away in scornful silence. Sophocles' play* Ajax *portrays the madness and suicide of Ajax after he has been denied the armor. Aeschylus also wrote a play, now lost, entitled* The Decision about the Armor.

1. Ajax

[1] I would like to have the same people judge me as were present during the events. For I know I would then need only to remain

silent and there would be nothing more for this man (Odysseus)[148] to say. But the fact is that those who were present during the actual events are absent now and you who know nothing of them are judging me. What sort of justice (*dikē*) would there be when the jurors know nothing, and have their information from speeches (*logoi*), although the events took place in reality (*ergon*)?[149] [2] It was I who rescued the body of Achilles from the battle, while this man took the armor, knowing that the Trojans were more anxious to get the corpse than the armor; for if they could get that, they could maltreat the body and obtain the ransom they paid for Hector.[150] As for the armor, they would not have dedicated it to the gods but would have hidden it away [3] out of fear of this good (*agathon*) man, for he earlier robbed their temple at night, stole the statue of the goddess and displayed it to the Achaeans as if he had done a fine deed.[151]

I think I should get the armor so that I can give it back to Achilles' friends, whereas this man wants it so that he can sell it; he would not dare use it, for no coward would use such distinguished armor, knowing that it would reveal his cowardice. [4] But it's all the same; although those who set up the contest claim to be kings, they turned over to others a decision about *aretē*, while you who know nothing are undertaking to judge a case about which you know nothing. Well, I know this, at least, that no king who is a competent judge of *aretē* would turn over this decision to others, any more than a good doctor would allow someone else to diagnose a disease.

[5] If I were contending against a man like myself, it wouldn't matter if I were defeated; but no two men could be more different than he and I. There is nothing he would do openly, whereas I would not venture to do anything in secret. I could not endure

---

[148] Neither Ajax nor Odysseus ever mentions the other by name. They commonly refer to each other by expressions such as "this man."

[149] The opposition word/deed (*logos/ergon*) is common in Thucydides and forensic oratory; see also *Ajax*, section 7 (below).

[150] In Book 24 of the *Iliad* Priam pays Achilles a large ransom for the corpse of his son Hector, which Achilles has maltreated.

[151] The story of Odysseus' theft of the statue of Athena from Troy was told in the (now lost) *Little Iliad*, an epic poem concerned with the fall of Troy (cf. Apollodorus, *Epitome* 5.13). In most versions the episode took place after Achilles' armor had been awarded to Odysseus.

having a bad reputation, even if it meant suffering terribly, whereas he could endure even being hanged, if he could make a profit. [6] Look how he allowed slaves to whip him and beat him across the back with sticks and punch him in the face, and then, dressed in rags, he slipped into the enemy's walls at night, robbed the temple, and returned. He admits he did this; maybe he'll even be able to persuade you it was a noble deed. So does this rogue, this temple-robber think he deserves to own the arms of Achilles?

[7] I ask you, therefore, you judges and jurors[152] who know nothing, to examine deeds (*erga*) rather than words (*logoi*) when you decide about *aretē*. War is decided by deeds, not words, and it is impossible to answer the enemy with a speech:[153] you must fight in silence and either win or be enslaved. Consider this carefully, for if you do not judge well, you will learn that compared with a deed a speech has no strength; [8] nor can a man bring you benefit simply by speaking; rather, you will learn very clearly that many long speeches are given because people cannot do anything. So either admit that you do not understand the points being debated and stand aside, or judge the issue correctly (*orthōs*). Judge it openly, moreover, not secretly, so that you know that those who judge must also pay the penalty if they do not judge correctly. Then perhaps you will realize that you are not here to judge speeches but simply to give an opinion. [9] I leave it to you to reach a decision about me and my affairs, and I urge you all not simply to conjecture. This concerns a man who came to Troy unwillingly, not willingly,[154] and me, who always stand in the front rank, alone and unprotected.

2. Odysseus

[1] I rise to answer not you alone, but everyone else here as well, for I have done the army more good than all of you. I would have

---

[152] Judges and jurors were not separate roles in Athenian courts, where a single body of men decided everything. Antisthenes indulges in the rhetorical practice (much favored by Gorgias) of using pleonasm – two terms where one will do.

[153] *Antilegein*, here translated "answer with a speech," can in other contexts mean "oppose" or "contradict," and the expression used here, *ouk estin antilegein*, "it is impossible to contradict (anyone)," has been attributed to Protagoras (fr. 25).

[154] Odysseus feigned madness in order to avoid going to Troy but was tricked (by Palamedes) into revealing his sanity.

said this to you even if Achilles were still alive, and I say it now that he is dead. For in every battle you have fought I have been there with you, and I have also taken risks on my own, of which you know nothing. [2] In battles involving the whole army no more was gained even by a good individual effort; but in situations where I took risks entirely on my own, if I should succeed, I would accomplish our entire objective, whereas if I failed, you would only lose one man – me. For our purpose in coming here was not to fight the Trojans but to recover Helen and capture Troy. [3] These considerations prompted my ventures. For where it was prophesied that Troy could not be taken unless we should first capture the statue that had been stolen from us, who else but I was going to bring the statue here? Yes, the very one you call a temple-robber. You don't know anything if you call the man who rescued the statue of the goddess a temple-robber, and do not use this word for Alexander, who originally stole it from us. [4] So, while everyone is praying for the capture of Troy, you call me a temple-robber for trying to discover how to accomplish this? Well, if it's a good thing (*kalon*) to capture Troy, surely it's a good thing to discover the key to doing so. Everyone else is grateful, but you criticize me, since you are too ignorant to understand how you benefitted. [5] I don't blame you for your ignorance – like everyone else you suffer this condition involuntarily – but because you cannot be persuaded that these very acts for which you reproach me are your salvation; thus you also threaten to harm these people if they vote me the armor. I suppose you'll often make many threats before you actually do anything; but to judge from what is likely (*eikos*), I think your bad temper will result in some harm to yourself.

[6] Well, you rebuke me for cowardice because I have done harm to the enemy, but in fact you are the foolish one for toiling openly and in vain. Do you think you are better because you did this with everyone else? And then you talk to me about *aretē*? In the first place you don't even know how to fight, but attack in anger like a wild boar. Some day you may kill yourself, falling on something.[155] Don't you know that a good (*agathon*) man is not supposed to suffer harm from anyone – himself, a companion or

---

[155] Traditionally (and in Sophocles' *Ajax*) Ajax commits suicide by falling on his sword.

the enemy? [7] Like a child, you're happy because these people call you brave; but I say you are the biggest coward of all and the most afraid of death. First, they call you invulnerable only because you have armor that is impenetrable and invulnerable. But what would you do if an enemy who has the same sort of armor should attack you? That would be a fine sight, if neither of you was able to do anything. Second, do you think there is a difference between having armor like this and sitting inside a wall, since you claim to be the only one not protected by a wall? In fact, you're the only one who has put a wall around himself, by carrying a seven-layered shield.[156] [8] I, on the other hand, without any armor at all, went not just up to the enemy's walls, but inside them, and although the enemy's sentries were awake, I captured them and their weapons. I am thus the leader and the protector of you and all the rest; I know the situation in the enemy camp as well as here, not because I send someone else to reconnoiter but because I go myself. Like the captain, who watches day and night so he can save his crew, I keep you and everyone else safe. [9] I didn't avoid any danger I thought was shameful, if it allowed me to do harm to the enemy, nor did I take risks when someone would see me just for appearances' sake. But if I could harm the enemy by being a slave or a beggar or a rogue, I would take on the role even if no one was watching. War always favors actions not appearances, both day and night.[157] I have no set armor in which I challenge the enemy to fight, but I am always ready to fight, against one or against many, with any weapons anyone wishes. [10] When I am wearied by fighting, I don't hand over my arms to others, as you do, but when the enemy stop fighting, then I attack them, at night, with whatever weapons will damage them the most. Nightfall has never taken me out of action, though it has often made you glad to stop fighting; but I am working for your safety while you snore, and I am always harming the enemy with these weapons, fit for a slave – rags and lash-marks – which allow you to sleep in safety. [11] Do

[156] Ajax's unique seven layered ox-hide shield is described in *Iliad* 7.219–223 as "like a tower." Several other points in Odysseus' speech allude to passages in Homer.

[157] The Greek of this sentence forms an almost perfect tragic couplet in iambic trimeter. Antisthenes may be citing a tragedian. Similarly, the next sentence from "I am always" to "against many" nearly forms a single iambic trimeter.

you think you are brave because you carried Achilles' corpse out of battle? But if you couldn't carry it, two men would have, and then perhaps they too would be in contention with us over *aretē*. I could use the same argument against them, but what would you say to them? Or would you not be concerned about having two opponents and be ashamed to admit being more cowardly than only one? [12] Don't you know that the Trojans' concern was to capture the armor, not the corpse? For they were going to return the latter but intended to dedicate the former to the gods in the temple. It is not disgraceful to fail to recover corpses but rather to fail to hand them over for burial. Thus you brought back something uncontested, whereas I deprived them of something in dispute.

[13] You are sick with jealousy and ignorance, two evils that are directly opposed; for one makes you desire excellence (*ta kala*) but the other prevents you from attaining it. Your experience is all too human: because you are strong, you think you are also brave; you do not realize that strength is not the same thing as courage and knowledge in matters of war, or that ignorance is the greatest evil for those who suffer from it. [14] And so, I think that if there is ever a poet who is wise in matters of *aretē*, he will make me a man of much endurance, much intelligence, much contrivance,[158] and a city-sacker, and he will say that I alone captured Troy. But as for you, I think he will liken your nature to that of sluggish mules and grazing cattle, who let others rope them and yoke them.

---

[158] These three compound adjectives all have the prefix *polu-* ("much, many"). We are told (Caizzi, fr. 51; Giannantoni, fr. 188 – see Bibliographic Note, § B.4) that Antisthenes examined at length the meaning of another Homeric adjective for Odysseus, *polutropos* or "man of many ways" (*Odyssey* 1.1, etc.).

PART V
SOPHISTS

Protagoras

Protagoras was born in Abdera around 485 and enjoyed a career of forty years as a professional teacher. He traveled widely and was richly paid for his efforts. The tradition that he was a student of Democritus is probably false, although he too came from Abdera. Most scholars also doubt the story that Protagoras was tried in Athens and condemned for atheism.

We translate here all of the generally accepted fragments, as well as texts in which Protagoras is paraphrased or closely imitated. We have shown only as much of the context as is needed for comprehension. Irrelevant intrusions of context have been omitted without comment. Some passages contain only a word or phrase that is a quotation from Protagoras; in such cases we have underlined the quotation and supplied the necessary context in normal print. We have included titles of works by Protagoras that are well attested and are interesting in their own right. We have also included passages that probably represent teachings of Protagoras that have been filtered through the teachings of other thinkers; these passages are labeled "reconstruction."

In a few cases we print passages that have long been associated with Protagoras, even though we are not convinced that their content is due to Protagoras. In such cases we preface our designation with the comment "doubtful." We have arranged the material by subject: first his profession, then political theory and ethics, then theory of knowledge, and finally diction or correct speaking.

1. *On being a sophist (Plato,* Protagoras *316d3–317c1,* PARAPHRASE)

I say that the sophistic profession (*technē*) is very old, but that the men who practiced it in the old days were afraid of the odium

attached to it, and disguised their profession under various covers:
some used poetry, as did Homer and Hesiod and Simonides, others
used religious rites and prophecies, as did Orpheus and Musaeus,
along with their followers. I've noticed that some even used athletics,
as did Iccus of Taras and, nowadays, Herodicus of Selymbria
(formerly of Megara), and he's second to none as a sophist. Aga-
thocles used music as his cover here in Athens, and he was a
great sophist; so did Pythocleides of Ceos and many others. All
these, I claim, used these professions as screens because of their
fear of resentment. But I do not go along with any of them on
this. I don't think they achieved what they intended – they didn't
fool the people who had power in the cities – which was the only
reason they had those covers, since ordinary folks hardly notice
anything anyway, but just sing along with the men in real power.
Now trying to run away without actually running away, but getting
found out – that's a really stupid thing to do, even in the attempt,
and it's certain to make people angrier than ever. They think you're
a rascal if you run away, besides whatever else they think. So I
have taken exactly the opposite road to theirs, and I admit that
I'm a sophist and I educate people. This admission is a better
precaution, I think, than their denial. I've thought out other precautions too, so that, god willing, I'll have nothing terrible happen
to me through admitting I'm a sophist.

2. *(Plato,* Protagoras *348e6–349a4, PARAPHRASE)*

Socrates: While others hide this profession, you advertise yourself
openly to all the Greeks, calling yourself a sophist, proclaiming
yourself a teacher of education and of *aretē*, the first to believe he
deserves to be paid for his teaching.

3. *On his teaching (Plato,* Protagoras *318a6–9, POSSIBLE QUOTATION)*

Young man, this will be your reward if you study with me: on the
day you come to me, you will go home a better man, and the next
day the same. And every single day you will become progressively
better.

4. *(Plato,* Protagoras *318d7–319a7, PARAPHRASE and POSSIBLE
QUOTATION)*

Protagoras: If Hippocrates[159] comes to me he won't have the experience he would have if he studied with some other sophist. The others ruin young men, you know; those young men had been running away from specialized knowledge (*technē*), but the other sophists take them and throw them back into specializations against their will, teaching them arithmetic and astronomy and geometry and music (and here Protagoras gave a sharp look at Hippias), but if he comes to me he won't learn about anything but what he came for. And that is good judgment (*euboulia*) about domestic matters, so that he may best manage his own household, and about political affairs, so that in affairs of the *polis* he may be most able both in action and in speech.

Socrates: Am I following what you say? I think you mean political knowledge (*technē*),[160] and you promise to make men good citizens.

Protagoras: That is exactly what I proclaim.

5. (*DK 3, QUOTATION*)

Teaching requires natural talent and practice; one must begin learning in early youth.

6. (*DK 10, QUOTATION*)

There is no specialized knowledge (*technē*) without practice, and no practice without specialized knowledge.

7. (*Plato,* Protagoras *351a1–b2, RECONSTRUCTION*)

Power (*dunamis*) and strength are not the same: power can come from knowledge, but it could also come from inspiration or anger; strength, on the other hand, is due to natural ability and the good nurture of bodies. It's the same in this case: daring and courage are not the same, and it turns out that all courageous people are daring, but not all daring people are courageous. For daring can

---

[159] Hippocrates, a prospective student of Protagoras, has asked Socrates to ask Protagoras what he teaches. He bears no relation to the famous author of the medical treatises.

[160] I.e., the knowledge of how to run a *polis* or city.

come to human beings from special knowledge (*technē*),[161] but also from inspiration or anger, as can power; whereas courage comes from natural ability and the good nurture of souls.

8. *Myth: Origin of the* polis *(Plato,* Protagoras *320c7–322d5,* POSSIBLE QUOTATION)

Selections 8, 9, and 10 are three sections of a single speech given in Plato's Protagoras. *Selection 8 (the Myth) uses Protagorean style and language, and is probably authentic; 9 and 10 are more likely to be paraphrases of Protagorean teaching, as the language of these is more Platonic. The myth gives a Protagorean twist to a story known from Hesiod, fr. 1 and Aeschylus, frs. 1–3.*

Once upon a time there were gods, but there were still no mortal species. And when the appointed time came for the birth of these 320d species, the gods shaped them within the earth, using a mixture of earth and fire and whatever compounds are made from fire and earth. And when they were about to lead them forth into the light, they assigned Prometheus and Epimetheus[162] the task of giving to each species the powers and equipment that would be appropriate to it. And Epimetheus begged Prometheus to let him make the distribution: "When I have finished," he said, "you may inspect." And after persuading Prometheus of this, Epimetheus made the distribution. Strength without speed he attached to some animals, 320e but he equipped the weaker animals with speed. To some he gave weapons, and he gave other powers of survival to those he had left without natural weapons: some that were tiny he protected by giving them wings to fly, or homes to dwell in underground; others he made of enormous size, so that their size alone would make them safe. The rest he treated in the same way, making his 321a distribution fair and equal. He devised all this with care that no species would ever vanish. And when he had provided ways of avoiding the destruction of one species by another, he developed means of comfort against the weather, clothing them with thick hair and tough skin sufficient to ward off the cold of winter and

---

[161] The thought behind this is that if you know how to do specialized work, you will approach your task with more confidence.

[162] The names mean "Forethought" and "Afterthought" respectively.

strong enough for the burning heat of summer, intending that these same things would be appropriate natural bedding for each species when it went to sleep. And for shoes he gave them hooves or 321b tough skin where no blood flows. After that he provided nourishment in different ways for different species: forage from the earth for some, fruits of trees for others, and roots for a third group. And there were those he set to devouring other animals for their food, but he gave them a low rate of fertility, while he made their prey highly prolific, and so preserved the race from destruction.

Now Epimetheus was not very clever, so he did not notice that he had given away all the powers he had to animals who lacked reason and language, while he still had the human species to equip. 321c He had no idea what to give them. While he was puzzling over this, Prometheus came to inspect the distribution, and saw the other animals cared for in every way, but human beings naked and unshod, coatless and unarmed. And already the appointed day was here, on which the human species also had to come forth from the earth into the light. Now Prometheus had no other means for saving the human species, so he stole from Hephaestus and Athena 321d their specialized knowledge and skill (*entechnon sophia*) along with fire – for no one could acquire or use such knowledge without fire – and he endowed the human race with this. That is how human beings came to know how to stay alive; but they did not know how to form cities. For that knowledge was in the keeping of Zeus, and Prometheus had no time left to break into the citadel where Zeus lived – besides, the watchmen Zeus had were terrifying. But Prometheus did secretly enter the shared workshop where 321e Athena and Hephaestus practiced their own specialized knowledge (*technai*), and he stole the fire-based knowledge of Hephaestus and the other knowledge of Athena and gave them to the human race. With that came a rich supply of the means of livelihood for human beings; but they say that the penalty for theft eventually caught up 322a with Prometheus, and all because of Epimetheus.

Because humanity shared in this divine gift, they alone among animals believed in gods, owing to their kinship with the gods; and they began to set up altars and images of gods. Next they quickly acquired the knowledge of making sound into articulate words, and discovered housing and clothing and shoes and bedding and nourishment from the earth.

Thus equipped, then, human beings originally had scattered dwellings rather than cities; they were therefore weaker in every 322b way than the wild beasts, who were killing them off. Although their practical knowledge (*demiourgikē technē*) was sufficient to provide nourishment, it was no help in fighting off the beasts – for human beings did not yet have political knowledge (*politikē technē*), and military knowledge is a part of that. They tried to band together and save themselves by founding cities. But when they were banded together, they would treat each other unjustly because they did not have political knowledge, and the result was that they would scatter again and be destroyed.

Zeus, therefore, taking fear that our race would be entirely killed 322c off, sent Hermes to bring Respect and Justice (*aidōs* and *dikē*) to the human race, so that Respect and Justice would bring order to cities and be the communal bonds of friendship.

Then Hermes asked Zeus in what way he should give Justice and Respect to human beings: "Shall I distribute these in the same way as specialized knowledge was distributed? That was distributed in the following way: one person who has medical knowledge is sufficient for many private people, and so it is with the other crafts. Should this be the way I distribute Justice and Respect among human beings, or should I give them to everyone?"

"To everyone," said Zeus, "and let all share in them. For there 322d would be no cities if only a few people shared in them as they do in the other kinds of specialized knowledge. And lay down a law from me that he who is not able to share in Respect and Justice be killed as a disease of the city."

9. *Explanation of the myth: All human beings must share in* aretē. *(Plato,*
   Protagoras *322d5–324d1,* PARAPHRASE *or* RECONSTRUCTION)

Socrates has challenged Protagoras to defend his assumption that aretē
can be taught (318b–d). This is his reply. It is continuous with selection 8.

Well, Socrates, that explains why people in Athens and elsewhere believe that when they are discussing *aretē* in carpentry or any other practical skill, only a few experts should advise them, and if 322e someone else tries to offer advice, they don't allow it, as you say – and I'd say that is reasonable (*eikos*). But when they come for

advice on *aretē* in running the city, which must proceed entirely 323a
through Justice and Soundness of Mind,[163] they allow every man
to take part – and that is reasonable too, for it is fitting for everyone
to share in this *aretē*, or there would be no cities. The story I told
explains that.

So that you won't suppose I'm trying to fool you when I say
that we all really do think every man has a share in Justice and
the rest of political *aretē*, consider this evidence. You are right about
other forms of *aretē*: if someone claims he's a good flute-player when
he isn't, or that he has any other specialized knowledge when he
doesn't, people either laugh at him or get angry, and his family 323b
come and try to bring him to his right mind, as if he were a
madman. But it's different in the case of Justice and the rest of
political *aretē*: if a person who is known to be unjust tells the truth
about himself in front of many people, then they think he is crazy
to have done what in the other case they thought showed a sound
mind – namely, telling the truth. In fact, people say that everyone
ought to call himself just, whether he is or not; and if someone
doesn't pretend to be just, they say he's crazy, on the grounds that
there cannot possibly be anyone who does not in some way or
other share in Justice, or else he cannot exist among human 323c
beings.[164]

I have said all this, then, to show that it is reasonable to accept
every man as an adviser about this *aretē*, because people think
everyone takes part in it. I turn now to the next point, which is
to show that people consider this *aretē* to be teachable, and they
think that anyone who acquires it does so by diligence, not by
natural inheritance or spontaneously. When people think someone
has bad qualities through chance or natural inheritance, they are 323d
never angry at him, never rebuke him or try to teach or punish
him in order that he should be otherwise. Instead, they pity him.
How could anyone be so stupid as to try such tactics on people
who are ugly or small or weak? Everyone knows, I think, that

---

[163] Here soundness of mind (*sōphrosunē*) takes the place of respect (*aidōs*) as the
second political virtue. *Aidōs* appeared in Protagoras' myth as a link with the
story as told by Hesiod (fr. 1), but Plato's interest is evidently in soundness of
mind. Also, where 8 uses *dikē*, 9 now uses *dikaiosunē*. See the Glossary on both
terms.

[164] Conveniently ambiguous between "not be in human society" and "not be counted
as a human being."

qualities like these, whether good or bad, are due to chance or natural inheritance.

When, on the other hand, someone fails to have good qualities that are thought to come from diligence and training and teaching, when in fact he has just the opposite qualities – bad ones – that is when people are angry, and that is when they punish and rebuke him. Injustice is one of these bad qualities, and so is impiety and so, in a word, is everything that is opposite to political *arete*. And so the reason any one person is angry at another and rebukes him is clearly that political *arete* is thought to be acquired by diligence and learning. 323e

324a

Just think what punishment can do for wrongdoers, Socrates, and you will see that human beings believe they should provide for the acquisition of *arete*. No one punishes a wrongdoer with any other thought or concern than that he has done wrong, unless he wreaks vengeance like a beast, for no reason.[165] But if someone has a reason (*logos*) to set about punishing another, he does not take vengeance out of any concern for the wrong that is past, since what has been done cannot be undone.[166] Instead, he uses punishment for the sake of the future, so that both the wrongdoer and anyone who sees him punished will be deterred from doing wrong again. And because he has this purpose in mind, he has in mind also the idea that *arete* is the product of education; at least he punishes for the sake of deterrence. This, therefore, is the opinion of all who seek punishment or vengeance, whether privately or in public; and human beings in general *do* seek vengeance and punish those they think have done wrong. Athenians especially do this – your fellow citizens; it follows from this argument that the Athenians too are among those who think *arete* is something to be acquired and taught. 324b

324c

It is reasonable, then, that your fellow-citizens accept a bronze-worker or shoemaker[167] as adviser on matters of politics and that

---

[165] Cf Aristotle, *Rhetoric* 1.10.17, 1369b12–14: "There is a difference between vengeance (*timoria*) and punishment (*kolasis*); punishment is for the sake of the one who receives it, while vengeance is for the sake of the one who gives it, so that he may get satisfaction."

[166] See our fragment **6** of Agathon making just this point (*Other Tragic Fragments*, above).

[167] These are the examples Socrates used in his original challenge to Protagoras' assumption that virtue can be taught (319d3).

they think *aretē* something to be taught and acquired – this I have
demonstrated for you, Socrates, and quite sufficiently in my 324d
view.

10. *Argument that* aretē *can be taught (Plato,* Protagoras *324d2–328c2,*
RECONSTRUCTION)

Protagoras is made to respond to Socrates' objections at 319b–320b.

There remains the difficulty you raised about men who are good:
why it is that good men teach their sons all the subjects that have
teachers, and give them all other skills, but when it comes to their
own excellence, the [political] *aretē* in which they excel, they fail
to make their sons better than anyone else.[168] On this point,
Socrates, I shall no longer be telling you a story (*mythos*), but an
argument (*logos*). Think about this: is there, or is there not, some
one thing in which all citizens must share if a city is to exist at 324e
all? This, if anything, will resolve that difficulty of yours. If there
is this one thing, and it is not carpentry or bronze-work or pottery 325a
but Justice and Soundness of Mind and Piety – this is one thing,
and, in a word, I call it a man's *aretē* – if this is what everyone
must share in, if this is what everyone must follow in doing whatever
else he wants to learn or do, or else not do it at all, if anyone
who does not share in this – whether man, woman, or child –
must be schooled or punished until the punishment makes him
better, and if anyone who does not respond to punishment and
education must be thrown out of the city or killed as incurable – 325b
if all that is so, just think: wouldn't it be amazing if, despite this
fact of nature, good men had their sons taught everything else,
but not this? We have already proved that they think this can be
taught both publicly and in private.[169] And since it *can* be taught
and nurtured, do they really have their sons taught other things,
where the penalty for ignorance is not death, but where the penalty
is death or exile for their sons if they are not taught and nurtured
in *aretē* – and besides death, the confiscation of property and, in 325c
a word, the overthrow of virtually the whole family – are you saying
that they do *not* have this subject taught, that they do *not* take

---

[168] E.g. Pericles (319e3, ff.; cf. *Meno* 93a).
[169] At 324c.

every care for this concern? You must think that they *do*, Socrates. Starting from early childhood, and for as long as they live, they teach and admonish their children. As soon as a child knows the meanings of words, his nurse and mother and pedagogue and even 325d his father are fighting hard to make the child turn out to be as good as possible. With every deed and every word they are teaching him and showing him – "this is right and that is wrong," "this is good and that is awful," "this is pious and that's impious," and "do this, don't do that." If he obeys willingly, that's fine. If not, they straighten him out with threats and blows, as if he were a board that had gone warped and crooked. After that, when they send him to school, they put much more weight on their concern 325e that the children learn good conduct (*eukosmia*) than that they learn to read and write or play music.

The teachers take this to heart; and when the children have learned the alphabet and are ready to read (as before, when they understood speech), then the teachers put works of good poets before them to read at their benches, and require them to learn 326a by heart poems that are full of good advice, and stories and songs in praise of good men of old, so that the child will be eager to emulate them, and will yearn to grow up to be a man like them. Musicians do much the same when they teach the lyre; they try to foster Soundness of Mind, and they keep the youngsters out of mischief. Besides that, once the children have learned to play the lyre, they are taught more poetry by good lyric poets. Then the 326b music-teachers set those poems to the music of the lyre, and make sure that rhythm and harmony dwell in the souls of the children, so that they will grow more gentle and their speech and their behavior will improve as they gain grace in rhythm and harmony, for all human life needs the grace of harmony and rhythm. On top of all that, parents send their sons to a physical trainer, so that their bodies will grow strong enough to serve those good minds they now have, so that bodily weakness will not force them 326c into cowardice in war or any other situation.

Now, the parents who are best able to do all this do it most thoroughly. The richest people are the most able, and their sons begin going to teachers at the earliest ages, and leave off at the latest.

When children leave their teachers, the city in its turn requires them to learn its laws and to live by the example they set, so that 326d they'll not do whatever they feel like, now that they're on their own. The city is exactly like a writing teacher who lays down lines with a stylus for boys who aren't good at writing yet, and requires them to write within the lines he laid down when he gave them their writing-tablets.[170] That's how the city lays down the laws that were discovered by the great lawgivers of the past, requires its citizens to rule and be ruled in accordance with these laws, and punishes anyone who goes outside the laws. The name for punishment of this kind, in Athens and everywhere else, is *straightening*, 326e since justice *makes straight*.

In view of all this diligent private and public concern for *aretē*, are you still surprised that it can be taught, Socrates? Is this still hard for you to understand? You ought not to be surprised; the real surprise would be if it were not teachable.

Why then do many sons of good fathers turn out poorly? You need to understand, now, that this is not at all surprising, if what I said before is true: if cities are to exist at all, there must be no one who is a complete layman on this subject of *aretē*. If what I 327a said is so – and it is so, more than anything – well, think of any other practice or subject you choose. Suppose there could be no city unless all of us were flute-players, each of us as good as he could be, and that everyone taught flute-playing to everyone else, privately and in public, and punished those who did not play well, and suppose no one guarded his knowledge of flute-playing from other people – just as, now, no one guards or hides away his knowledge of what is just and lawful, as other experts do with the 327b tricks of their trades. (I think that practicing *aretē* and justice towards each other is to our advantage; that's why everyone is so eager to teach everyone else what is just and lawful.) Now suppose it was flute-playing that we were so totally eager to teach to other people ungrudgingly: Socrates, do you think that the sons of good flute-players would be good flute-players any more than the sons of bad ones? I think not. If somebody's son turned out to have

---

[170] The analogy is to horizontal lines drawn by a teacher on the student's writing tablet. The passage rings in Greek with repetitions of *gram-* and *graf-*, which are untranslatable puns on *line* and *letter*.

great natural ability for flute-playing, he would grow up to count 327c
for something; but if he lacked natural ability, he'd lack fame.
Often a poor flute-player would come from a good one, and often
a good one from a poor one. But then, as flute-players, all of them
would be good enough, at least in comparison with complete laymen
who know nothing of flute-playing. That, believe me, is how it is
in regard to Justice: take a person you think is very unjust: if he
has been brought up among laws and men he is actually just; in
fact, he's an expert at the practice of justice if he's to be judged
against people who've had no education, no law-courts, no laws, 327d
and nothing to force them to care about *aretē* in every circumstance – savages rather like the ones Pherecrates the poet presented
at the Lenaia last year.[171] Really, if you wound up among such
people as those man-haters in his chorus, you'd be pleased if you
ran into Eurybatus and Phrynondas [proverbial scoundrels], and
you'd weep with longing for the bad people here.

But as it is, Socrates, you're spoiled: *everyone* is a teacher of 327e
aretē so far as he is able, and so you don't notice any of them.
It's as if you were looking for a teacher of the Greek language [in 328a
Greece]: you wouldn't notice a single one![172] And even if you
looked around for someone who could give further instruction to
a craftsman's son in the special knowledge he had learned as best
he could from his father and his father's friends and fellow-
craftsmen, even then, Socrates, I don't think you would find a
teacher for the son of an expert very easily, though it's quite easy
to see that there are teachers for those who know nothing at all.
That's how it is with *aretē* and with everything else. So if any one
of us is even a little bit better at helping others advance towards 328b
aretē, he should be welcomed. I believe that I am one of these,
that I do a better job than others do in helping a person become
fine and good, and that I am worth the fee I charge and even
more, as the pupil himself judges. That is why I have set up this
system for determining my fee: when someone has studied with
me, he pays the sum I charge if he's willing; if not, he goes to a 328c
temple, makes an oath as to how much he declares the lessons to
be worth, and pays that much.

[171] This comedy, *Agrioi* (*Savages*), was performed in 420.
[172] Cf. Plato, *Alcibiades I* 111a1–4; on the thesis that all are teachers of virtue, cf.
the remarks of Meletus (*Apology* 24e) and Anytus (*Meno* 93a).

11. *Good is a relative term (Plato, Protagoras 334a3–c6, PARAPHRASE)*

Protagoras volunteers an account of "good" and "advantageous" that goes beyond what was called for in Socrates' questions.

I know many things that are unbeneficial to humans – foods and drinks and drugs and thousands of other things – and others that are beneficial. Some are neither beneficial nor harmful to humans, but are beneficial for horses, some only for cattle, and others for dogs. Some aren't good for any of them, but are for trees. And some are good for the roots of the tree, but harmful to the shoots; manure, for example, is good if applied to the roots of all plants, but if you want to put it on the sprouts and young twigs it destroys them all. And, again, olive oil is very bad for all plants and most inimical to the hair of animals other than humans; but is helpful for human hair and the rest of the body. But so various and many-sided a thing is the good, that even when we human beings use oil, it is good for the outside parts of the body, but the same oil is very bad for our insides. Because of this, all doctors forbid weak people to use oil, except for the smallest dash of oil in dishes they are going to eat, just enough to quench the harshness that comes to the attention of the nostrils from foods and relishes.

12. *(Plato, Protagoras 351d4–7, RECONSTRUCTION)*

Protagoras gives his reason for not adopting Socrates' premise of hedonism.

There are some pleasant things that are not good; and, again, there are some painful things that are not bad, while some are, and there's a third set that are neither, not good and not bad.

13. *(Plato, Theaetetus 166d6–8, RECONSTRUCTION)*

This and the following passage come from a speech in which Protagoras is imagined to be replying to Socrates' objections.

But this is the man *I* call wise: when one of us has bad things appear and be to him, the wise man can change that and make good things appear and be to him.

14. *(Plato,* Theaetetus *167c4–5,* RECONSTRUCTION*)*[173]

Whatever each city judges to be just and fine, these things in fact are just and fine for it, so long as it holds those opinions.

15. *A human being is the measure (DK 1,* QUOTATION*)*

A human being is measure of all things, of those things that are, that they are, and of those things that are not, that they are not.

16. *The man–measure quotation (passage* **15***) is said to occur in each of the following titles:* Truth[174] *and* The Downthrowing [Arguments].[175] *A related title is* On Being *(DK 2).*

17. *(Plato,* Theaetetus *152a6–8,* PARAPHRASE*)*[176]

Each thing is to me such as it appears to me, and is to you such as it appears to you.

18. *(Plato,* Theaetetus *167a7,* RECONSTRUCTION*)*

Socrates, speaking for Protagoras:

It is not possible to think what is not.

19. *(Plato,* Theaetetus *166c4–6,* RECONSTRUCTION*)*

Socrates, speaking for Protagoras:

Each of us has his own private perceptions, and what appears exists only for that person to whom it appears.

20. *Obscurity and the gods (DK 4,* QUOTATION*)*

Concerning the gods, I am not in a position to know either that they exist or that they do not, nor can I know what they look like,

[173] Cf. *Theaetetus* 168b5, 172b2–6, 177d1–2, 179a5.
[174] Plato, *Cratylus* 391c6; *Theaetetus* 171c6.
[175] Sextus Empiricus, *Against the Mathematicians* 7.60.
[176] Cf. *Cratylus* 386c2–5.

for many things prevent our knowing – the subject is obscure (*adēlon*) and human life is short.

21. *PROBABLE QUOTATION*[177]

It is manifest to you who are present that I am sitting; but to a person who is absent it is not manifest that I am sitting; whether or not I am sitting is obscure.

22. *(Aristotle,* Metaphysics *B 2, 997b35–998a4,* PARAPHRASE*)*

Nothing perceptible is as straight or as round as the geometers say, for, as Protagoras said in refuting the geometers, the circle does not touch the ruler at a single point.

23. *(DK 5) The title of a work:*

"Contradictions."

24. *(Diogenes Laertius 9.51,* QUOTATION*)*[178]

On every subject there are two *logoi* [speeches or arguments] opposed to one another.

25. *(Diogenes Laertius 9.53,* DOUBTFUL QUOTATION*)*[179]

It is not possible to contradict.

26. *(Plutarch,* Against Colotes *4, 1108f. = DK 68 B 156, line 14,* PROBABLE QUOTATION*)*

Each thing is no more such than such.

---

[177] From Didymus the Blind's Commentary on the *Psalms*, a papyrus text published in 1969 (see Bibliographical Note, § B.5).

[178] Cf. the imitation of this in Aristophanes, *Clouds*, lines 112–114.

[179] Cf. Plato, *Euthydemus* 286c.

27. *(Aristotle,* Rhetoric *2.24, 1402a23* = DK 6b, PROBABLE QUOTATION)

Making the weaker *logos* stronger.[180]

28. *Correctness of speech (Plato,* Protagoras *338e7–339a1,* PARAPHRASE)

I think the greatest part of education for a man is to be clever (*deinos*) about verses; by that I mean to be able to grasp which of a poet's lines are composed correctly (*orthōs*), and which are not, to know how to distinguish them, and to give a reason (*logos*) when questioned.[181]

29. *(Plato,* Cratylus *391c3,* PROBABLE QUOTATION)

Correctness (*orthotēs*) concerning [words].[182]

30. *(Plutarch,* Life of Pericles *36.3,* POSSIBLE QUOTATION)

When an athlete unintentionally struck Epitimus the Pharsalian with a javelin and killed him, Pericles spent an entire day with Protagoras puzzling over whether one should believe that the javelin or the javelin-thrower or those who arranged the contest were more to blame, according to the most correct account (*logos*).

31. *(Plato,* Phaedrus *267c6,* QUOTATION)

Correctness of diction [*orthoepeia* – a term we are told Protagoras used in his teaching of oratory].

---

[180] *Hēttōn* ("weaker") and *kreittōn* ("stronger") have a wide range of meanings, including "worse" and "better" in a moral sense. Aristophanes uses these as the names of the opposed *logoi* who debate in the *Clouds* (889–1104). Cf. Herodotus 8.93, where he reports that Themistocles' entire speech before the battle of Salamis opposed the stronger/better to the weaker/worse and urged the Greeks to choose the stronger. The practice of making the weaker case stronger in a speech was attributed to several sophists (Cicero, *Brutus* 30).

[181] Protagoras illustrates this method by finding two statements that are contradictory in a poem by Simonides, and arguing that one of them must be incorrect.

[182] Cf. the use of this phrase in Gorgias, fr. 3.

32. *(Aristotle,* Sophisticis Elenchis *14, 173b17,* PARAPHRASE*)*

If "wrath" and "helmet" are masculine, then one who says "destructive" [in the feminine form, modifying either of these words] makes a mistake.[183]

33. *(Aristotle,* Poetics *19, 1456b15,* PARAPHRASE*)*

One sort of inquiry concerns the modes of diction which should be known by an actor or one whose profession it is [to know such things]: for example, what is a command and what is a prayer or a statement or a threat or a question or an answer or whatever. But no criticism worth our concern is brought against poetry for knowledge or ignorance of these things. For who would suppose the poet erred where Protagoras criticizes him, for giving a command although he thought he was praying when he said, "Sing, goddess of the wrath"?[184]

---

[183] Both words are grammatically feminine. The allusion is to the first two lines of the *Iliad*, in which Homer prays the goddess to sing of the destructive wrath of Achilles. Cf. Aristophanes' parody of this teaching in the *Clouds*, lines 658 ff.

[184] *Iliad* 1.1; cf. Gorgias, fr. 11.

Gorgias

Gorgias came from Leontini in Sicily. All sources report that he lived more than 100 years, c. 480–375. In 427 he came to Athens as an ambassador from Leontini and reportedly created a sensation with his rhetorical style.[185] *He had many other interests in addition to rhetoric, for which he is best known. The material we translate includes two complete speeches attributed to mythological characters, a fragment of a funeral oration, a later summary/paraphrase of a philosophical treatise, and miscellaneous fragments and reports of his views. None of these can be dated, except perhaps for* On Not Being, *which was reportedly written in the eighty-fourth Olympiad (444–441).*

Gorgias' teaching was closely associated by Plato with rhetoric, and he apparently disclaimed teaching all other subjects, including virtue. We arrange the material loosely by subject matter: first rhetoric, then ethics, metaphysics, and science.

1. Encomium of Helen (DK 11)

According to the principal version of the myth (as found in Homer), when the Trojan prince Alexander (Paris) was a guest in the house of Menelaus, king of Sparta, he took advantage of Menelaus' absence to abduct his wife Helen and take her back to Troy with him. Menelaus raised a Greek army to recover Helen, hence the Trojan War. There were many other versions of the story, including some in which Helen did not go to Troy at all.[186]

---

[185] Diodorus Siculus 12.53.1–5.
[186] Most notably, the palinode of Stesichorus (see Plato, *Phaedrus* 243), Euripides, *Helen*; and Herodotus 2.118–120.

[1] For a city the finest adornment (*kosmos*) is a good citizenry, for a body beauty, for a soul wisdom, for an action *aretē*, and for a speech truth; and the opposites of these are indecorous. A man, woman, speech, deed, city or action that is worthy of praise should be honored with acclaim, but the unworthy should be branded with blame. For it is equally error and ignorance to blame the praise-worthy and praise the blameworthy. [2] The man who speaks correctly what ought to be said has a duty to refute those who find fault with Helen. Among those who listen to the poets a single-voiced, single-minded conviction has arisen about this woman, the notoriety of whose name is now a reminder of disasters. My only wish is to bring reason to the debate, eliminate the cause of her bad reputation, demonstrate that her detractors are lying, reveal the truth, and put an end to ignorance.

[3] That the woman I speak of is by nature and birth the foremost of the foremost, men or women, is well known by all. Clearly her mother was Leda and her father in fact a god, but in story a mortal: Zeus and Tyndareus. One was thought to be her father because he was, the other was reported[187] to be because he said he was; one was mightiest of men, the other tyrant of all. [4] Born from such as these, she equaled the gods in beauty, not concealed but revealed. Many were the erotic passions she aroused in many men, and her one body brought many bodies full of great ambition for great deeds; some had abundant wealth, some the glory of an old noble lineage, some the vigor of personal valor, and some the power of acquired wisdom. All came for love that desires to conquer and from unconquerable desire for honor. [5] Who it was or why or how he took Helen and fulfilled his love, I shall not say. For to tell those who know something they know carries conviction, but does not bring pleasure. Now that my speech has passed over the past, it is to the beginning of my future speech that I proceed and propose the likely reasons for Helen's journey to Troy.

[6] Either she did what she did because of the will of fortune and the plan of the gods and the decree of necessity, or she was seized by force, or persuaded by words, ⟨or captured by love⟩. If she left for the first reason, then any who blame her deserve blame

---

[187] Following MacDowell's text (see Bibliographical Note, § B.5).

themselves, for a human's anticipation cannot restrain a god's inclination. For by nature the stronger is not restrained by the weaker but the weaker is ruled and led by the stronger: the stronger leads, the weaker follows. Now, a god is stronger than a human in strength, in wisdom, and in other respects; and so if blame must be attached to fortune and god, then Helen must be detached from her ill repute.

[7] If she was forcibly abducted and unlawfully violated and unjustly assaulted, it is clear that her abductor, her assaulter, engaged in crime; but she who was abducted and assaulted encountered misfortune. Thus, the undertaking undertaken by the barbarian was barbarous in word and law and deed and deserves blame in word, loss of rights in law, and punishment in deed. But she who was violated, from her country separated, from her friends isolated, surely (*eikotōs*) deserves compassion rather than slander. For he did and she suffered terrible things. It is right to pity her but hate him.

[8] If speech (*logos*) persuaded and deluded her mind, even against this it is not hard to defend her or free her from blame, as follows: speech is a powerful master and achieves the most divine feats with the smallest and least evident body.[188] It can stop fear, relieve pain, create joy, and increase pity. How this is so, I shall show; [9] and I must demonstrate this to my audience to change their opinion.

Poetry (*poiēsis*) as a whole I deem and name "speech (*logos*) with meter." To its listeners poetry brings a fearful shuddering, a tearful pity, and a grieving desire, while through its words the soul feels its own feelings for good and bad fortune in the affairs and lives of others. Now, let me move from one argument to another. [10] Sacred incantations with words inject pleasure and reject pain, for in associating with the opinion of the mind, the power of an incantation enchants, persuades, and alters it through bewitchment. The twin arts of witchcraft and magic have been discovered, and these are illusions of mind and delusions of judgment. [11] How many men on how many subjects have persuaded and do persuade how many others by shaping a false speech! For if all men on all subjects had memory of the past, ⟨understanding⟩ of the present,

---

[188] Gorgias has a materialist theory of speech, derived perhaps from Empedocles.

and foresight into the future, speech would not be the same in the same way;[189] but as it is, to remember the past, to examine the present, or to prophesy the future is not easy; and so most men on most subjects make opinion an adviser to their minds. But opinion is perilous and uncertain, and brings those who use it to perilous and uncertain good fortune. [12] What reason is there, then,[190] why Helen did not go just as unwillingly under the influence of speech as if she were seized by the violence of violators? For persuasion expelled her thought – persuasion, which has the same power, but not the same form as compulsion (*anankē*). A speech persuaded a soul that was persuaded, and forced it to be persuaded by what was said and to consent to what was done. The persuader, then, is the wrongdoer, because he compelled her, while she who was persuaded is wrongly blamed, because she was compelled by the speech. [13] To see that persuasion, when added to speech, indeed molds the mind as it wishes, one must first study the arguments of astronomers, who replace opinion with opinion: displacing one but implanting another, they make incredible, invisible matters apparent to the eyes of opinion. Second, compulsory debates with words,[191] where a single speech to a large crowd pleases and persuades because written with skill (*technē*),[192] not spoken with truth. Third, contests of philosophical arguments, where it is shown that speed of thought also makes it easy to change a conviction based on opinion. [14] The power of speech has the same effect on the disposition of the soul as the disposition of drugs on the nature of bodies. Just as different drugs draw forth different humors from the body – some putting a stop to disease, others to life – so too with words: some cause pain, others joy, some strike fear, some stir the audience to boldness, some benumb and bewitch the soul with evil persuasion.

[15] The case has been made: if she was persuaded by speech, her fortune was evil, not her action. The fourth reason, I discuss in my fourth argument. If it was love that did all these things, she will easily escape blame for the error that is said to have occurred.

---

[189] Text uncertain, but the sense clearly is "the same as it is now."
[190] The text of this and the next sentence is corrupt, though the general sense is clear. We follow MacDowell's suggestions (note *ad loc.*).
[191] This expression probably designates speeches in law courts.
[192] See Plato, *Gorgias* 449d–466a.

For whatever we see has a nature, not the one we wish, but whatever each happens to have. And by seeing the mind is molded even in its character. [16] As soon as men in war arm their bodies against the enemy with armor of bronze and iron – some for defense, some for attack – if the sight sees this, it is shaken and shakes the mind, so that men often flee in panic from danger that lies in the future. And[193] the truth of law is firmly established through the fear that comes from sight, which, as it comes, causes acceptance of what the law judges honorable and justice establishes as good. [17] Some indeed, who have seen fearful things, have lost their present purpose in the present moment, so thoroughly does fear extinguish and expel thought; and many have fallen into useless labors, terrible diseases, and incurable madness, so thoroughly does sight engrave on the mind images of things that are seen. Many frightening things are omitted here, but those omitted are similar to those mentioned. [18] Further, whenever painters fashion one perfect bodily form from many colors and bodies, they delight the sight; the creation (*poiēsis*) of statues and the production of works of art provide a sweet sickness for the eyes. So by nature sight grieves for some things and longs for others, and many things make many people desire and long for many deeds and many bodies. [19] So if Helen's eye, pleased by Alexander's body, transmitted to her soul an eagerness and striving for love, why is that surprising? If love is a god, with the divine power of gods, how could a weaker person refuse and reject him? But if love is a human sickness and a mental weakness, it must not be blamed as mistake, but claimed as misfortune. For it came, as it came, snared by the mind, not prepared by thought, under the compulsion of love, not the provision of art (*technē*).

[20] How then can the blame of Helen be considered just? Whether she did what she did, invaded by love, persuaded by speech, impelled by force or compelled by divine necessity, she escapes all blame entirely.

[21] With my speech I have removed this woman's ill repute; I have abided by the rule laid down at the beginning of my speech; I have tried to dispel the injustice of blame and the ignorance of

---

[193] There is considerable dispute over the text of this sentence; we follow Buchheim, who adheres to the ms. version.

opinion; I wished to write this speech for Helen's encomium and my amusement.

2. *Defense of Palamedes (DK 11a)*

Palamedes was a minor Greek hero at Troy, best known for his intelligence and inventiveness. He was the subject of plays by Aeschylus (10–11) and Sophocles (19–20), that are now lost. According to tradition, Odysseus, out of jealousy because Palamedes outwitted him when he was trying to avoid joining the expedition to Troy, devised a charge of treason against Palamedes by hiding a sum of gold in his tent and claiming that this was the bribe Palamedes had received. The false charge was successful and Palamedes was put to death.[194]

[1] The determination of a death sentence is not the business of the prosecution and the defense, for nature (*phusis*) sentences all mortals to death with a clear vote the day they are born. What is at risk here is honor and dishonor: whether I may die with justice or be forced to die under the greatest reproaches and most shameful accusations. [2] Of these two possibilities, you are completely in control of the one and I of the other: I the master of justice and you of force. If you wish, you can kill me easily, for you have this under your control, while I happen to have no control over it.

[3] Now, if my accuser Odysseus made this accusation because of his concern for Greece, either in the clear knowledge that I was betraying Greece to the foreigners, or at least in the opinion that I was doing so, he would be the best of men. For how could he be otherwise, if he is saving his homeland, his parents, and all Greece, and is punishing a wrongdoer besides? But if he concocted this charge through envy, fraud, or wickedness, that would make him a complete rascal, just as other motives would make him quite superior.

[4] Where should I begin my speech on these matters? What should I say first? To what part of my defense should I turn? An unsupported accusation produces an obvious sense of panic; and this panic necessarily deprives me of every resource for speech unless I learn something from the truth itself and the present

---

[194] Cf. Alcidamas' *Odysseus* (fr. 3) for a version of Odysseus' speech in the case.

necessity; for chance brought me these teachers, more risky than resourceful. [5] My accuser accuses without certain knowledge; this I know for certain, since I know clearly that I personally have not done any such thing, and I do not know how anyone could know as a fact something that did not happen. If he makes his accusation thinking this is so, I have two arguments to show he is not speaking the truth: I would not have been able to undertake such deeds, even had I wished; and I would not have wished to do them, even had I been able.

[6] I proceed first to the argument that I was unable. There must have been some first beginning to the treason, and this beginning would have been a discussion (*logos*), for there must be discussion before actions are planned. But how could there have been a discussion without some meeting taking place? How could there have been a meeting unless that man[195] sent someone to me or someone went from me to that man? A written message does not arrive without a bearer. [7] But this can occur only by conversing. Well then, suppose I am in his presence, and he in mine. How could we speak? Who is with whom? A Greek with a foreigner? How would we listen or talk? Are we one-to-one? But we will not know each other's words. Are we with an interpreter? Then there would be a third person, a witness to things that need to be kept hidden.

[8] But grant that this happened, even though it did not. Afterwards we would have had to give and receive a pledge. What was the pledge? An oath? Who would trust me, if I was a traitor? What about hostages? Who were they? I might have given my brother, for instance, for I had no one else, and the foreigner would have given one of his sons, for these would be the most trustworthy pledges I could give him or he me. But if these transactions had occurred, they would have been obvious to all of you. [9] Someone will say that we secured the agreement with money that he gave and I received. Well, would it have been a small sum? But it is not likely that anyone would take a small sum for a large service. A large sum? Then what was the means of conveyance? Would one man have brought it or many? If many brought it, there would have been many witnesses to the plot; but if one man brought it,

---

[195] That is, the Trojan with whom Palamedes purportedly conspired.

he could not have brought a very large sum. [10] Did they bring it by day or night? [At night] there are many guards close together, and one could not get through undetected. Was it by day? But light is hostile to such activities. All right, did I go out to accept the money, or did he bring it in here? Either way is impractical. If I had accepted it, how would I have hidden it from the men inside or outside [the camp]? And where would I have put it? How would I have guarded it? If I used it, I would have been discovered; but if I did not use it, what good would I have had from it?

[11] Still, grant that it all happened, even though it did not: we met, we spoke, we understood each other, I took money from them, I was not seen, I hid it. Then, of course, the goal of these actions had to be fulfilled, but this was even more difficult than the actions I have discussed. For in accomplishing this I acted either on my own or with others. Well, it was not a project for one man. With others then? With whom? Quite clearly with my associates. Are these free men or slaves? The free men I associate with are you. Who of you, then, knows about it? Let him speak. But surely it is not credible that I would use slaves. For they make accusations willingly to gain freedom and because they have to [when tortured].[196] [12] As for the deed, how would it have occurred? Clearly, enemies had to be brought in who were stronger than you, which is impossible. How could I have brought them in? Through the gates? But the leaders were in charge of them: it was not my job to open and close them. Over the walls with a ladder? No, since they were guarded everywhere. So did I go through a hole in the wall? This would have been obvious to all. In a camp men live outdoors under arms, and in those circumstances everyone sees everything, and everyone is seen by everyone. It was thus completely impossible for me to do any of these things in any way.

[13] Let us together consider this too: What could I reasonably hope to gain by doing these things – if I really was capable of doing them all? No one wants to face the greatest risks and wickedly do the greatest evil for nothing. So, why did I do it? (I keep returning to this point.) In order to be a tyrant? Over you or the foreigners? It would be impossible to rule over you: you are too numerous and have all the greatest advantages: distinguished ances-

---

[196] For the torture of slaves, see below, n. 223.

tors, substantial wealth, glory, strength of spirit, and dominion over cities. [14] Over foreigners then? Who would betray them? And by what power would I, a Greek, take over foreigners, one man ruling many? By persuasion? By force? They certainly would not willingly be persuaded, nor do I have the power to force them. Is someone perhaps willing to betray them to another who is willing, and to pay for this treason? But only a real fool would give credence or belief to this. For who would choose slavery over kingship, the worst over the best? [15] Someone might say that I undertook this crime in my passion for wealth and money. But I have a moderate amount of money and need no great wealth. People need large sums if they have large expenses: not if they have control over natural pleasures, but rather if they are slaves to pleasure and are trying to gain honor [or "public office"] from wealth and magnificence. None of this applies to me, and I offer my past life as a persuasive witness that I am telling the truth. You are witnesses to this as well, for you are my associates and so you know these things. [16] Moreover, a man who is even moderately sensible would not undertake such an action for the sake of honor. For honor results from *aretē*, not from wickedness; so how could honor be given a man who betrays Greece? Besides, I happened not to lack honor; for I was honored for the most honorable quality by the most honorable men – by you for my wisdom. [17] No one would do these things for his own security; for a traitor is an enemy to everyone: law, justice, the gods, and most people; for he disobeys the laws, dissolves justice, destroys most people and dishonors the divine. Such a life is full of the greatest dangers and has no security. [18] Well, did I wish to help my friends or harm my enemies? Someone might commit a crime for these reasons. But for me it was just the opposite: I was harming my friends and helping my enemies. Thus the action involved no beneficial gain, and no one does wrong because he wants to suffer loss. [19] The last possibility is that I acted to escape some fear or trouble or danger. But no one would say that any of these applies in my case. Only two motives lie behind every human action: either to gain profit or avoid loss. To commit a crime for any other reason is madness. It is quite clear that I would be hurting only myself if I did this; for in betraying Greece, I would betray myself, my parents, my friends, my ancestors' reputation, their sacred rites, their tombs,

and the great country of Greece. I would have entrusted what
matters most to most of us to the very people we have wronged.
[20] Consider this too. Wouldn't my life be unlivable if I did
this? Where could I turn? To Greece? So that I could be punished
by those I had wronged? Would any of those who had suffered
leave me alone? Would I have to remain among foreigners, giving
up all the most important things, deprived of the highest honor,
living in infamous disgrace, abandoning all the *aretē* I had earlier
toiled so hard to achieve? And this would have been my own doing.
This is the height of shame for a man – to cause his own misfortune.
[21] Furthermore, I would also not be trusted by the foreigners.
How could I be, when they knew I had done something most
untrustworthy, betraying my friends to my enemies? Life is not
livable without trust. Someone who has lost his money or fallen
from power or fled his country might regain these, but once
someone has lost trust, he can no longer gain it. What I have said
proves that I could not and would not have betrayed Greece.

[22] Next I wish to speak to my accuser. What in the world do
you put your trust in, a man like you accusing a man like me? It
is worth finding out just what sort of man you are, saying the sort
of things you do – unworthy man addressing the unworthy. Do
you accuse me because you have precise knowledge or just an
opinion? If you know, did you see the crime, or participate in it,
or hear about it from someone else? If you saw it, tell these men
the place, the time, when, where, and how you saw it. If you
participated, you are guilty of the same charges. If you heard about
it from a participant, whoever he is, let him come forth, appear,
testify. The accusation will be more trustworthy, if supported by
testimony. As it is, neither of us has a witness.[197] [23] Perhaps you
will say it is fair that you not provide witnesses for things that
happened (so you claim), but that I provide them for things that
have not happened. But it's not fair; for surely it is impossible to
testify to things that did not happen. For things that happened,
however, it is not only possible, but easy, and not only easy, but
you can find false witnesses as well as true ones, whereas I could
not possibly find either of these. [24] It is thus clear that you do
not have knowledge of the facts of your accusation. The only thing

---

[197] In Alcidamas' speech (fr. 3) Odysseus presents witnesses (section 7).

left is that you have merely an opinion without knowledge. Well then, most audacious of all men, do you dare to prosecute a man on a capital charge trusting only in an opinion, a most untrustworthy thing, without knowing the truth? How do you know he has done such a deed? All men have opinions about everything, and you are no wiser than others in this regard. One must not trust those who have an opinion but those who know; nor should one think opinion is more trustworthy than truth, but the reverse – truth is more trustworthy than opinion.

[25] In your speech you accused me of two quite opposite qualities, cleverness (*sophia*)[198] and madness, which the same man cannot possess. For when you say I am skillful, devious, and resourceful, you accuse me of cleverness; but when you say I betrayed Greece, you accuse me of madness. For it is madness to undertake impossible, ineffectual, and indecent deeds that harm one's friends and help one's enemies, and make one's own life most disgraceful and hazardous. How, then, could anyone trust a man who would say completely opposite things about the same men in the same speech on the same subject? [26] I would like to hear from you: do you regard clever men as foolish or sensible? If foolish, your argument is unusual but not true. If sensible, then surely sensible men are not expected to make enormous mistakes, or prefer evils to present goods. So then, if I am clever, I did not err; if I erred, I am not clever: in either case you would be wrong.

[27] Although I could countercharge you with committing many great crimes, old and new, I do not wish to. For I wish to be acquitted of this charge because of my own virtues, not your vices. That is all I have to say about you.

[28] As for you judges, I wish to say something invidious, but true about myself; this would be intolerable from someone not accused but is fitting for an accused man. I am now before you undergoing a scrutiny and giving an account of my past life.[199] So I ask this of you: if I remind you of some of the fine things I have done, do not resent what I say. Please understand that since I am falsely accused of terrible crimes, it is necessary for me to

---

[198] In this passage we translate *sophia* as "cleverness" and *sophos* as "clever"; Gorgias is playing on the ambivalent overtones of the words, which traditionally meant "wisdom/wise" or "skill/skilled."

[199] A reference to the *euthunai* (see Glossary).

mention some good things [about me] to you who already know the truth. And this is most pleasant for me. [29] First, then, and second and most important, my past life has been faultless throughout, from beginning to end, and free of all blame. For no one could truly make any accusation of wickedness about me to you. Even the accuser himself has provided no proof for what he has said. In effect, therefore, his speech is unsubstantiated slander. [30] But I would say – and in so speaking I would not be lying, nor could I be refuted – that I am not only faultless but also a great benefactor of you and the Greeks and all men, not only those now living but those to come. For who else would have made human life rich when it was poor, bringing order out of disorder? Who else would have discovered military tactics, most important for success? Or written laws, guardians of justice? Or writing, the instrument of memory? Weights and measures, facilitators of commercial transactions? Number, the guardian of possessions? Beacons, the strongest and swiftest messengers? Or, finally, draughts, the painless pastime of leisure? Why do I remind you of these? [31] To make clear that I give my attention to such matters and to provide an indication that I refrain from shameful and evil deeds. For it is impossible to give one's attention to such things as these while attending to those other activities. And I think that since I did you no wrong myself, I should not be wronged by you. [32] Nor do I deserve to be ill treated by young or old on account of my other pursuits. For I cause no pain to the old, am not unhelpful to the young, do not envy the fortunate, and have compassion for the unfortunate. I neither scorn poverty nor honor wealth above *aretē*, but *aretē* above wealth. I am not useless in councils or lazy in battles but carry out my assignment and obey those in charge. It is not my business to praise myself, but the present situation and the accusations made against me have compelled me to defend myself in every way.

[33] My last words to you are about you, and when I have said them, I shall end my defense. Pity and entreaties and the intercession of friends are useful when judgment takes place before a mob. But among you, who are the foremost of the Greeks in fact and in reputation, I should not persuade you with the aid of friends or entreaties or pity. I must escape this charge by making justice very clear and showing you the truth, not by deceiving you. [34] You must not pay

more attention to words than to deeds, or prefer accusations to proofs, or consider a short time to be a wiser judge than a long time, or think slander more credible than experience. In all things good men should take great precautions against committing an error, and even more so when matters are irremediable, for these can be controlled by foresight, but are incurable by hindsight. Such things are at issue whenever men judge a man on a capital charge, as is now the case for you. [35] So if it were possible to make the truth of actions clear and evident to listeners through words, a decision based on what has been said would now be easy. But since this is not so, safeguard my body, wait for a while longer, and make your decision with truth. You run a great risk that by seeming to be unjust you will cast off one reputation and take on another; but good men prefer death to a shameful reputation, for the one is the end of life, the other a disease for life. [36] If you kill me unjustly, it will be evident to many; for I am not unknown, and your wickedness will be known and evident to all Greeks. For this injustice you, not the accuser, will be blamed in everyone's eyes, since the outcome of the trial is in your hands. There could be no greater error than this; for if you judge unjustly, you will not only err against me and my parents, but by so doing you will be in charge of a terrible, ungodly, unjust, unlawful deed: you will kill a comrade in arms, your helper and Greece's benefactor. You will be Greeks killing a Greek, with no proof of evident injustice or credible accusation.

[37] My case has been stated and I shall stop. It would be reasonable to remind you briefly of what has been stated at length, if you were inferior jurors; but it is not right even to think that the foremost among the foremost, Greeks selected from Greeks, would not pay attention to or remember what I have said.

3–5. *Funeral oration*

In this speech Gorgias reportedly praised certain Athenians for their bravery in war. Not being an Athenian, Gorgias would not actually have delivered a funeral oration in Athens; this may be a rhetorical exercise.

3. *(DK 6)*

For what was absent from these men which ought to be present in men? And, what was present which ought not to be present? May I be able to speak what I wish and may I wish to speak what I ought, avoiding divine retribution and escaping human envy. For these men attained an *aretē* that was divine and a mortality that was human, often preferring gentle fairness to obstinate justice and correctness of speech to precision of law, regarding this as the most divine and universal law: to speak, to be silent, and to act as one ought and when one ought,[200] and especially exercising two needed faculties, intelligence ⟨and strength⟩, using one for deliberation and the other for accomplishment, helping those who unjustly suffered misfortune, chastising those who unjustly prospered, stubborn in the pursuit of the beneficial, good tempered toward what was fitting, restraining the thoughtlessness ⟨of the body⟩ with the thoughtfulness of the mind, insolent toward the insolent, orderly toward the orderly, fearless toward the fearless, and terrible among the terrible. To testify to these things they set up trophies over their enemies, glories for Zeus and ornaments for themselves. Not inexperienced in natural war-strength, customary passions, armed strife, and honor-seeking peace, they were reverent toward the gods by their justice, reverent toward their parents by their care, just toward their fellow citizens by their fairness, and respectful to their friends by their faithfulness. Therefore, although they have died, longing for them has not died, but it lives, though they do not live, immortal in bodies that are not immortal.

4. *(DK 5b)*

Triumphs over the foreigners demand festive songs; but those over Greeks, laments.

5. *(DK 5a)*

Gorgias called Xerxes "the Zeus of the Persians;" and vultures, "living tombs."[201]

---

[200] Although the word is not used here, there seems to be a reference to Gorgias' idea of *kairos*, or "the opportune" (moment, expression, etc.).

[201] The expressions in 5–6 are cited as examples of Gorgias' metaphors, which at the time were considered "poetic," as were the long compound words in 7. Poetic features are characteristic of early rhetorical prose.

6. *(DK 16)*²⁰²

The deeds are green and full-blooded; you sowed these things shamefully and reaped a bad harvest.

7. *(DK 15)*

Beggarly-poet-flatterers; false-oath-swearers; and good-oath-swearers.

8. *(DK 8)*

Our contest²⁰³ requires two *aretai*: boldness and wisdom: boldness to withstand danger, and wisdom to understand the riddle. For like the herald at Olympia, speech *(logos)* summons whoever wishes [to compete], but crowns the one who is able.

9. *(DK 12)*

One must defeat the seriousness of one's opponents with laughter and their laughter with seriousness.

10. *(DK 23)*

Tragedy produces a deception in which the one who deceives is more just than the one who does not, and the one who is deceived is wiser than the one who is not.

11. *(DK 27)*

Threats were mingled with entreaties and laments with prayers.²⁰⁴

---

²⁰² Frs. 6 and 7 are cited as examples of Gorgias' vivid experiments with language: metaphors and neologisms; the three expressions in 7 are each a single Greek word.

²⁰³ The contest *(agōnisma)* is probably one of rhetorical competition. A "riddle" may have been set as the subject of some sophistic debates.

²⁰⁴ This fragment refers to Agamemnon's exhortations to his troops *(Iliad* 4.250). It indicates the application of rhetorical criticism (here, the classification of speech acts) to the study of Homer (cf. Protagoras, fr. 33).

12. *(DK A21)*[205]

I especially admire Gorgias for this, Socrates: you would never hear him promising this [i.e., that he is a teacher of *aretē*]; in fact, he laughs at others he hears making such promises. He thinks one should make men skillful at speaking.

13. *(DK A27)*

In the other professions all knowledge more or less concerns handicrafts and similar activities; but in rhetoric there is no such handicraft. All of its activity and accomplishment comes through words. I thus judge that the art of rhetoric is concerned with words – and as I say, my assertion is correct.

14. *(DK A8b)*[206]

No mortal has yet found a nobler profession (*technē*) than Gorgias:
   To train the soul for the contests of *aretē*.
His statue stands in the vale of Apollo,
   A tribute not to wealth, but to the piety of his character.

15. *(DK 19)*[207]

First, if you want the *aretē* of a man, it is easy to say. The *aretē* of a man is this: to be competent in public affairs, and in one's actions to help friends and harm enemies and to take care not to suffer such harm oneself. And if you want the *aretē* of a woman, it is not difficult to explain: she must manage the household well, preserving the possessions within and being obedient to her hus-

---

[205] We include here two Platonic reports (12 = *Meno* 95c; 13 = *Gorgias* 450b–c) about Gorgias' activity. Generally we quote only actual fragments, but the substance of these reports, that Gorgias claimed only to teach the *technē* of speaking and did not teach *aretē*, is so emphasized by Plato that many scholars have felt that Gorgias must have said something to this effect (though perhaps not intending the same implications as Plato understands from this claim). Against Plato's reports should be set 14 (cf. 8).

[206] A verse inscription from Olympia of the early fourth century, commemorating a statue that may have been erected at the time of Gorgias' death.

[207] A response by Meno to Socrates' question, "What is *aretē*?" (Plato, *Meno* 71e), which claims to present the views of Gorgias (cf. Aristotle, *Politics* 1.13.10).

band. Different too is the *aretē* of a child, both female and male, and that of an old man, both free man and slave, as you wish. There are very many other *aretai*, so that there is no difficulty in speaking about what *aretē* is. For there is an *aretē* for each of us for each function in each activity and period of life.

16. *(DK 22)*

A woman should be known to many by reputation, not by appearance.

17. *(DK 20)*

Cimon[208] acquired money for use and used it for honor.

18. *On Not Being (DK 3)*[209]

[979a] Gorgias says: (a) [Anything you might mention][210] is nothing; (b) if it were something, it would be unknowable; and (c) if it were something and knowable, it could not be made evident to others.

(a) *That it is nothing*

[*Our source summarizes the argument as follows: If it is, then necessarily it is neither one nor many, neither unborn nor born.*[211] *It follows that it is nothing, because if it were something, it would be one of these. He tries to show that it is neither one nor many using Melissus' arguments, and that it is neither unborn nor born using Zeno's,*[212] *after his own*

---

[208] A famous Athenian general who died in 450.

[209] There are many problems with the Greek text; see Bibliographical Note, § B.5.

[210] Throughout the argument the subject of the Greek verb *to be* is left open. We have supplied "it" in order to achieve readable English. In most cases, the place after the verb *to be* is also left open, but sometimes it is "something." We have supplied this where necessary, as it makes for a more readable text, and does not beg the question as to whether or not *to be* here is to be read as always having strong existential import.

[211] The verb *gignomai*, translated as "be born," can also mean "come to be," "become."

[212] Melissus was a philosopher and general on Samos in the middle of the fifth century. His account of being is one of Gorgias' chief targets. Zeno was a philosopher of the fifth century and the author of a number of paradoxes. See Barnes, *Early Greek philosophy*, and Kirk, Raven, and Schofield (eds.), *The presocratic philosophers* (Bibliographical Note, § A.5).

first proof, which shows that it is not possible for it either to be or not to be.]

If not being is not being, then not being would have no less being than being does itself, since not being *is* being, while being also is being, with the result that things no more are than are not. If, on the other hand, not being is something, then its opposite, which is being, would not be. For if not being were something, then it would be fitting for being not to be. On this reasoning, it would be nothing unless it were the same thing to be as it is not to be. But if they are the same thing, then the same reasoning would entail that it [i.e., the open subject] is nothing. For not being is not anything, and neither is being, if in fact being is the same as not being. . .

[979b20] If there is anything, it is either unborn or born. If it is unborn, [*he concludes on the principles of Melissus that*] it is unlimited. But the unlimited could not be anywhere [i.e. in anything], for it could not be in itself or in anything else. Otherwise there would be two unlimited things: the one that is inside and the one that it is in.[213] And if it is nowhere [i.e. not in anything], it is nothing (according to Zeno's arguments about space). For this reason, then, it is not unborn; but neither is it born. For nothing could be born from being or from not being. If being were to be changed, it would no longer be being; and in the same way, if not being should be born, it would no longer be not being. Besides, however, it cannot be born from ⟨not⟩ being. For if not being is not anything, then, since it is nothing, nothing could be born from it; but if not being is something, then it [i.e., the open subject] could not be born from not being for the same reason that it could not be born from being. So if there is anything, it is necessarily either unborn or born, and since both of these are impossible, it follows in fact that it is impossible for there to be anything.

Furthermore, if there is anything, it is one or more [in number]. And if there is neither a one nor a many, there would be nothing. And there could not be a one, since what is truly one [i.e. the number one] is incorporeal insofar as it has no magnitude. But if

---

[213] There cannot be two unlimited things, since unless each were a limit to the other, they would be the same.

there is not a one, there will be nothing at all. For if there is not a one, there could not be a many; and if there is neither a one nor a many, there is nothing.

[980a] Besides, [*he says*] nothing can be changed. For if anything were to be changed, it would not be the same as it had been; but what is [something] would then be what is not [that thing], and so what is not would have come to be. Further, if anything changes and, while being one, is moved, then the thing that is would not be continuous but would be divided and not in that [same] place. As a result, if it moves everywhere, it is divided everywhere, and in that case, it does not exist anywhere, since it would be deprived of being in any place in which it is divided.

(b) *That it is unknowable*

So then there is nothing. ⟨But if there is anything, it is unknowable.⟩ ⟨If it could be known⟩, then whatever could be thought must have being, and whatever has no being (if it really has none) could not be thought. But if this were so, no one would say anything false – not even if he were to speak of chariots racing in the sea; for then all these things would really be the case. And whatever is seen or heard will also be the case, because each of them is thought. But this would not make that [to be the case]. In fact, just as there is no more reason for things we see to be the case (merely because we see them), so things we see are no more likely to be the case than are things we have in mind. There, [I concede,] many people would see the same things, exactly as here many people would think the same things also; but why is it any more evident that such things are the case? The nature of true things is not evident [to the senses]; so that even if they are the case, these things would not be knowable, at any rate not by us.

(c) *That it could not be made evident to others*

Even if they were knowable, how could anyone make them evident to another? How could someone express in words what he has seen? Or how could such a thing become evident to someone who has heard the other speak of it, but has not seen it himself? [980b] Just as vision does not recognize sounds, so hearing does not hear colors, but sounds. And a speaker speaks, but what he says is not a color or a thing. Thus, if someone does not have a notion of something, how could he acquire a notion of it from someone else by a word or by some sign different from the thing, except by seeing it if it is a color, or by ⟨hearing it if it is a sound⟩? For to begin with, someone who speaks does not say ⟨a sound⟩ or a color, but a word, so that a color cannot be thought, nor can a sound, but it is only possible to see a color and hear a sound.

Even if one accepts the possibility of knowing something and speaking what one knows, how could the hearer have the same notion as the speaker? It is impossible for the same thing at the same time to exist in several persons separately, for then the one thing would be two. Even if in fact the same thing were in several persons, there is no reason why it should appear the same to them, unless they are all the same in every way and in the same place. And if they were in the same place, they would be one, and not two. But it is apparent that even the same person does not perceive the same things at the same time, but different things with his hearing than with his sight, and differently now than in the past, so that it is scarcely possible for one person to perceive the same thing as another.

In this way, therefore, if anything is knowable, no one could make it evident to another both because things are not words and because no one has the same thing in mind as another.

19. *(DK 26)*

Being is unclear if it does not meet with belief, and belief is weak if it does not meet with being.

20. *(DK 4)*[214]

Color is the effluence of things which is commensurate with, and perceptible to, sight.

21. *(DK 5)*

[An explanation of combustion from a burning-glass]: because of fire passing through the pores.

---

[214] A response by Meno to Socrates' questioning (Plato, *Meno* 76d), which (like **15**) claims to present the views of Gorgias.

Prodicus

Prodicus came from the island of Ceos; he was probably born around 470 and died some time after 400. There is an amusing picture of him in Plato's Protagoras *(315c–d), lying on a couch. Socrates often refers to Prodicus as his teacher, and some have speculated that Socrates' concern with the precise meanings of words like "justice" may owe something to Prodicus' work on distinctions. In addition to fr.* 1, *there are also references to Prodicus' fondness for distinguishing between near synonyms in* Protagoras *339e–341d,* Meno *75e,* Euthydemus *277e, and Aristotle,* Topics *2.6, 122b22.*

1. *(Plato,* Protagoras *337a–c; DK A13)*

During an interlude in the discussion between Socrates and Protagoras, Prodicus contributes the following.

Those who are present at these discussions should be an impartial but not an egalitarian audience; for these are not the same. You must hear both sides impartially but not give them equal weight; rather, give more weight to the wiser and less to the more foolish speaker. For my own part, moreover, I think you two, Protagoras and Socrates, should agree to debate but not to quarrel; for friends debate with friends in a cordial spirit, but enemies and adversaries quarrel with one another. In this way we will have the best discussion, for you speakers will be esteemed, and not praised: esteem is truly in the minds of the listeners without deceit, whereas praise is often falsely given in words that run counter to one's actual opinion. In this way, too, we listeners may derive the most enjoyment, not pleasure: we derive enjoyment from learning and taking part in intellectual activity with the mind, but pleasure comes from eating or experiencing some other pleasant activity with the body.

2. (DK 7)

Desire doubled is love; love doubled becomes madness.

3. (DK 6)

They [the sophists] are on the borderline between philosophers and politicians.

4. *The Choice of Heracles (Xenophon,* Memorabilia *2.1.21–33; DK 2)*

This speech is from a work entitled Horai *or* Seasons, *perhaps meaning "the right season or time." It is uncertain what relationship this speech bears to Prodicus' original words. Xenophon has Socrates deliver the speech, introducing it with "Prodicus the wise . . . speaking more or less as follows, as best I remember it." After finishing he adds, "In this way Prodicus set forth the education of Heracles by Virtue, but he adorned his thoughts with more elegant expressions than I."*

When Heracles, no longer a child, was just becoming an adult – at that time when young men are becoming independent and are beginning to show whether they will direct their lives down the path of Virtue (*aretē*) or the path of Vice (*kakia*) – he went off and sat down in a peaceful spot, not sure which path he should choose. [22] And two tall women appeared to approach him. One was pleasing to look at, and, evincing a naturally free spirit, a pure complexion, a respectful look in her eye, and a modest bearing, she was dressed in white. The other was plump and soft and clearly well-fed, her natural color heightened with powder and rouge, her bearing made to look unnaturally tall, her eyes open to all, and dressed so that her full maturity was evident. She frequently checked her appearance, looked to see whether anyone was watching her, and glanced back at her own shadow. [23] As they approached Heracles, the first woman continued in the same manner but the other, wanting to get ahead, ran up to Heracles and said, "I see, Heracles, you cannot decide which path to take for your life. If you make me your friend and come with me, I will lead you along the path of pleasure and ease; you will taste every delight and avoid all trouble in life. [24] First, you will think no more of wars or business affairs, but will need to consider only what delicious food or drink you might find, or what sights or sounds would delight you, what aromas or textures would please you, which young boys you would most enjoy having affairs with, how you might sleep most softly, and finally, how you might have all this with the least possible trouble. [25] And if you ever suspect that the supply of these goods may be scarce, do not fear that I might lead you to obtain them by working or suffering in body or in spirit. Rather, you will make use of what others work to produce and you will not be deprived of any source of profit, for I give my associates the opportunity to obtain goods from every quarter." [26] When Heracles heard this, he asked, "What is your name, Madam?" She replied, "my friends call me Happiness, but my enemies get stirred up and call me Vice."

[27] At that moment the other woman came up and said, "I have come to you, Heracles, because I know your parents and I carefully observed your nature during the course of your education. From this I am confident that if you turn to my path, you will accomplish many fine and noble deeds, and you will know that I am to be still more honored and distinguished for the benefits I bestow. I will not deceive you with preludes about pleasure, but will relate truthfully how the gods have really arranged things in the world. [28] The gods give nothing really good or honorable to mortals without diligence and toil. If you want the gods to favor you, you must serve the gods; if you wish to be loved by friends, you must be good to your friends; if you desire honor from a city, you must benefit that city; if you think all Greece should admire you for your *aretē*, then you must work for the benefit of Greece; if you want the earth to bear you abundant fruit, you must cultivate the earth; if you think you should get rich from cattle, you must tend to your cattle; if you are eager to grow great through war and want to be able to liberate your friends and conquer your enemies, you must learn the skills (*technai*) of warfare from those who have mastered them and then practice their correct use. And

finally, if you want to be physically powerful, you must accustom
your body to serving the mind and train it with sweat and toil."
[29] Here Vice interrupted: "Consider what a long, hard path
to enjoyment this woman is showing you, Heracles. I will lead you
down a short, easy path to happiness." [30] And Virtue answered,
"What good can you offer, you wretch? What do you know about
pleasure, when you are not willing to do anything for these things?
You don't even wait until you desire pleasures, but take your fill
of everything before you desire it, eating before you are hungry
and drinking before you are thirsty. To enjoy your food, you
prepare fancy dishes; to enjoy your drink, you buy expensive wine
and in the summer you run around looking for ice; to sleep soundly,
you use not only soft bedding but a bedstead and mattress as well.
You desire sleep not because you've been working but because you
have nothing to do. You force yourself to have sex before you want
it, with all sorts of devices, and using men as women. In this way
you teach your friends to be wanton all night and sleep during the
best part of the day. [31] Though immortal, you have been cast
out by the gods and have no honor among good men. You never
hear that most pleasant sound, your own praise, and you never see
that most pleasant sight, your own good works, for you have never
accomplished any. Who would believe anything you say? Who would
grant you something you wish? Who with any sense would join
your enthusiastic following, whose young members lose the strength
of their bodies, while older ones lose the faculties of their minds?
In their youth they grow fat without work, but they pass through
old age withered and ailing. They are ashamed of what they have
done and worn out by what they are doing. Pleasures they ran
through in their youth; hardship they put off until old age. [32] I,
on the other hand, keep company with gods; I keep company with
good men. No fine deed, human or divine, is done without me. I
am honored above all others both by gods and by those mortals
who ought to honor me: craftsmen welcome me as a partner,
masters as a faithful guardian of their houses, servants as a kindly
helper, peacemakers as a helpful assistant, warriors as a steadfast
ally, and friends as their finest companion. [33] My friends enjoy
their food and drink without trouble, for they wait until they truly
desire them. They sleep more sweetly than those who do not work,
and when they awaken they do not complain, nor do they neglect

their duties on account of this. The young are delighted to be praised by their elders; the old are proud to be honored by the young. They remember their past deeds with pleasure and enjoy the success of their present activities. Because of me they are dear to the gods, loved by their friends and honored by their city. And when their appointed end has come, they do not lie forgotten and dishonored, but they flourish, remembered in song, forever after. All this is yours, Heracles, you son of excellent parents; with hard work you will gain the most blessed happiness."

5. *On Nature (DK 5)*

The sun and the moon and rivers and springs and everything else that benefited our lives were called gods by early people because they are beneficial. The Egyptians, for example, deified the Nile.

6. *(DK 4)*

Phlegm is the part of the humors that has been inflamed and, as it were, overcooked.

Hippias

Hippias of Elis was born before the middle of the fifth century. He was frequently appointed to represent Elis as an ambassador and traveled widely for professional reasons as well. He was richly paid for his lessons on a variety of topics, including mnemonics, speech rhythms and harmonies, astronomy, mathematics, ethics, and history. He did original work in mathematics, and was known for a more technical approach to teaching than that of Protagoras. He visited Athens regularly, is the principal character in the two Platonic dialogues named after him, and appears also in the Protagoras. *He appears to have been a supporter of the idea that nature is opposed to custom.*

1. *Hypothesis to Sophocles'* Oedipus Tyrannos *(DK 9)*

The poets after Homer have this peculiarity: they call kings before the Trojan war "tyrants," although this word was given to the Greeks rather late, in the time of Archilochus according to the sophist Hippias. For Homer says that Echetus – who was the most lawless of all – was a king and not a tyrant: "to Echetus the king, destroyer of men."[215] They say that tyrants are named after the Tyrrhenians, some of whom were terrible robbers.

2. *Plutarch,* Lycurgus *23 (DK 11)*

Hippias the sophist says that Lycurgus[216] himself was very military, and had experience of many campaigns.

---

[215] *Odyssey* 18.85.
[216] The legendary lawgiver of Sparta (see Introduction).

3. *Stobaeus 3.38.32; from Plutarch's* On Slander *(DK 16)*

Hippias says that there are two envies: just envy occurs when one envies bad men who are honored; unjust envy when one envies good men. Envious people suffer twice as much harm as others do, for they are pained not only by what harms themselves, as others are, but also by the goods that come to other people.

4. *Stobaeus 3.42.10; from Plutarch's* On Slander *(DK 17)*

Hippias says that slander is an awful thing. He uses this word because there is no punishment written in the laws for slanderers as there is for thieves.[217] But they steal what is the best possession, friendship, so that although *hubris* does do evil, it is more just than slander because it is not out of sight.

5. *Custom and nature (Plato,* Protagoras *337d–338b)*

The following is Plato's version of a brief speech designed to resolve a dispute between Socrates and Protagoras concerning the conduct of their discussion, delivered to an audience of sophists and their followers from many parts of the Greek world. The speech is probably a parody, but if so, is revealing about Hippias' style and views.

I believe that you men who are present here are all kinsmen, family members, and fellow citizens by nature (*phusis*) though not by custom (*nomos*). For by nature like is kin to like, but custom is a tyrant over human beings[218] and forces many things on us that are contrary to nature. It would be disgraceful for us, then, who know the nature of things and are the wisest men of Greece and have gathered now at this citadel of wisdom in Greece in this, the greatest and most prosperous house in that very city – surely it would be disgraceful for us to display nothing worthy of that reputation, but to disagree among ourselves like the most contemptible people! Therefore I beg and advise you, Protagoras and Socrates, to let us, as umpires, help you agree to a compromise.

---

[217] In Athens (but perhaps not in other cities) there was a law against specific kinds of slander.
[218] Cf. Pindar, fr. 1.

Socrates, do not hold to that precise form of discussion that uses very short answers if it is not pleasing to Protagoras, but relax and loosen the reins of discourse so that we will find the discussion more elegant and seemly. And, Protagoras, do not stretch every rope, give your ship to the winds, and sail off into a sea of words beyond sight of land. Instead, both of you cut a middle course. So do this, then: take my advice and appoint someone to be referee, chairman, and president, to see that your speeches are of moderate length on both sides.

Antiphon

Antiphon was an Athenian orator and sophist,[219] *who was born around 480. In 411 he was one of the leaders of a coup that brought the oligarchy of the Four Hundred to power (pp. 130–131); when this government collapsed and democracy was restored, Antiphon was tried, convicted, and executed for treason. He was a popular legal adviser to others and his final speech in his own defense was much admired.*

In addition to the speeches he composed for others to deliver, three of which survive complete, Antiphon wrote three Tetralogies *for hypothetical homicide cases. Since these raise general rhetorical, legal, and philosophical issues, we translate them here. A common idea in the* Tetralogies *is that a killer suffered religious "pollution" or "defilement" (*miasma*) which could be transmitted to others. The concept of pollution is much less important in the speeches delivered in court and apparently did not play a significant role in Athenian law.*

In Athenian law a homicide case could normally be prosecuted only by a relative of the victim. Each side spoke twice, first the plaintiff and then the defendant.

The main "sophistic" works of Antiphon were Truth, *in two books, and* Concord; *the latter addresses more mundane issues and may have been intended for a less specialized audience. Less well attested are a collection of* Proems, *or typical introductory remarks for speeches in lawsuits, and an* Art of Rhetoric.

---

[219] Some scholars maintain there were two different Antiphons, an orator and a sophist; others doubt the authenticity of the *Tetralogies*.

1. *In his own defense*

Antiphon delivered this speech in his own defense when charged with leading the oligarchic coup in 411. Although he was convicted and executed, the speech was highly praised by Thucydides (8.68) and others. Only a few fragments of the speech survive, including some papyrus fragments discovered in 1907. We translate the only fragment with continuous text (fr. 3 in the Teubner text by Thalheim, [Leipzig, 1914]); it shows an uncompromising attitude toward the jurors reminiscent, in some ways, of Socrates' defense (as reported by Plato).

⟨What was supposed to be my motive for conspiring against the democracy? Was it⟩ a public office where I had handled large sums of money and faced an accounting (*euthunai*) that I feared? Or because I had been disenfranchised, or had done you some wrong, or feared an impending trial? Surely I had no such motive, since I faced none of these situations. Well, were you depriving me of property? Or ⟨was I in danger because of⟩ wrongs done to you by my ancestors? . . . ⟨People generally⟩ desire a different form of government from the one they have because they wish either to escape punishment for crimes they have committed or to take revenge for what they have suffered and not suffer in return. But I had no such motive.

My accusers say that I used to compose speeches for others to deliver in court and that I profited from this. Under an oligarchy I would not be able to do this, whereas under a democracy I have long been powerful because of my knowledge of the art of speaking. I would be worthless in an oligarchy, but very valuable in a democracy. Surely then I am not likely (*eikos*) to desire an oligarchy. Do you think I cannot figure this out or cannot understand what is to my own advantage?

2. First Tetralogy

In this hypothetical case we are to assume that a man was assaulted and killed at night. His attendant, who was a slave, also died from the assault, but lived long enough to implicate the defendant, a long-time enemy of the victim. The main interest of the case is the use of arguments involving eikos *("likelihood"), a concept that was much debated by early writers on rhetoric (see Glossary).*

2a. *Plaintiff's first speech*

[1] In the case of crimes planned by ordinary people, it is not difficult to convict someone, but when those with both natural ability and previous experience, who are at that point in their lives when their mental facilities are at their height, commit a crime, it is difficult to obtain knowledge or proof of their crime. [2] Because of the great risk involved they pay very careful attention to their own safety in planning their actions and do not undertake anything without first guarding themselves against all possible suspicion. You should recognize this fact and give full credence to whatever conclusion you find most likely (*eikos*). For our part, in undertaking these homicide proceedings we are not letting the guilty one go free in order to prosecute an innocent man. [3] We know well that since the whole city is polluted by the killer until he is [successfully] prosecuted, if we wrongly prosecute an innocent man, we are guilty of impiety, and retribution for your error [in convicting him] will also recoil on us. Since the entire pollution thus reverts to us, we shall attempt to show you as clearly as possible from the facts at our disposal that he killed the man.

[4] ⟨Common criminals are unlikely to have killed the man,⟩[220] for no one who took the most extreme risk of endangering his life would give up the gain he had secured and had in hand; and yet the victims were found still wearing their cloaks. Nor would someone who was drunk have killed him, for he would have been recognized by his fellow drinkers; nor again in a quarrel, for they wouldn't be quarreling in the middle of the night in a deserted place. And no one would have killed him by accident when aiming at someone else, for then his attendant wouldn't have been killed too. [5] So all other suspicions are allayed, and the kind of death he died shows that it was deliberately planned. Who then is more likely to have attacked him than one who has already suffered great harm [from him] and expects to suffer even more? And that man is his old enemy, the defendant, who has prosecuted him many times on serious charges but never gained a conviction. [6] In

---

[220] The bracketed words are not in our manuscripts but something like this must have been in the original text. An important activity of "common criminals" or "muggers" (*kakourgoi*) was stealing cloaks, since a man's cloak was normally the most valuable thing in his possession when he went around town.

return, however, the defendant has been prosecuted even more often and on more serious charges; he has never once been acquitted and has lost most of his property. In the latest case the defendant was indicted[221] for theft of sacred property and faced a fine of two talents.[222] Since he knew full well he was guilty, since he had previous experience of his opponent's power, and since he harbored resentment from the earlier incidents, in all likelihood he formed this plan and in all likelihood he killed the man to defend himself against this hostile action. [7] Desire for revenge made him unmindful of the danger, and fear of impending disaster fired him with greater eagerness to attempt the crime. By this action he hoped both to kill the man without being caught and also to be released from the indictment, since no one else would prosecute that case and it would be forfeited. [8] And even if he were caught, he reckoned it more honorable to gain his revenge and suffer the consequences than like a coward to take no action and let himself be ruined by the impending prosecution. And he knew very well he would be convicted in that case, for otherwise he wouldn't have thought this trial offered him a better chance.

[9] These then are the considerations that forced him to commit this unholy crime. As for witnesses, if many had been present, we would have presented many here. But since only his attendant was present, those who heard him speak will testify. For he was still breathing when we picked him up and questioned him, and he said he recognized this man alone among those who attacked them. Since, then, his guilt is established both by arguments from likelihood and by people who were present, it would be neither just nor advantageous for you to acquit him. [10] Not only would it be impossible to establish the guilt of those who plan crimes if they are not proven guilty either by the testimony of those present or by arguments from likelihood, but it is to your disadvantage if this polluted and unholy person should either enter into the precincts of the gods and sully their holiness or share the tables of innocent men and infect them with this defilement. Acts such as these cause harvests to fail and affairs in general to miscarry. [11] This man's punishment is thus your own concern: attribute his impiety to him

---

[221] I.e., by the procedure of *graphē* (see above, n. 130).
[222] A talent was a very large sum; see Glossary.

alone and you will insure that his misfortune remains his own private affair while the city remains untainted by it.

2b. *Defendant's first speech*

[1] I don't think I'm wrong to consider myself most unfortunate of all men. Others suffer misfortunes, but if their troubles are caused by a storm, these cease when good weather returns, and if they fall sick, the danger passes when they recover their health, and if any other misfortune assails them, a reversal of fortune brings relief. [2] But in my case, when this person was alive he was ruining my estate, and now that he is dead, even if I am acquitted, he has added substantially to my pain and anxiety. For my bad luck has gone so far that showing my own purity and innocence will not be enough to save me from ruin: unless I can also find the true killer and establish his guilt, though they [my prosecutors] are unable to find him in their quest for revenge, then I shall be the suspect and shall be wrongly convicted of murder. [3] They claim that my cleverness, on the one hand, makes it hard to establish my guilt, but my foolishness, on the other hand, allows them to infer from my actions that I did the deed. For if the enormous hostility between us leads you now to consider me the likely suspect, then it would be even more likely that before the crime was committed I would foresee that I was the obvious suspect; and in fact if I learned of anyone else planning to kill him, I would even prevent him from acting rather than commit the murder myself and willingly incur the obvious suspicion that would result. For if the deed itself pointed clearly to me, I would be doomed, and even if I escaped detection, I knew full well I would incur this suspicion. [4] I am thus in the miserable position of being forced not only to defend myself but also to reveal the true killers. An attempt must be made, nonetheless, for there is likely to be nothing more bitter than necessity. I have no other way to proceed than from those arguments the prosecutor used in absolving others of the crime when he claimed that the nature of the death points to me as the murderer. For if their ostensible innocence makes the crime appear to be my doing, then it is only right that any suspicion cast on them should make me seem innocent.

[5] It is not unlikely, as they claim, but likely that people wandering around in the middle of the night would be killed for their cloaks. That the cloaks were not removed proves nothing, for if the killers did not remove them in time but left them there because they were frightened by the approach of others, then they were acting prudently; they were not crazy to prefer their own safety to considerations of profit. [6] If he wasn't killed for his cloak, perhaps he noticed others doing something wrong and was killed so he wouldn't report the crime. Who knows? There are also many others who hated him almost as much as I: isn't one of these more likely to have killed him than I? It was clear to them that I would be suspected, and I knew full well that I would be blamed in their place. [7] As for the attendant's testimony, how can it deserve your credence? Terrified by the danger, he was not likely to recognize the killers, but it is likely he was persuaded to agree with his masters. Since the testimony of slaves in general is untrustworthy – otherwise we wouldn't torture them[223] – how can it be right for you to believe this witness' testimony and destroy me?

[8] If anyone thinks arguments from likelihood carry as much weight against me as the truth, by the same reasoning he should consider it more likely that I would pay close attention to the safety of what I planned and would take care not to be present at the crime rather than let this man recognize me as he was being killed. [9] Unless I was out of my mind, I did not consider this crime any less dangerous than the indictment I was facing, but rather far more dangerous, as I shall demonstrate. If I was convicted in that case, I knew I would lose my property but I wouldn't be deprived of my life or my city. I would survive, and even if I had to borrow money from friends, I wouldn't have come to the ultimate harm.[224] But if I'm convicted and put to death in this case, I shall leave behind an unholy disgrace for my children; or if I go into exile,[225] an old man without a country, I'll be a beggar in a foreign

---

[223] The Athenians allowed the testimony of slaves in court only after they had been tortured in the presence of representatives of both parties. In this case circumstances obviously make this impossible and the "testimony" would be legally permissible, but the defendant seeks to cast doubt on its credibility.

[224] A common euphemism for death.

[225] Exile is often referred to as an alternative penalty to death in homicide cases. The speaker may refer to the possibility of leaving the city before his second speech; see 2d.1 below; cf. 4d.1 with n. 239.

land. [10] So all their accusations are unconvincing. If it is likely, but not a fact, that I killed the man, then the right course by far is for you to acquit me. [In that case] I clearly would have been defending myself against an enormous injustice, or it wouldn't have seemed likely that I killed him. Your proper task, however, is to convict true killers, not those who have a reason to kill.

[11] Thus in every way I am absolved of the charge and shall neither defile the holiness of the gods if I enter their sacred precincts, nor offend them if I persuade you to acquit me. But it is those who prosecute me, an innocent man, while letting the guilty one go who are to blame for the failure of harvests. It is they who urge you to offend against the gods, and so they ought rightly to suffer all the punishment they say I deserve. [12] That's what they deserve, so put no credence in their arguments. But consider my previous activities and you will know that I made no plan and sought no improper advantage. On the contrary, I have contributed generously to many special levies, outfitted many triremes, underwritten the costs of splendid dramatic productions,[226] lent money to many friends, and guaranteed many large debts as well. I have acquired my property, moreover, by hard work, not litigation; I have fulfilled my duties to gods and men. Do not impute to one such as I any unholy or disgraceful deed. [13] If the victim were still alive and were prosecuting me himself, I would not only defend myself; I would also demonstrate that he and his helpers have no concern for justice but are bringing this case for personal enrichment. I pass over these matters more out of decency than justice, but I implore you, gentlemen, you who judge and oversee the greatest matters, take pity on my misfortune and provide a cure for it; do not join in their attack and allow them to subject me to this lawless and godless destruction.

2c. *Plaintiff's second speech*

[1] He wrongs misfortune when he uses her to mask his crimes and seeks to expunge his defilement. He deserves no pity from

---

[226] In lieu of regular taxation Athens relied on several different kinds of "contributions" by rich citizens. The special levies were raised only in wartime; regular contributions, called "liturgies," included the equipping of triremes (warships) on an annual basis, and the underwriting of various musical and dramatic productions that were presented at public festivals throughout the year.

you, for he brought disaster on the victim against his will and willingly assumed this risk for himself. I already showed in my earlier speech that he killed the man. I shall now try to refute the claims he made in his defense.

[2] If the killers had seen others approaching and had fled leaving the victims there without removing their cloaks, then those who discovered them would have gotten a clear story from the servant, who was still conscious when they found him even if his master was already dead, and they would have reported the culprits to us so that this man would not be blamed. Or if anyone else had been observed committing a crime and had killed the victims so that they wouldn't be recognized, then the other crime would have been reported at the same time as this murder and suspicion would have fallen on those others [3] And I don't know how those who were in less danger would have plotted against him more than those who had more to fear. For the latter, their fear and the great wrong they had suffered overcame their caution, whereas for the former the dangerous and disgraceful nature of the crime outweighed their previous differences and tempered the vehemence of their spirit, even if they contemplated such action. [4] They are wrong to say you should give no credence to the attendant's evidence. Slaves who give the sort of evidence he did are not tortured but are set free. In cases where they deny a theft or conspire with their masters to conceal a crime, then we consider their testimony truthful only under torture [5] And he is no more likely to have been absent than present: he would run the same risk absent as present since anyone captured at the scene would have established his guilt as the planner, whereas the execution of the crime would have suffered since none of his agents would be as eager for it as he. [6] I shall also show that in his view the indictment posed not a smaller but a far greater risk than this trial. Let's assume he had the same expectation of conviction or acquittal in each case. Now he had no hope of avoiding trial on the indictment as long as this man was alive, for he would never persuade him to settle the case,[227] whereas he hoped to avoid trial in this case since he thought he could kill the man without being

---

[227] The Greek says simply "he would never persuade him," but "persuasion" in this context implies paying money in order to reach an out-of-court settlement.

caught. [7] He is wrong if he thinks you shouldn't suspect him because he's the obvious suspect. If the risk of suspicion was enough to deter this man from attacking when he faced the gravest danger, then no one at all would have planned the murder: anyone in less danger than the defendant would also be less likely than he to attempt the crime, since the fear of incurring suspicion would still outweigh the danger he was facing. [8] The special levies and dramatic productions are a good indication of his prosperity but not of his innocence. On the contrary, it is precisely his fear of losing this prosperity that makes it likely that he committed this unholy murder. And when he says that it is not those who are likely to have killed but those who have actually killed, who are murderers, he is correct about those who have actually killed, if it was clear to us who his actual killers were. But if the killers are not evident, then, since his guilt is established by likelihood, this man and no other would be the killer; for such things are not done in the presence of witnesses, but secretly.

[9] Since, then, he is clearly convicted as the killer on the basis of his own defense, his plea amounts to nothing less than that you transfer his own defilement onto yourselves. We, on the other hand, ask for nothing; we simply inform you that if this man's guilt is not established by either likelihood or witnesses, then it is no longer possible to convict any defendant. [10] If you acquit him wrongly, the dead man's spirit will not seek to take revenge on us but will weigh on your consciences; for knowing exactly how he died, you know that the tracks of suspicion lead clearly to this man, and since the attendant has given reliable testimony, how can it be right to acquit him? [11] With this in mind, assist the victim, punish the killer and purify the city. You will achieve three good results: fewer men will plot crimes, more men will observe their religious duties, and you will free yourselves from this man's pollution.

2d. *Defendant's second speech*

[1] Behold! I willingly put myself in the hands of misfortune,[228] though they say I am wrong to blame her, and of their hostility,

---

[228] See above, n. 225.

since although I fear the enormity of their slander, I have confidence in your intelligence and in the truth of my actions. Since they prevent me from lamenting my present misfortune before you, I don't know where else to seek refuge. [2] The accusations they raise are pure invention, if one may call it invention rather than malice. They pretend to want prosecution and execution for the murder, but they reject all grounds for true suspicion and call me the murderer simply because they don't know who killed him. Their assignment is to punish the killer, but they clearly seek the opposite, to kill me unjustly. [3] My proper course is only to defend myself against the attendant's testimony. I am not obliged to reveal or convict the true killers, only to answer the charge against me. Nevertheless, I must do more if I am to make it entirely clear to you that these men are plotting against me, and that I am innocent of all suspicion. [4] I ask then that my misfortune, which they use to slander me, turn to good fortune; I think you should bless me with an acquittal rather than pity me after a conviction.

They assert that anyone who happened on them while they were being beaten, rather than leave the scene, would be more likely to investigate exactly who the killers were and report them when they reached home. [5] But I don't think any man is so reckless that he wouldn't turn and run away if in the middle of the night he came upon a corpse still quivering, rather than risk his life to learn the identity of the criminals. And since they probably did what was likely, it would not be reasonable to acquit those who killed them for their cloaks, and I am removed from suspicion. [6] Whether or not any other crimes were reported at the same time as their murder, who knows? No one took the trouble to look into this. And since there is no information about a report, it is not hard to believe he was killed by these criminals. [7] Why should you give more credence to the attendant's testimony than to that of free men? If the latter are judged to have testified falsely, they lose their civic rights and are fined, but this man, who furnished no proof and was not tortured – how will he be punished? Indeed, what proof could there be? Since he faced no danger in testifying, it's not surprising he was persuaded by his owners, my enemies, to lie against me. But it would be a sacrilege if this untrustworthy testimony should cause you to ruin me. [8] They also assert that it is more credible that I was present at the scene of the murder than that I was absent, but I shall prove my absence not as a matter of likelihood but as a fact. I offer you all my slaves for torture,[229] male and female; if it does not become clear that I was at home in bed that night and did not go out anywhere, then I admit I am the murderer. It was no ordinary night, for the man died the day of the Dipoleion.[230] [9] They allege that my prosperity makes it likely that I killed him, since I was afraid of losing it, but the situation is quite the opposite. It is those in misfortune who stand to gain by stirring up trouble (*neōterizein*),[231] since a general upheaval can be expected to alter their own impoverished state. Those who are prosperous, on the other hand, benefit from preserving the social order and protecting their present fortunes, for when conditions change, their prosperity soon turns to adversity. [10] Although they claim to establish my guilt on the basis of likelihood, they then assert that I am the man's killer not in likelihood but in fact. The likelihood has been shown to be more in my favor, however, for the witness against me has been proven to be unconvincing, and he offers no proof. I have shown that the evidence supports me not him, and the tracks of the murder have been shown to lead not to me but to those who are being set free by my opponents. Since on examination their entire case has proven unconvincing, my acquittal would not mean that criminals cannot be proved guilty, but my conviction would mean that no defense is sufficient to acquit those who face prosecution. [11] They prosecute me so unjustly, claiming to be pure while they seek to murder me in unholy fashion and then calling my actions unholy though I only urge you to respect the gods. Since I am innocent of all charges, for myself I implore you to respect the righteousness of those who have done no wrong, whereas on behalf of the dead man I remind you to seek retribution and urge you not to convict an innocent man while you let the guilty go free. For if I die, no one will any longer look for the true killer. [12] With these considerations in mind, acquit me in accordance

---

[229] See above n. 223. In an actual case this challenge would probably have been issued before the trial began.

[230] An annual summer festival in honor of Zeus.

[231] *Neōterizein*, literally "to make new," implies the fomenting of revolution. This passage reveals the aristocratic prejudice that the poor were most likely to overthrow the government, even though both revolutions in fifth-century Athens were the work of oligarchs overthrowing a democratic government.

Antiphon

with the laws of gods and men. Do not change your mind and recognize your mistake only later, for later regret is no cure for such mistakes.

3. Second Tetralogy

The hypothetical situation is stated in 3a.1: A youth throws a javelin during practice and hits a boy who was at that moment picking up javelins for the throwers. These facts are accepted by both sides. The dispute is whether the thrower should be found guilty of unintentional homicide, a charge normally punishable by exile, perhaps for a year. The defense argues that the boy was responsible for his own death. In some ways the case resembles one of involuntary manslaughter in American law. Cf. the case discussed by Protagoras (fr. 30).

3a. *Plaintiff's first speech*

[1] When the facts are agreed on by both sides, the sentence is determined by the laws and by those who voted for them, who have final authority over our government. But if there should be disagreement on any matter, it is your duty, citizens, to decide. Now I do not think even the defendant will disagree with me in this case; for my boy, struck in the side on the training field by a javelin thrown by this youth, died on the spot. I therefore charge him not with intentional but with unintentional homicide. [2] For me, however, he produced just as great a loss unintentionally as if he had acted intentionally, and he has burdened the spirit not of the dead man but of those still living. I ask you then to pity the parents' loss of their child, to grieve for the unseasonable end of the deceased, to banish the killer from the places restricted by law,[232] and to recognize that he has brought pollution on the whole city.

3b. *Defendant's first speech*

[1] It is now quite clear that misfortune and need lead even those who mind their own business into litigation and force normally

---

[232] Athenian law specified several public places, including the law courts and the *agora*, as off limits to those formally accused or convicted of homicide.

quiet men to become bold and in general to speak and act against their true nature. Unless I am greatly mistaken I am not and have no desire to be such a man, but I am now forced by this very misfortune to defend myself[233] in an unaccustomed manner in matters whose precise meaning I understand only with difficulty, and I am even more perplexed how I should explain it to you. [2] Forced by cruel necessity I seek refuge, jurors, in your pity. If you think I speak with greater than usual subtlety, I ask you not to judge my defense, because of circumstances mentioned by my opponent, by appearance rather than truth. For the appearance of things favors those who speak well but the truth favors those who act in a just and righteous manner.

[3] I thought it would be good for both of us if I taught my son things that brought the greatest benefit to the community, but the result has been quite different from this expectation. For the youth, not through insolence (*hubris*) or lack of self-control (*akrasia*), but practicing with his friends on the playing field, threw his javelin but did not kill anyone, according to the truth of what he did, but he is now blamed for someone else's self-injury, which he did not intend. [4] Now, if the javelin had hit and wounded the boy because it carried outside the boundaries of its proper course, then we would have no argument (*logos*) against the charge of homicide. But because the boy ran under the trajectory of the javelin and placed himself in its path, one of them was prevented from hitting its target whereas the other was hit because he ran under the javelin. And now he hits us with the blame, though it is in no way ours! [5] Since the boy was hit because of his running under, the youth is unjustly charged, for he hit no one who was standing away from the target. If it is clear to you that the boy was not hit standing still, but intentionally running under the trajectory of the javelin, then it is shown even more clearly that he died on account of his own error, for he would not have been hit if he had stood still and had not run.

[6] Since, as you know, it is agreed by both sides that the killing was unintentional, one could decide even more clearly who was

---

[233] The defense (speeches 3b and 3d) is spoken by the father of the defendant, who is not old enough to defend himself. The father often speaks as if he himself is on trial, which in a sense he is, since a conviction would probably, in practice, force him to accompany his son into exile.

the killer by establishing which of the two made the mistake. For those who make a mistake in accomplishing what they have in mind to do are the agents of unintentional acts, and those who do or suffer anything unintentional are responsible for the sufferings that result. [7] Now the youth made no mistake affecting anyone, for he was practicing what was assigned, not what was prohibited: he was throwing his javelin on the throwing field, not where others were exercising; and he did not hit the boy because he missed his target and threw toward the bystanders. Rather he did everything he had in mind to do correctly and accomplished nothing unintentional, but he suffered by being prevented from hitting his target. [8] The boy, on the other hand, wished to run out but mistook the right moment when he could run and not be hit; so he fell into something he did not want. Unintentionally erring against himself he experienced his own proper misfortune and punished himself for his mistake, thus getting his just deserts. We had no wish for and took no pleasure in his fate but share his pain and suffering. Since the error is ascribed to him, the act is not ours but his who made the mistake; and since the suffering afflicts the doer,[234] it relieves us of the blame and punishes the doer at the very moment of his error. [9] We are also acquitted by the law on which he relies in prosecuting me for murder, which prohibits killing unjustly or justly.[235] Because of the dead boy's own error the youth is acquitted of killing him unintentionally, and because the plaintiff does not even charge him with killing intentionally, he is acquitted on both counts, intentional and unintentional killing.

[10] Since we are thus acquitted by the truth of the actions and by the law under which they prosecute, it is not right that because of our daily activities we should be thought to deserve such troubles. This youth will suffer unholy evils if he is burdened with errors that are not his, while I, who am just as innocent as he is (but not more), shall encounter much greater misfortune than he. For his destruction will make the rest of my life unlivable, and my childlessness will be a tomb while I still live. [11] Take pity on this young man, whose misfortune is not his fault, and on this old man, wretched me, whose suffering was unexpected. Do not vote

---

[234] A reference to the common Greek proverb "the doer suffers."
[235] I.e. intentionally or unintentionally.

for conviction and consign us to a miserable fate, but respect the gods and acquit us. The victim is not unavenged for the misfortune that befell him, and it is not right for us to endure a share of his errors. [12] Have respect, therefore, for the righteousness and justice of these actions; acquit us as is pious and just; and do not cast us two, father and son, most wretched of men, into an untimely disaster.

3c. *Plaintiff's second speech*

[1] I think this man has shown by actions, not words,[236] that great need can compel anyone to speak and act against his nature. In the past he was never the least bit disrespectful or daring but now he is compelled by misfortune herself to make statements I never imagined he would utter. [2] I was so foolish I did not imagine he would even respond; otherwise I would not have given only one speech instead of two and deprived myself of half of the prosecution. And if he were not so bold, he would not have this double advantage over me, for he can give one speech in defense against my one speech and have his one speech of accusation go unanswered. [3] With such an advantage over us in his words and an even greater advantage in his actions, he makes this impious request that you accept his defense completely. I, on the other hand, have done nothing wrong but have suffered terrible miseries and now suffer even more terribly. I take refuge in your pity, in fact not in word, gentlemen, you who punish unholy deeds and distinguish them from holy ones, and I make this request: where the facts are evident do not let yourselves be persuaded by a wicked subtlety of words to think that the truth of actions is really false. [4] For subtlety is persuasive rather than true, while truth will be spoken with less deceit but also with less power. If I put my trust in justice, I can ignore the defendant's arguments, but I distrust the cruel hand of divinity and dread the possibility not only of losing the benefit of my son but also of seeing him branded a murderer by you. [5] For my opponent has the audacity and the insolence

---

[236] The contrast between *logos* and *ergon* ("word" vs. "deed" or "action," "pretense" vs. "actuality," etc.), which occurs frequently in Thucydides, is especially prominent in this speech.

to claim that his son, who both threw and killed, neither wounded nor killed; and he asserts that my son, who did not lay a hand on the javelin and never thought of throwing it, thrust the javelin through his own ribs, missing the whole earth and all the other people on it. I think I could be more convincing if I brought a charge of intentional homicide than this man is when he asserts that the youth neither threw nor killed.

[6] For the boy was summoned at just the right moment by the training master, who was in charge of picking up the javelins for the throwers, but because of the thrower's lack of self-control, he fell into this youth's hostile missile and died miserably, though he had made no mistake affecting anyone. But the youth made a mistake about the right moment for picking up the javelins, and far from being prevented from hitting his target, he hit a most miserable and bitter target. He did not kill him intentionally, but it would be more accurate to say he killed him intentionally than that he neither threw nor killed. [7] Although he killed my son without intending to no less than if he had intended to, he denies having killed him at all and claims not to be convicted by the law prohibiting just and unjust homicide. But who threw the javelin? To whom should the killing be attributed? To the spectators or the attendants, whom no one accuses of anything? There is no mystery about the death; indeed it is all too clear to me. The law is quite correct, I say, in prescribing that those who kill be punished, for it is right that one who kills unintentionally fall into troubles he did not intend, whereas it would be wrong if the victim were to be left unavenged, since the damage is done, unintentionally no less than intentionally. [8] Nor is it right for him to be acquitted just because his error was unfortunate. If the misfortune occurred without any divine involvement, the person who erred ought rightly to suffer the result of his error; but if a divinely inspired defilement attached itself to the agent for some impious act, it would not be right to hinder divine retribution.

[9] They also argue that because they have led an exemplary life, they should not be thought to deserve trouble. But how could our suffering be deserved, if we are punished with death for leading no less fine a life? Moreover, when he claims that he made no mistake and maintains that those who make mistakes should suffer the consequences, not those who make no mistake, he is arguing

our case. For it would be wrong if my son, who made no mistake affecting anyone but was killed by this youth, should be unavenged. And I too, who am even less guilty of error than he, will suffer dreadfully if I do not obtain from you the revenge granted me by law. [10] I shall now demonstrate on the basis of their own statements that he is not innocent of the mistake or the unintentional homicide but that both of these belong to both the boy and the youth together. If it is just to treat the boy as his own killer because he ran under the trajectory of the javelin and did not stand still, then the youth is not innocent of the blame either, but only if the boy had died while the youth was standing still and not throwing his javelin. So the killing was caused by both of them, and since the boy's mistake affected himself and he has punished himself more severely than his mistake deserved (for he is dead), how is it right that the youth, his accomplice and partner in an error affecting those who did not deserve it, should escape without penalty?

[11] Since, then, on the basis of the defendants' own defense speech the youth shares in responsibility for the killing, it would be unjust and ungodly for you to acquit him. We have already been ruined by their mistake; if we are convicted of murder, we would be subjected by you to not holy but unholy sufferings. And if those who have brought death upon us are not banished from the appropriate places, you would be showing disrespect to the gods by acquitting those who are unholy. Since the entire defilement of everyone will be on you, you must exercise great caution. If you convict him and banish him from the places restricted by law, you will remain innocent of any charges; if you acquit him, you are guilty. [12] For the sake of your righteousness, then, and the laws, take him off and punish him. Do not yourselves take on a share of this person's defilement, but for us the parents, already living in this tomb because of him, make this disaster at least seem lighter.

3d. *Defendant's second speech*

[1] It's likely the prosecutor was thinking about his own speech and did not understand my defense. Your task is to recognize that we litigants are likely to judge the matter from our own point of

view and each of us is likely to assume his case is just; you, however, must view the actions of the two parties with a righteous mind, [2] for the truth of these actions is to be discerned from what each side says. For my part, if I have said anything false, I agree that whatever I have said correctly can also be discredited and judged unjust; but if what I have said is true but I have spoken subtly and very precisely, then it is only fair that your hostility should be directed not at me the speaker but at him [the boy] whose actions I am describing. [3] First, I want you to understand that a man is not a killer if someone claims he is but only if he is proven to be. The defendant here agrees that the actions occurred as we have stated but he disagrees on the question of the killer, although it is impossible to show who the killer is in any other way than from the actions.

[4] He complains bitterly that his son is being slandered if he is shown to be a killer when he did not throw any javelin or even think of throwing one, but he is not addressing my argument. I do not claim the boy threw a javelin or hit himself with it, but that by going under the javelin's blow he was killed not by the youth but by himself; for it was not by staying where he was that he died. And since this running across the field was the cause of his trouble, if he ran out because he was called by the training master, then the training master would have killed him, but since he ran out on his own impulse, then he has been killed by himself. [5] I do not want to begin a new argument before making it even clearer whose act it was. The youth no more missed his target than any one of those practicing with him, nor is it through any error of his own that he has done anything of which he is accused, whereas the boy did not act in the same way as his fellow spectators but ran out into the path of the javelin. This shows clearly that it is by his own error that he encountered more extraordinary misfortunes than those who stayed where they were. The thrower would not have missed his target if no one had run out under his javelin; the boy would not have been hit if he had stayed with the spectators. [6] I shall now demonstrate that the youth has no greater part in the killing than his fellow javelin-throwers. If the boy died because of the youth's javelin-throwing, then all those practicing with him would share responsibility for the act, for they avoided hitting him not because they did not throw their javelins but because he did

not run under any of their javelins. The young man made no greater mistake than they, and like them would not have hit the boy if he had stayed in his place with the spectators. [7] The boy is guilty not only of error but also of carelessness. When the youth looked around and saw no one running across the field, how could he have taken care not to hit anyone? The boy, on the other hand, saw the javelin-throwers and could easily have taken care that no one hit anyone; for he could simply have stood still. [8] As for the law they cite, we should praise it, for it correctly and justly punishes those who kill unintentionally with unintended sufferings. Since the youth made no mistake, it would not be just for him to be punished for someone else's mistake. It is enough for him to bear the burden of his own mistakes. But since the boy was destroyed by his own mistake, the moment he erred, he punished himself. And since the killer is punished, the death is not unavenged.

[9] Since, then, the killer has already been punished, you will not be burdened with the victim's spirit if you decide to acquit, but only if you convict. Since the boy himself bears the consequences of his own mistakes, his spirit will not seek revenge, but the youth is innocent of all fault, and if he is killed, his spirit will be a greater burden on those who convict him. If by our speeches the boy is revealed to be his own killer, the blame lies not on us who speak, but on the facts of what he did. [10] Since the arguments have correctly established that the boy is the killer, the law absolves us of any blame but convicts him who killed. Do not, then, cast us into troubles we do not deserve, and do not lend assistance to them in their misfortunes by rendering a verdict contrary to the divinity. In accordance with religion and justice, remember that this unfortunate event occurred because of his running under the trajectory of the javelin and acquit us, for we are not to blame for the killing.

4. Third tetralogy

The hypothesis is that two men, who have been drinking, have a fight. One of them is badly hurt and dies some days later after being tended by a doctor (see 4b, where "many days later" may well be an exaggeration). Athenian law considered a person guilty of intentional homicide even if his intent was only to hurt, not to kill, and so the defendant argues that he was only defending himself against the victim, who started the fight.

4a. *Plaintiff's first speech*

[1] The law has quite correctly established that prosecutors in homicide cases should make every effort to make their case and present their witnesses in accordance with justice, not letting the guilty go free or bringing the innocent to trial. This custom is quite correct, [2] for when the god wished to make the human race, he brought forth the first of us humans and provided the earth and the sea for our sustenance so that we would not die from lack of basic necessities before dying of old age. Since god placed such a high value on our life, whoever kills someone unlawfully sins against the gods and violates the rules of human society. [3] Thus the victim, deprived of god's gift, is likely to leave behind as god's instrument of vengeance the ill will of avenging spirits, which unjust prosecutors or witnesses will take into their own homes; and since they have joined with the killer in his sin, they will have a pollution that is not properly theirs. [4] If we, who are the avengers of those who are killed, prosecute an innocent man out of personal hatred, then, because we are not gaining revenge for the victim, we will be afflicted by the avenging spirits of the dead; because we unjustly put to death an innocent man, we are liable for the penalties for murder; and finally, because we persuade you to do something unlawful, we also bear the responsibility for your error. [5] Fearful of such consequences I for my part bring the sinner to you and thus remain free from such charges. For your part if you give this trial the full attention it deserves in view of the considerations I have mentioned and assign the criminal a penalty appropriate for the suffering he has caused, you will keep the entire city free from pollution.

[6] If he had killed the man unintentionally, he would deserve some forgiveness, but since in arrogance (*hubris*) and uncontrolled (*akolasia*) drunkenness he killed a man older than he, striking and throttling him until he had taken away his last breath of life, he is liable to the penalties for murder. And since he violated all the rules governing the treatment of the elderly, it is only right that he also receive all the punishment appropriate for such criminals.

[7] The law quite correctly hands him over to you for punishment. You have heard the witnesses who were with him in his drunkenness. You must take action against the lawlessness of this injury, punish his arrogance as the suffering he caused deserves, and deprive him in turn of the spirit that planned this deed.

4b. *Defendant's first speech*

[1] I'm not surprised they have kept their speech short, for the danger they face is not that they might suffer harm but that they might satisfy their hatred by ruining me unjustly. But I think it's reasonable that I'm upset at them for wanting to put this case, in which the victim was more responsible for his own death than I, on the level of the most serious crimes. He began the fight by drunkenly attacking a man much more sober than he, and thus he is responsible not only for his own misfortune but also for this accusation against me. [2] In my view their accusation is neither just nor godly. He hit me first, and even if I had defended myself with a sword or a rock or a stick, I still would do no wrong, for justice requires that those who start a fight be repaid not in the same degree but much more severely. So if I returned with my hands the blows I had received from his hands, what wrong did I do? [3] All right. But his response will be that "the law prohibiting just and unjust killing shows that you are liable for the penalties for homicide; for the man is dead." For the second and third time I answer, "I did not kill." If the man had died on the spot as a result of the blows, then his death would be attributable to me, though it would be a just death, for justice requires that those who started a fight be repaid not in the same degree but much more severely. [4] But in fact he was entrusted to the care of a bad doctor and died many days later because of the doctor's incompetence, not because of the blows.[237] Other doctors warned him that although he could be cured, he would die if he was going to follow that course of treatment. And yet he hurled this unholy charge at me even though you, his advisers, caused his death.

---

[237] In Athens a doctor could not be prosecuted for homicide if a patient died after receiving treatment.

[5] I am also acquitted by the law under which I am being prosecuted, since it provides that the planner of a death is a killer.[238] But how could I have planned to kill him if he didn't plan to kill me? In defending myself against him I used the same means as he, and I gave the same as I got. Clearly he planned the same against me as I planned against him. [6] If someone thinks he died from the blows and considers me to be his killer, he should consider the counterargument that the blows were caused by the one who started the fight. This shows clearly that he is responsible for the death and not I, since I would not have defended myself if I hadn't been struck by him. Since I am thus acquitted both by the law and by the fact that he started the fight, in no way am I his killer. The victim is the killer, and if it was unfortunate that he died, he was the victim of his own misfortune, since he had the misfortune to start the fight. Likewise, if he died through thoughtlessness, then it was his own thoughtlessness, since he wasn't thinking well when he struck me.

[7] I have demonstrated that I am accused unjustly; I now wish to show that my accusers are themselves liable for all the charges they are making. In plotting to murder me even though I am innocent of all blame, and in depriving me of the life god gave me, they sin against the god; in plotting my death unjustly, they violate the rules and become in fact my murderers; and in persuading you to put me to death in this unholy fashion, they also become murderers of your righteousness. [8] For these reasons may god punish them. You, on the other hand, must consider your own interest and be willing to acquit rather than convict me, for if I am wrongly acquitted and get off because you were not correctly informed, then I will set the dead man's spirit on him who didn't inform you and not on you. If I am wrongly convicted by you, however, I will inflict the wrath of the avenging spirits on you, not on him. [9] Understanding then that the offense against god is theirs, and keeping yourselves innocent of all blame, acquit me as

---

[238] Athenian law provided that the "planner" or instigator of a homicide was liable to the same treatment as the actual killer. There was considerable flexibility in the concept of "planning"; Antiphon wrote a speech, "On the Chorus-Boy" (not translated here), for a man accused of "planning" an accidental death because he was the general supervisor of the men directly involved in the accident.

is just and godly. In this way all our citizens would remain completely pure.

4c. *Plaintiff's second speech*

[1] It doesn't surprise me that this man's words match the unholy deeds he has committed, and I understand that in your desire to learn the precise significance of these events you would put up with hearing from him arguments that deserve to be rejected out of hand. For although he agrees he struck the blows that led to the death, he denies being the victim's murderer and instead, though he lives and breathes, he accuses us, who seek only proper revenge, of being his murderer. I wish to show that the rest of his defense has arguments similar to these.

[2] His first argument is that although the man died from his blows, he didn't kill him, because by law the one who started the fight should be held responsible for the events and the victim started the fight. First, you know that the young are more likely than the old to get drunk and begin a fight. Young men are inclined to give rein to their anger, since they are proud of their birth, they are at the peak of their physical strength, and they have little experience of wine. With old men, on the other hand, their previous experience of drunken behavior, their weakness in old age and their fear of the strength of the young tend to make them control themselves. [3] The deed itself indicates that he did not defend himself in the same way but in exactly the opposite way, for he killed the man with the full force of hands then at their peak, whereas the victim was unable to defend himself against the stronger man and died leaving no mark of any attempted defense. And if he killed with his hands and not with a sword, he is all the more the killer in that his hands are more a part of him than a sword. [4] He has the audacity to assert that someone who started the fight but didn't kill is the killer rather than the person who killed; for it is the former, he says, who planned the death. But I would say just the opposite. If our hands are the servants of our intentions, then he who hit but didn't kill was only the planner of the blow, but he who struck the fatal blow was the planner of the death; for the man is dead as a result of what he did, not through his own mistake but through the mistake of the striker. For he did more

than he wished and through his own misfortune killed a man he didn't wish to. [5] I am surprised that in claiming he died at the hands of the doctor he also says that we killed him by advising that he be entrusted to the doctor, since if we had not turned him over, he would say that he had died from our failure to give him care. Moreover, even if he died at the hands of the doctor (which he did not), the law prevents the doctor from being declared his killer; and since we turned him over to the doctor only because of this man's blows, who else would be his killer but the man who forced us to employ the doctor?

[6] Although it is clearly established by every argument that he killed the man, he is not content with defending himself for his ungodly actions, but he has the audacity and the insolence to claim that we who are proceeding against this man's defilement have ourselves committed outrageous and unholy acts. [7] Of course it's fitting, considering the sort of things he has done, that he should say these things and even worse than these. For our part, we have demonstrated clearly how he died, that there is agreement about the blow that caused his death, and that the law puts the murder on him who struck the blow. We now charge you on behalf of the dead man to appease the wrath of the avenging spirits by this man's death and make the city free of this defilement.

4d. *Defendant's second speech*

[1] The defendant has left,[239] not because he recognizes his own guilt but because he fears the prosecutors' aggressiveness. For us, his friends, it is more righteous to defend him while still alive than when he is dead. To be sure, it would be best for him to make his own defense, but since he thought it would be safer, we, who would be most grieved by his loss, must defend him.

[2] In my opinion the injustice concerns him who started the fight. The prosecutor uses unlikely arguments in claiming that this man started it; for if it were as natural for the young to be aggressive (*hubrizein*) and the old to act with restraint (*sōphronein*),

---

[239] If the defendant went into exile before his second speech, his relatives would speak for him and the jurors would still deliver their verdict for conviction or acquittal. Antiphon may use this device here to suggest the weakness of the defendant's case.

as it is natural that we see with our eyes and hear with our ears, the case would not need your judgment, for their age alone would convict young men. But since many young men act with restraint and many elderly men become violent when drunk, this argument does not support the prosecutor any more than the defendant. [3] Moreover, since this argument supports us equally, on this point we have the entire advantage, for the witnesses say the deceased started the fight, and since he started it, the defendant is blameless on all the other charges against him. For if it is the case that, by striking a blow and forcing you to seek the care of a doctor, the striker rather than the one who killed him[240] is the murderer, then the one who started the fight is in fact the murderer, for he compelled both his adversary to strike back in self-defense and the one who was then struck to go to the doctor. It would be an awful experience for the defendant if he is to be the murderer instead of the immediate killer and instead of the man who started the fight, even though he himself neither killed nor started the fight. [4] Nor indeed is the defendant any more the planner of the death than the prosecutor. For if the man who started the fight had intended to strike but not kill and the one who defended himself had intended to kill, then the latter would be the planner; but in fact he too intended to strike but not kill, but he missed his mark and struck a blow with unintended results. [5] He was thus the planner of the blow, but how could he have planned the death, since he struck with unintended results? The error too belongs properly to the man who started the fight rather than to the one who hit back; for the latter was only seeking to return the blow he suffered when he was forced into his error by his assailant, whereas the former, since everything he did or suffered resulted from his own lack of self-control, is responsible for both his own and the other man's error; thus it is just that he be the murderer. [6] I shall now demonstrate that the blows he struck in self-defense were not stronger than but considerably inferior to those he suffered. The victim stopped at nothing in his arrogance and drunkenness, with no thought of self-defense, whereas this man sought

---

[240] I.e. the doctor. The argument concerns the chain of causation: if we move responsibility from the immediate cause of death (the doctor) to an earlier cause (the striker), then we should also move it back to an even earlier cause (the starter of the fight).

only to avoid suffering and ward off the blows; what he suffered was involuntary and what he did in trying to avoid suffering himself was less than what he who started the fight deserved and so was not really an action at all. [7] Even if because of his own greater strength the blows he struck were stronger than those he suffered, it is not just for you to convict him for that reason; for large penalties are prescribed everywhere for the one who starts a fight, but nowhere is any penalty written for one who defends himself. [8] The argument about the prohibition of just and unjust killing has already been answered: the man did not die from the blows but from the doctor's care, as the witnesses have testified. The misfortune (*tuchē*) thus belongs to the one who started the fight not the one who defended himself; for the latter acted and suffered unintentionally and became involved in someone else's misfortune, whereas the former did everything intentionally. His very own actions led to this outcome, and in his own misfortune he went wrong. [9] That the defendant is not liable on any of the charges has now been shown. And if someone thinks the action and the misfortune are attributable to both parties jointly, and decides on the basis of the arguments presented that there is no more reason to acquit the defendant than convict him, even in that case it is right to acquit rather than convict him. For it is unjust for the plaintiff to gain a conviction without showing clearly that he has been wronged, and it is not righteous to convict a defendant unless the accusation has been plainly proven.

[10] Since in this way the defendant has been entirely cleared of the charges, the request we make on his behalf is more righteous: in your attempt to punish the killer do not put an innocent man to death. If you do, the dead man's spirit will still be just as much an avenging spirit towards those guilty of the crime, and the unholy destruction of this man will double the pollution of the avenging spirits against those who killed him.[241] [11] Stand in fear of this and consider it your duty to free the innocent man from the blame.

[241] I.e. in addition to the spirit of the original victim, the defendant, if unjustly convicted, will also haunt those guilty of unjustly killing him, namely the plaintiff and the jurors. In this conclusion the speaker draws on rhetorical commonplaces without regard to the facts of this particular case, in which the defendant is already in exile and thus would not be put to death or leave avenging spirits. Moreover, only one man is guilty of the original homicide (according to the defense), namely the victim himself, and he has already been punished in full.

As for the polluted killer, you can leave him for time to reveal and for the relatives to punish. In this way you would do what is best for men and gods.

Truth

5. (DK 1, M 67)[242]

Someone who says one thing does not in fact have one thing in mind, nor does one thing exist for him, neither something that the one who sees best sees with his sight nor something that the one who knows best knows with his mind.[243]

6. (M 68)

Men consider things they see with their sight more credible than things for which an examination of the truth leads into the unseen (*aphanes*).[244]

7. (DK 44, M 91)[245]

7a. [col. 2] ... ⟨the laws (?)[246] of nearby communities⟩ we know and respect, but those of communities far away we neither know nor respect. We have thereby become barbarous toward each other, when by nature (*phusis*) we are all at birth in all respects equally capable of being both barbarians [i.e. foreigners] and Greeks.

We can examine those attributes of nature that are necessarily in all men and are provided to all to the same degree, and in

---

[242] For Antiphon's fragments, in addition to DK numbers we include references to Morrison's translation (see Bibliographical Note, § B.5).

[243] The sense is rather obscure and we try to stick close to the Greek. Antiphon seems to mean that a single spoken word does not refer to a single object in the speaker's mind or in the real world; no such object could be seen by the person with the best eyesight or known by the person with the best mind.

[244] This fragment is often assigned to a courtroom speech (fr. 35 in the Teubner text by Thalheim [Leipzig, 1914]); cf. Protagoras, fr. 21.

[245] A papyrus discovered since DK's text and Morrison's translation has added some new text and led to a rearrangement of the previously known fragments (see Bibliographical Note). The order of 7a and 7b is reversed in DK and M.

[246] The intelligible papyrus text begins in mid-sentence; an alternative suggestion for "laws" is "gods."

these respects none of us is distinguished as foreign or Greek. For we all breathe the air through our mouth and through our nostrils, and we laugh when we are pleased [col. 3] in our mind or we weep when we are pained, and we take in sounds with our hearing, and we see by the light with our sight, and we work with our hands and we walk with our feet. . . [col. 4] They agreed . . . laws . . .[247]

7b. [col. 1] . . . Justice (*dikaiosunē*), therefore, is not violating the rules (*nomima*) of the city in which one is a citizen. Thus a person would best use justice to his own advantage if he considered the laws (*nomoi*) important when witnesses are present, but the consequences of nature (*phusis*) important in the absence of witnesses. For the requirements of the laws are supplemental but the requirements of nature are necessary; and the requirements of the laws are by agreement and not natural, whereas the requirements of nature are natural and not by agreement. [col. 2] Thus someone who violates the laws avoids shame and punishment if those who have joined in agreement do not notice him, but not if they do. But if someone tries to violate one of the inherent requirements of nature, which is impossible, the harm he suffers is no less if he is seen by no one, and no greater if all see him; for he is harmed not in reputation (*doxa*) but in truth (*alētheia*).

I inquire into these things for the following reason, that most things that are just according to law are inimical to nature. For rules have been made for the eyes, what they should [col. 3] and should not see, and for the ears, what they should and should not hear, and for the tongue, what it should and should not say, and for the hands, what they should and should not do, and for the feet, where they should and should not go, and for the mind, what it should and should not desire. Thus the things from which the laws dissuade us are in no way less congenial or akin to nature than the things toward which they urge us. For living and dying both belong to nature, and for humans living is the result of advantageous things, whereas dying is the result of disadvantageous things. [col. 4] The advantages laid down by the laws are bonds on nature, but those laid down by nature are free. Thus things

---

[247] The scanty remains of column 4 suggest that it contained remarks on the early history of humans. The gap between 7a and 7b was probably about three columns.

that bring pain do not, according to a correct account (*orthos logos*), help nature more than things that bring joy. Nor would things that bring pain be more advantageous than things that bring pleasure; for things that are in truth advantageous ought not to harm but to benefit. Thus things that are advantageous to nature[248] . . .

. . . and those who [col. 5] defend themselves when attacked and do not themselves begin the action, and those who treat their parents well even when they have been badly treated by them, and those who let their opponent swear an oath when they have not sworn one themselves.[249] One would find many of the things I have mentioned inimical to nature; and they involve more pain when less is possible and less pleasure when more is possible, and ill treatment which could be avoided. Thus, if the laws provided some assistance for those who engaged in such behavior, and some penalty for those who did not but did the opposite, [col. 6] then the tow-rope of the laws would not be without benefit. But in fact it is apparent that the justice (*to dikaion*) derived from law is not sufficient to assist those who engage in such behavior. First, it permits the victim to suffer and the agent to act, and at the time it did not try to prevent either the victim from suffering or the agent from acting; and when it is applied to the punishment, it does not favor either the victim or the agent; for he must persuade the punishers[250] that he suffered, or else be able to obtain justice by deception. But these means are also available to the agent, ⟨if he wishes⟩ to deny[251] . . . [col. 7] . . . the defendant has as long for his defense as the plaintiff for his accusation, and there is an equivalent opportunity for persuasion for the victim and for the agent.

7c. [col. 1] . . . to testify truthfully for one another is customarily thought to be just (*dikaios*) and to no lesser degree useful in human affairs. And yet one who does this will not be just if indeed it is just not to injure (*adikein*)[252] anyone if one is not injured oneself; for even if he tells the truth, someone who testifies must necessarily

---

[248] There is a gap of eight lines (about a sentence or two) in the papyrus.

[249] That is, they allow the opponent to swear what is possibly a false oath but refuse to swear a false oath themselves: cf. Aristotle; *Rhetoric* 1.15.27–32, 1377a.

[250] I.e. the jurors.

[251] There is a gap of four lines here.

[252] In this section there is an untranslatable ambiguity in *a-dikein* (lit. "not be just"), which can mean "commit injustice" or "injure."

injure another somehow, and will then be injured himself, since he will be hated when the testimony he gives leads to the conviction of the person against whom he testifies, who then loses his property or his life because of this man whom he has not injured at all. In this way he wrongs the person against whom he testifies, because he injures someone who is not injuring him; and he in turn is injured by the one against whom he testified in that he is hated by him [col. 2] despite having told the truth. And it's not only that he is hated but also that for his whole life he must be on guard against the man against whom he testified. As a result he has an enemy who will do him whatever harm he can in word or deed.

Now, these are clearly no small wrongs (*adikēmata*), neither those he suffers nor those he inflicts. For it is impossible that these things are just and that the rule not to injure anyone nor to be injured oneself is also just; on the contrary, it is necessary either that only one of these be just or that they both be unjust. Further, it is clear that, whatever the result, the judicial process, verdicts, and arbitration proceedings are not just, since helping some people hurts others. In the process those who are helped are not injured, while those who are hurt are injured.

8. (DK 2, M 70)

For in everyone the mind rules the body, with regard to health and disease and all other things.

9. (DK 15, M 83)

The decay of the wood would come to be alive.[253]

10. (DK 10, M 78)

For this reason he [god?] does not need anything nor does he expect anything from anyone, but he is without limit (*apeiros*) and without need.

---

[253] Cf. Aristotle, *Physics* 2.10, 193a, where Antiphon is said to have argued that if you plant a piece of a bed in the ground and it decays and puts out a shoot, the shoot would be wood, not bed.

11. *(DK 14, M 82)*

Stripped of a starting-point, it[254] would have arranged many fine things badly.

12. *(DK 29, M 101)*

When there are showers and winds opposing each other in the air, then the water is brought together and thickened in many places. And any of the colliding bodies that are overpowered are thickened and brought together, squeezed by the wind and its force.

13. *(DK 30, M 102)*

Burning and melting the earth, it [the sun?] makes it wrinkled.

Concord

14. *(DK 48, M 135)*

Man, who on the one hand claims to have the most god-like form of all creatures, . . .

15. *(DK 51, M 130)*

All of life is wonderfully easy to find fault with; it has nothing unusual or great or awesome, but rather everything is small and weak and short-lived and mixed with great pains.

16. *(DK 52, M 131)*

It is not possible to take back one's life like a checker-piece.

17. *(DK 49, M 123)*

Well then, suppose his life progresses further and he desires marriage and a wife. That day, that night is the beginning of a new

---

[254] Without a context the subject of the verb is unknown. Diels suggests "nature," Morrison "intellect."

spirit, a new destiny. For marriage is a great contest (*agōn*) for a man. If she does not happen to be congenial, how should he cope with this misfortune? It's a bother to divorce her:[255] to make one's friends into enemies, men with the same thoughts, the same lives, whom you respect and who respect you. But it's also a bother to keep such a possession, to bring home pains when you think you are acquiring pleasures.

But come, let's not speak of evil but of the most congenial of all situations; for what is sweeter for a man than a wife after his own heart? And especially what is sweeter for a young man? But, of course, in that very same place where pleasure resides, somewhere close by there is also pain. For one cannot traffic in pleasures alone, but they are accompanied by pains and struggles. Even victories in the Olympian or Pythian games or other such contests, or intellectual accomplishments, in fact all pleasures tend to be the result of much pain. For honors and prizes, the bait that the god has given people, impose on them the necessity of great toil and sweat. If I had a second body to take care of, as I take care of myself, I would be unable to live, so great is the trouble I give myself caring for my body's health and its daily subsistence and its reputation and respect and honor and good name. What then if I had another such body that I cared for in the same way? Isn't it clear that if a man has a wife after his own heart, she will give him no less affection and no fewer pains than he gives himself, when he cares for the health of two bodies and their daily subsistence and their respect and honor?

Well then, suppose he also has children. Everything is now full of concerns and the youthful bounce is gone from one's mind and one's face is no longer the same.

18. (DK 60, M 117)

First among human activities, I think, is education. For whenever someone correctly begins something, no matter what it is, it is also likely to end correctly. Whatever seed one plants in the earth, one should expect the harvest to be similar; and whenever one plants

---

[255] See n. 52 above.

an excellent education in a young body, it will live and thrive for its entire life, and neither rainstorm nor drought will destroy it.

19. *(DK 62, M 119)*

Whomever a person is with for most of the day, he himself must necessarily become similar to that person in his own character.

20. *(DK 61, M 118)*

There is nothing worse for people than unruliness (*anarchia*). In former times men knew this and accustomed their sons from the beginning to be ruled and do what they were told, so that when they reached manhood and their circumstances changed, they would not get carried away.

21. *(DK 66, M 139)*

Taking care of the old is similar to taking care of the young.

22. *(DK 50, M 129)*

Life is like watch-duty during the day that lasts only a single day, on which we look up at the light and pass it on to others who succeed us.

23. *(DK 53a, M 133)*

There are those who do not live their present life but prepare themselves with great eagerness as if they were going to live some other life, not the present one. In such fashion they do not notice that time has gone.

24. *(DK 53, M 132)*

Those who work and are thrifty and endure hardship and accumulate things enjoy just the sort of pleasure one would expect them to enjoy. But those who diminish and use up [their resources] suffer pain just as if they were losing their own flesh.

25. *(DK 54, M 134)*

There is a story that one man saw another acquiring a lot of money and asked him to lend it to him at interest, but he refused. He was the sort of man who did not trust or help anyone, but he took the money and stored it somewhere. And someone saw him doing this and stole it. Some time later the man who hid the money went and did not find it. Greatly pained by this misfortune, especially because he had not granted the man's request for the money, which would then have been safe and would also be adding interest, he met the man who had wanted to borrow and began lamenting his misfortune: he had made a mistake and was sorry he had not agreed but had refused the man's request, since now all his money was gone. But the man told him not to worry but to put a stone in the same place and then think that he still had the money and hadn't lost it. "Since you were making no use of it at all when you had it, don't think now that you are missing anything." Whatever someone has not used and is not going to use, he suffers no more and no less harm whether he has it or not. For when god does not wish to give someone unqualified good, he gives him financial wealth but makes him poor in good judgment, and by taking away the one, he deprives him of both.

26. *(DK 59, M 125)*

Someone who has neither desired nor chosen shameful or evil things is not showing self-control (*sōphrōn*); for there is nothing that he himself has overcome in making himself orderly.

27. *(DK 70, M 144)*

One who is gentle and moderate and doesn't cause trouble is "easy on the reins."

28. *(DK 64, M 137)*

Recent friendships impose constraints; old friendships impose more constraints.

29. *(DK 65, M 138)*

Many people have friends and don't know it, but they make acquaintances who flatter wealth and fawn on good fortune.

30. *(DK 58, M 124)*

One is more prudent (*sōphrōn*) if, when he is about to attack his neighbor, he is afraid he might fail to accomplish what he wants and achieve what he does not want. Because he is afraid, he delays, and because he delays, the intervening time often deflects his mind from what he intended; and this cannot happen if he has already acted, but only if he is delaying. Whoever thinks he will do his neighbor harm and not suffer himself is not prudent. Hope is not entirely a good thing; for such hopes have plunged many into irremediable disaster, and whatever they expected to do to their neighbors, they are seen to suffer the same things themselves. Prudence in a man is determined by nothing other than if he blocks the immediate pleasures of the emotions and has been able to control and conquer himself. But whoever wishes to give rein to his anger immediately, chooses the worse instead of the better.

31. *(DK 56, M 127)*

He would be a coward if he is bold with his tongue and makes haste in his desire when the danger lies far in the future, but hesitates when the matter is at hand.

32. *(DK 57, M 128)*

Sickness is a holiday for cowards.

33. *(DK 63, M 136)*

They listen, knowing the arrangement[256] . . .

---

[256] Perhaps the arrangement of a speech; cf. fr. 11 above.

Proems

34. *(M 159)*

I am prosecuting this case (*graphē*) because, by Zeus, I have suffered many wrongs at this man's hands and also because I have seen you and the rest of the citizens suffer even more wrongs.

35. *(M 160)*

But if my case appears stronger and at the same time I offer precise evidence, . . .

36. *(M 161)*

And I, miserable man, who ought to be dead, am alive, laughed at by my enemies.

Art of Rhetoric

37. *(M 162)*

It is in accordance with nature for us to perceive things that are present and at hand and next to us, but contrary to nature to preserve a clear impression of them when they are gone.[257]

---

[257] Cf. **6** above, and Protagoras, fr. **21**.

Thrasymachus

Thrasymachus of Chalcedon (a Greek colony on the Bosporus) was an orator, active during the second half of the fifth century. We have no reliable information about his life. He is best known today from the vivid caricature Plato gives of him in the first book of the Republic. *Otherwise, ancient writers speak of him as a stylist, not a political theorist. For the suggestion that he may be the author of a speech we have assigned to Critias, see the discussion on Critias, fr. 26, in the Bibliographical Note (§ B.5).*

1. (DK 1)

*This excerpt is quoted by Dionysius of Halicarnassus (*Demosthenes 3*), who presents it as an example of the "mixed" style (combining the "plain" and "elaborate" styles). The overall level of generality has led some scholars to suggest that this is a display piece, not written for any specific occasion.*

I would have preferred, Athenians, to have taken part in the public life of the old days when young men could remain silent, since affairs did not compel them to speak in public and their elders were running the city correctly. But since the gods have assigned us to live in a time when we obey the rule of others in the city but endure its misfortunes ourselves, and since the greatest of these misfortunes have been brought not by the gods or fortune but by those in charge, I am compelled to speak. For a man is either senseless or excessively patient if he lets himself continually be abused by whoever wishes and takes the blame himself for the treachery and wickedness of others.[258]

Enough time has passed: instead of peace we face war and danger; even now we welcome yesterday and fear tomorrow; and instead of concord we have hostility and confusion among ourselves. Although others are arrogant and contentious in times of abundant good fortune, we were restrained during good times; but in bad times we have gone mad, when others ordinarily come to their senses. Why then should anyone hesitate to say what he knows, when he has no choice but to suffer under the present conditions, although he thinks he has an idea for preventing them in the future.

First then I will show that those politicians and others who argue with each other have unexpectedly met with the inevitable fate of those who speak thoughtlessly in their desire to win debates: they think they are stating opposed views and don't realize that in fact they are doing the same thing, for they include their opponents' arguments in their own speeches. Consider the aims of both sides from the beginning. First, the ancestral constitution[259] causes confusion, though it is very easy to understand and belongs to all citizens in common. We must listen to the words of our ancestors for whatever lies beyond our own understanding, and whatever the elders among us have seen, this we must learn from those with knowledge.

2. *(DK 2)*[260]

Shall we, who are Greeks, be slaves to Archelaus, a Barbarian?

3. *(DK 6a; Plato,* Republic *1, 338c)*

Justice *(to dikaion)* is nothing other than the advantage of the stronger.[261]

---

[258] For similar remarks see the opening of Critias, fr. **26**.

[259] The "ancestral constitution" was a conservative political slogan in Athens during the revolts of 411 and 404; see Ostwald, *Popular sovereignty* (Bibliographical Note § A.1), p. 367 n. 119 (with further references) and *passim*.

[260] From a speech "on behalf of the people of Larissa." Archelaus was king of Macedonia, 413–399. See Critias, fr. **26** below.

[261] In the rest of Book 1 Plato explores some variations on this statement; it is uncertain whether this fragment or anything else Plato has him say represents Thrasymachus' actual views.

4. *(DK 8)*[262]

The gods have no regard for human affairs, or they would not have overlooked the greatest of human goods, justice (*dikaiosunē*). For we can see that people make no use of this.

---

[262] Probably a paraphrase.

Evenus

Evenus came from the island of Paros and was active toward the end of the fifth century. Plato often speaks of him as a sophist (Apology 20b, Phaedo 60c–61c, Phaedrus 267a), but only a few fragments of his elegiac verse survive.

1. (W 1)

It is the habit of many to dispute (*antilegein*) about everything in
    the same way,
    but they do not yet have the habit of disputing correctly (*orthōs*).
Against these men one old saying is sufficient:
    "let that be your opinion; let this be mine."
But one would most quickly persuade intelligent men by speaking
    well,[263]
    for these men are easy to teach.

2. (W 3)

I think it not the least part of wisdom
    to know correctly what each man is like.

3. (W 4)

To have boldness together with wisdom is a great advantage,
    but by itself it is harmful and brings evil.

---

[263] There is an ambiguity, which may be intended, in *legein eu* between "speaking well" and "saying (something) good."

4. *(W 9)*

I say that training, my friend, lasts a long time; and in the end,
this is nature *(phusis)* for men.

Critias

Critias was a relative (probably cousin) of Plato's mother, from an old and wealthy Athenian family which, like most such families, traditionally favored close relations with Sparta; he seems to have been a vocal advocate of Spartan customs (see frs. 18–21). He is best known as one of the leaders of the Thirty, a group of oligarchs who with the support of Sparta staged a coup against the democratic government of Athens in 404–403. The Thirty had some reasonable goals but their regime soon turned brutal, and democrats regained power in 403. Critias was killed in the final battle at about the age of fifty. The moderate tone of his surviving fragments seems strangely incongruent with the cruelty and violence that characterized his last year. See the Bibliographical Note, § B.5, for details of the fragments in our selection.

Tragedies

Pirithus

Ancient sources ascribe Pirithus *to Euripides, but most scholars accept Critias' authorship.*

1. *(DK 21, S 10)*

Speaking with a well exercised mind, he was the first
to make his throw, and devised this *logos*:
"Fortune is an ally to those with good sense."

2. *(DK 22, S 11)*

A good character *(tropos)* is more certain than a law,
for a speaker could never distort it,
whereas he often abuses a law,
shaking it up and down with arguments *(logoi)*.

3. *(DK 23, S 12)*

Isn't it better not to live than to live wretchedly *(kakōs)*?

Rhadamanthys

4. *(DK 15, S 17)*

We have all sorts of passions in life.
One man longs to have a noble birth;
another has no thought for this but wishes
to be called lord of many possessions in the house;
another is pleased to speak unhealthy thoughts   5
and persuade his neighbors with his evil daring;
still others seek shameful profits ahead of what is fine in life.
Thus the lives of people go astray.
I do not want any of these,
but would prefer to have a glorious reputation.   10

Sisyphus

Ancient sources are divided in ascribing this fragment, some giving it to Critias, some to Euripides, whose satyr play Sisyphus *was produced in 415. Sextus, our main source for the fragment, reports that the last two verses came a little later than the main text.*

5. *(DK 25, S 19)*

There was a time when human life had no order
but like that of animals was ruled by force;
when there was no reward for the good *(esthlos)*,
nor any punishment for the wicked *(kakos)*.
And then, I think, men enacted laws   5

for punishment, so that justice (*dikē*) would be the ruler (*tyrannos*)
. . . and[264] *hubris* would be its slave,[265]
and whoever did wrong would be punished.
Next, since the laws
prevented people only from using violence openly,   10
but they continued to do so secretly, then I think
for the first time some shrewd, intelligent (*sophos*) man
invented fear of the gods for mortals, so that
the wicked would have something to fear even if
their deeds or words or thoughts were secret.   15
In this way, therefore, he introduced the idea of the divine (*theion*),
saying that "there is a divinity (*daimōn*), strong with eternal life,
who in his mind hears, sees, thinks, and
attends to everything with his divine nature.
He will hear everything mortals say   20
and can see everything they do;
and if you silently plot evil,
this is not hidden from the gods, for our thoughts
are known to them." With such stories as these
he introduced the most pleasant of lessons,   25
concealing the truth with a false account (*logos*).
And he claimed that the gods dwelt in that place which
would particularly terrify humans;
for he knew that from there mortals have fears
and also benefits for their wretched lives –   30
from the revolving sky above, where
he saw there was lightning, the fearful din
of thunder and the starry radiance of heaven,
the fine embroidery of Time, the skillful craftsman.
Thence too comes the bright mass of a star[266]   35
and damp showers are sent down to earth.
With fears like these he surrounded humans,
and using them in his account he settled
the divinity nobly in an appropriate place
and extinguished lawlessness with laws.   40

---

[264] One or two words are missing at the beginning of this line.
[265] Critias may be alluding to the discussion of *hubris* and *dikē* in Hesiod, *Works and Days* 213–285 (fr. 6).
[266] Perhaps a reference to a meteor.

. . .

thus, I think, someone first persuaded
mortals to believe there was a race of gods.

Tennes

6. *(DK 12, S 21)*

Alas, nothing is just (*dikaion*) in the present generation.

From unspecified tragedies

7. *(DK 28, S 24)*

It is terrible when someone with no sense thinks he has good
sense.

8. *(DK 27, S 23)*

Whoever works to please his friends in everything
he does with them ensures pleasure for the moment
but hostility in the future.

9. *(DK 29, S 25)*

It is better to have clumsy wealth
living in one's house than wise poverty.

10. *(S 22; cf. DK 26)*

Time is a drug for all anger.[267]

Other fragments

11. *(DK 32)*

I begin, you see, with the moment of a person's birth: how can
he develop the best and the strongest body? The prospective father

---

[267] This verse violates a metrical rule for tragedy ("Porson's bridge") and may be
from a comedy of some other poet. Diels therefore substitutes the unattributed
line that follows in our source (Stobaeus): "After the shadow, time ages very
quickly."

should exercise and eat healthily and impose a harsh regime on his body, and the future child's mother should exercise and strengthen her body.

12. *(DK 49)*

Once you are born, nothing is certain except death and the impossibility of proceeding through life without disaster *(atē)*.

13. *(DK 9)*

More people are good *(agathon)* through practice than by nature.

14. *(DK 40)*

If you yourself should train your mind so that it should be competent, you would in this way be least wronged by them.[268]

15. *(DK 39) Two separate fragments quoted by Galen in connection with perception and thought; cf. Antiphon, fr. 5.*

15a.

Neither what one perceives with the rest of his body nor what he knows with his mind.

15b.

People know, if they are accustomed to having a healthy mind.

16. *(DK 42)*

An irritable person is one who gets more annoyed, or gets annoyed more often, than others over small and large matters alike.

---

[268] The reference of "them" is unknown; suggestions are the bodily senses or the common people.

17. *(DK 48)*

The most beautiful form among males is the female, but among females the opposite.

18. *(DK 7)*

It was a Spartan wise man, Chilon, who said this: "nothing too much." All things are good (*kalon*) at the right time (*kairos*).

19. *(DK 37)*

In Sparta especially there are slaves and free persons. Since the Spartan mistrusts the Helots,[269] at home he removes the handle from their shields. On a campaign he cannot do this, because they must often be armed quickly, and thus he always carries his spear so that he will be stronger than the Helots, if they should try to revolt with their shields alone. The Spartans have also devised locks they think are strong enough to prevent any plots the Helots might devise.

20. *(DK 34)*

Apart from this, [consider] the smallest details in life: Laconian[270] shoes are the best and Laconian clothes are the most pleasant and useful. And the Laconian drinking-cup, the *kothon*, is the most convenient for campaigns and easiest to carry in a pack. Let me explain why it is good for the military. It is often necessary for a soldier to drink impure water. In the first place the appearance of the liquid in this cup is not easy to discern; secondly, the *kothon* has an inward-curving rim that traps impurities.

21. *(DK 6)*

It is the custom and accepted practice at Sparta
to drink wine from the same cup,

---

[269] A local people who had been conquered by Sparta and reduced to the status of serfs; see Glossary.
[270] I.e. Spartan.

not to give toasts mentioning anyone by name,
   and not to go around the circle of the group to the right[271]
. . .   5
   An Asian-born Lydian hand invented pitchers
and proposing toasts to the right and challenging
   by name whomever one wishes to toast.
Such toasts loosen their tongues
   for disgraceful stories and render their bodies   10
weaker, and a blinding mist sits on their eyes.
The memory inside melts away into forgetfulness,
the mind goes off its track, the servants' ways are uncontrolled,
   and the house is worn down, beset by expenses.
But Spartan youths drink only enough   15
   to bring them all to cheerful hopes,
friendly words and moderate laughter.
That much drinking is beneficial to body,
mind and property, and is well suited to the deeds of Aphrodite[272]
   and to sleep, a haven from toils,   20
and to Health, most delightful of gods for mortals,
   and to Self-control (*sōphrosunē*), neighbor to Reverence.
. . .
Toasts[273] offered beyond due measure bring delight
   for the moment but cause harm for all time.
The Spartan way of life is evenly balanced: 25
   they eat and drink in moderation so that they can still
think sensibly and work; and there is no day set apart
   for intoxicating the body with unrestrained drinking.

22. *(DK 2)*

The cottabus[274] is from Sicily, a fine accomplishment;
   we set it up as a target for the shots of wine drops.
And the wagon, too, is Sicilian, supreme in beauty and expense.
. . .

---

[271] As was the Athenian practice. A gap follows, probably of only one line.
[272] "The deeds of Aphrodite" was a common expression for sexual activity.
[273] These lines come later in the same poem.
[274] Cottabus was the name of a game in which wine drinkers threw the dregs
remaining in their cup at a target; it was also (as here) the name of the target.

the throne is Thessalian, a luxurious seat for one's limbs;   5
  and Miletus and Chios, island city of Oenopion,
excel in the beauty of the marriage-bed.
The Etruscans are supreme in their bowls, wrought in gold,
and all their bronzework that adorns a house for every use.
The Phoenicians invented letters, an aid to speaking;[275]   10
Thebes built the first chariot,
  and the Carians, servants of the sea, the first cargo ships.
The potter's wheel and the offspring of earth and oven,
  glorious pottery, most useful for the household, were
    invented
by her who set up the fine victory trophy at Marathon.[276]   15

23. *(DK 31)*

The Thessalians, it is agreed, have become the most lavish of the Greeks in their dress and their way of life. This is the reason why they brought the Persians in against Greece,[277] because they envied their luxury and lavishness.

24. *(DK 1)*

You who once wove songs with womanly strains,
sweet Anacreon,[278] Teos brought you to Greece:
a provocation at banquets, a seducer of women,
a rival to flutes,[279] a friend of the lyre, sweet and without pain.
Fondness for you will never grow old or die,   5
as long as the boy brings around water mixed with wine
in cups, distributing the toasts to the right,
and dance-troops of women tend to the all-night festivities,

---

[275] The meaning of the very rare word *alexilogos* (= "assisting *logos*") is unclear. Several alternative readings have been proposed.
[276] Probably Athena, though the goddess is an odd addition to the human inventors of the other crafts.
[277] Persia had a reputation for luxury; their forces invaded Greece in 480 and Thessaly joined their side.
[278] Anacreon (*c.* 560–500), from the island of Teos, was particularly known for his love poems.
[279] Perhaps a reference to the common presence at banquets of flute-girls, the Greek equivalents of geisha girls.

and the disk, daughter of bronze, sits at the high peak
of the cottabus,[280] [struck] by drops of wine.   10

25. *(DK 44)*

If he [Archilochus][281] had not spread his own reputation among
the Greeks, we would not have known that he was the son of the
slave woman Enipo, nor that he left Paros and went to Thasos
because of dire poverty, nor that when he arrived there he became
an enemy to the inhabitants, nor indeed that he maligned his
friends and enemies alike. In addition, we would not know that he
was an adulterer, had we not learned it from him, nor that he was
an arrogant lecher, and, what is more shameful even than these,
that he lost his shield. Thus Archilochus was not a good witness
on his own behalf, leaving behind this sort of fame and reputation
for himself.

26. *([Herodes], On the Constitution)*

*Whether written in the fifth century or later,[282] this speech addresses an
apparently historical situation: a threatened attack on the region of
Thessaly in northern Greece (perhaps on the city of Larissa) by Archelaus,
king of Macedonia 413–399. The speaker appeals to his audience to
form an alliance with Sparta so as to enlist their help in defending
against this attack. We know little about the government of Thessaly,
but it seems to have been a loose federation of cities in which shifts of
power were frequent. Traditional aristocracies ruled several cities and
tended to side with Athens; pro-Spartan oligarchic groups were thus
sometimes opposed to these aristocracies rather than to democratic forces,
as in other cities.*

[1] Why it is necessary for those of my age or not much younger
to speak about the present affair, I can explain; but I cannot learn
from anyone else and have not discovered myself what reason there

---

[280] See above, n. 274.
[281] Archilochus of Paros (first half of the seventh century) wrote poems on a wide
variety of topics. Many are purportedly autobiographical, including one of his
most famous poems in which he admits dropping his shield and retreating from
battle.
[282] See Bibliographical Note, § B.5.

could be for someone who has something to say to keep silent. [2] One might be able to accuse those who speak about another matter of not knowing the present affair, and charge them with lack of purpose or meddlesomeness. But matters of war are of common concern to everyone and it is most necessary and fitting that this generation be informed and speak about them. Indeed, those whom the danger touches most closely are most compelled to be concerned, and those whose duty it is to be concerned have good reason to inform themselves. [3] I have thus determined that it is necessary to speak and I see no excuse for keeping silent. For I would like you yourselves to be responsible for your own well being – with the gods; but if you conclude that it is pleasant to prosper by the help of others, I think events will transpire with the attention of some god. [4] For all the necessary preparations – persuading others with money and risking your lives – have been accomplished for you by fortune without trouble or money, and so perhaps your enemies will voluntarily give you satisfaction.[283] First I will show you it is good to heed those who are urging war, and second that it is necessary.

[5] If we knew how to recognize powers that are by nature hostile to this land, we would have recognized them and taken precautions before suffering any harm; we would have used every device to render them weaker and ourselves stronger, understanding that a power that is hostile by nature will remain peaceful only if it is unable to inflict harm. [6] But only from our misfortunes have we learned our lesson: this man, Archelaus, will never be our friend, nor will there ever be a reconciliation between us; for he is our enemy not because of any injury we have done him but because of his desire to injure us. He already possesses land our fathers acquired and gave to us; if we are weak, he will continue to hold it, but if we are strong, he will be forced to give it back. [7] This is one reason for his ill will towards us; in addition, although Greek cities are content to preserve their power for their descendants, this is not enough for tyrants, who always want to

---

[283] If the text is sound, the speaker must be sarcastic here. He seems to mean that because the procurement of allies, which would normally require financial expenditures and military risks, has been accomplished without any effort (i.e. Sparta is offering help of its own accord), perhaps some think the enemy will capitulate voluntarily as well.

keep adding neighboring lands to their dominion. [8] I don't think we will allow this easily and we'll block him from conquering others. That is why he is angry at us, because he wants to dash the hopes of those who rely on us. So by this one means he thinks he can conquer us and those whom he cannot conquer because of us.

[9] We used to be able only to imagine these matters, but we now have a clear understanding of them from direct experience. When he sees us engaged in factional strife (*stasis*), he knows that this is the point at which a city and its territory are most easily captured. He has not hesitated to attack all these cities with the help of the oligarchs (*oligoi*). [10] For he knew that if he had not attacked[284] the many when he arrived, he would not have accomplished his wish. For he was not going to rule the many by joining in the attack on the weaker side, for they had sufficient resources to defend themselves against him. But he thought if he could conquer the many with the help of the few, then he could easily rule everyone. Thus he naturally wanted us to engage in factional strife, and you are aware that if it is to his advantage, he will pursue this course.

[11] You will see how great an evil this is to us, though it is to his advantage, if you compare it to the greatest of other evils. For all agree that war is the greatest of all evils, just as peace is the greatest of goods, and yet *stasis* is as much a greater evil than war as war is than peace; for in an external war men die preserving their fatherland, but in a civil war they die killing each other, and neither the slayers nor the slain gain any glory. [12] When we fight others, we fight for our friends, and when we conquer others, we make new friends; but when we fight ourselves, we lose even those friends we already have. It would take a large amount of

---

[284] The negative is not in the ms. but this or some other emendation is probably necessary. According to this text, Archelaus' policy is to join the oligarchic faction in its struggle against the democrats; when the democrats are defeated, he easily rules the oligarchs, who are "weaker." If he joined the democrats, they could defeat the oligarchs but the democrats would then be strong enough to defend themselves against him. But the speaker may not have in mind the traditional division between oligarchs and democrats (see introductory note, p. 267 above). We know too little about the internal affairs of Thessaly to say just how the speaker's analysis would apply or if it is meant to apply: it is possible the remarks are tailored to a more generic *stasis*.

time to relate in detail all that can happen: pillaging of the country, destruction of property, pleasure for one's enemies, and misfortune for one's friends. [13] Once it begins, there is no easy escape from these evils, for negotiation becomes impossible. Those who live close by are not sorry to see a neighbor engaged in factional strife: if weaker, they will be less likely to be subjected to their rule; if of equal strength, they will become relatively stronger; and if already stronger, they can now subject them more easily.

[14] I do not know where else to find evidence for this, since we ourselves serve as evidence for others. For we have the most land of the Greeks and it provides the most produce for ourselves and our neighbors, but we clearly are not richer than those who import from us, for they store up imported goods for their own use, whereas we waste ours on others, using[285] public goods for private benefit and private goods in public affairs. [15] But isn't it terrible to nourish at public expense men who do not leave the city open to all of us? Besides this, our land is naturally suited for defense against invaders and is well stocked with a native fighting force and horses, and yet not only can we not prevent people from committing crimes, but we import hired soldiers to protect us, turning over our defense to foreigners! Our country's might is scorned and we ourselves are laughed at. [16] You were present yourselves and saw the man[286] who is responsible for all these and many other evils make his presentation to everyone, a presentation no one is hardened or cynical enough to recount without tears. Did he leave out any of the greatest evils? Didn't children see their fathers dying, wives their husbands, and fathers and mothers their children, some dying in their family's arms, others on enemy soil? [17] ⟨Didn't he describe⟩ houses being razed and property ⟨carried off⟩?[287] And isn't it worst of all when the one who does

---

[285] We retain the ms. reading. The reference of these remarks would presumably have been clear to the audience. Apparently certain merchants were accumulating profits which the oligarchs were using to influence public policy in favor of Archelaus.

[286] This is usually taken as a reference to Archelaus himself, but the characterization of him as being of the same tribe (section 17) is puzzling. More likely the speaker is referring to a local ally or spokesman for Archelaus, who recently presented Archelaus' case to the same audience. The case presumably portrayed the dire consequences of not bowing to Archelaus' wishes.

[287] The text of this sentence is faulty; the words in parentheses are mere guesses.

these things happens to share the same temples and belong to the same tribe, someone who should properly be defending his country in accordance with the law, not lawlessly destroying it? When the elderly view their old age, and orphans their youth as misfortune ...[288] [18] Surely we must inflict damage on the man responsible for these things. We have the power to repel aggression, avenge those who have died, and show pity for those who have suffered loss. The benefit is great: not only will we punish past deeds, but by this example we will teach others not to think that disagreement among us is a windfall for them, or that they can join with some of us in plotting against others. And if we do this, I have great hope that we will cease our factional strife when no one brings aid to those who engage in these plots.

[19] For these reasons, then, it is good for us that you have willingly agreed with those who ask you to join in the fighting. In what remains, we must consider why this is necessary. Archelaus did not join the Athenian attack on the Peloponnesus, and he neither stopped those who wanted to pass through his territory nor provided them with money.[289] Thus there is no reason for [Spartan] enmity except that he would not join their side against Athens but remained neutral. [20] Since Peloponnesians consider themselves justified in treating as an enemy those who do not join them in war,[290] let us take care that they do not make war on us for the same reason, if we are unwilling to join the Peloponnesians in war when asked. For he has not been wronged by the Athenians. [21] What argument do we have left? That we have not been wronged? Then we'll teach them to do the same thing as he, since there is not any wrong if whoever did it did no wrong. Well, shall we admit we have been wronged but say we do not wish to defend ourselves? Then we'll make those who wish to harm us completely fearless. [22] Well, [shall we say] that we want to [defend ourselves] but cannot? Who then will not despise our power, when we have other Greeks to help us but still cannot defend ourselves against

---

[288] The text is faulty; as it stands the sentence is incomplete.

[289] The speaker apparently refers to an episode in 424, before Archelaus became king. Some take this confusion as evidence that the speech does not belong to the fifth century.

[290] Cf. the Melian dialogue (Thucydides, fr. 5b), when the Melians' desire to remain neutral provoked the enmity of Athens.

our enemies? And would not the worst thing be if we are criticized a second time by the Greeks, first because we did not join them in the war against the Medes,[291] and second [if we do not join them in] the recently declared [war]? [23] And indeed, in that war we had good reason, for we wished to take risks for our land only together with them.[292] That was a fairer plan than to abandon our land and join them in fighting for theirs. But now what shall we say? They have come here and want to fight defending us and our land. [24] How terrible it would be if we, alone of the Greeks, will not let ourselves be counted in this alliance of Greeks! He himself has made clear the nature of such an act, for he wanted to become a Greek ally and was willing to pay them money, but he could not do it; and this shows two things: that it is good and that it is difficult [to become a Greek ally].

[25] That is enough said on these points, if someone wishes to dispute them. I have sufficient evidence from what I have already heard being said that my response to my opponents is the best possible one. No matter how strong their argument is, there is no more reason to fear it. [26] For they say that Archelaus, despite being the neighbor he is, is preferable to the Peloponnesians, for if we should wish, we could defend ourselves against him, but not against the Peloponnesians; and so [they argue] it is better to engage in civil strife (*stasis*) among ourselves than to be slaves to others. But for my part, if I had to choose between civil strife and slavery, I would deliberate carefully which I should choose; and I find that peace is in favor of the Peloponnesians. [27] But I am surprised that they contrast this situation with that one, for they are not comparing like with like. First, we have full knowledge of his activities but we can only guess at theirs, for we have direct experience of the former but we do not know if we will experience the latter. It's not fair: they are not angry about what has already happened but are more afraid of what they imagine will happen. [28] What precedent leads us to fear them? Don't we see that our closest Greek neighbors, the Phocians, are free, and the adjacent

---

[291] When the Persians (here called Medes) under Xerxes invaded Greece in 480, the Thessalians submitted without resistance.

[292] See Herodotus 7.172, where a similar excuse is given. The rest of the Greeks retreated south, leaving the Thessalians either to face Xerxes alone, abandon their land and retreat with the others, or come to terms with him.

Boeotians neither pay tribute to them [Sparta] nor is there a Spartan ruler there, and farther away the Corinthians are autonomous and manage their own affairs, and [so too] those next to them, the Achaeans, who have no greater population than we and do not live in cities,[293] and the Elians and the Tegeans and the other Arcadians, who are neighbors [of Sparta]? [29] But in those cities no one has yet found a Spartan ruler, just as there has not been a Macedonian here;[294] but we know that they everywhere have constitutions and laws and the people make common use of public goods.

[30] Perhaps someone might object that they establish oligarchy everywhere. Well, that is just the sort of government we have long desired and hoped for, but were deprived of after experiencing it only briefly – if it is really proper to compare those oligarchies to the one here; for where among them is there a city as small as ours in which a third of the people do not participate in public affairs?[295] [31] Someone who does not have weapons or any other means to engage in public service[296] is kept out of public affairs not by the Spartans but by fortune, and he is kept out until[297] he becomes an example. This is possible, as is the case with us. For I do not think that in all our hopes we would hope to be governed otherwise. Since they provide such examples as these, they have no reason to fear what is more terrible if it does not occur than if it does. [32] The Spartans are no more inclined by nature to attack us; they live far from us and they are not prepared for our kind of land, for where we are strong, they are quite different.[298]

---

[293] Like Thessaly and other less populated areas, Achaea (in the north-central Peloponnese) was primarily organized not into city-states (*poleis*) but into tribes (though neither area was entirely without *poleis*). The list of Sparta's autonomous allies moves steadily from Thessaly's immediate neighbors to Sparta's.

[294] Albini (following Wade-Gery) emends the ms. to remove the negative: "as there has been a Macedonian here." Since we do not know whether in fact there had ever been a Macedonian ruler in Thessaly, we retain the ms. reading.

[295] This seems to mean that under the short-lived Thessalian oligarchy two-thirds of the citizens were allowed to participate in the government, which was thus hardly a typical oligarchy.

[296] Oligarchic governments often restricted service in a Council or Assembly to those who could afford weapons or meet other financial criteria.

[297] The ms. text of the rest of this sentence and the next is probably corrupt, but since no better alternative has been suggested, we have done our best to translate it. The interpretation of this entire section is disputed.

[298] The Thessalians' special strength was their cavalry; the Spartans' their heavily armed foot-soldiers (hoplites).

Thus in the first place they have no good reason to plan an attack; but if they attempt one, they will not go unnoticed, and if we have advanced knowledge, we will not ignore them. Thus there is no way they will do well in attacking us.

[33] Now if someone makes the argument that Archelaus holds children [as hostages] and because of these children it is impossible to join the fighting, first of all I should be amazed that this man speaks about ten children but says nothing about the whole populace or the city, thus trying to remove the advantage from the many and transfer it to the few. If it were indeed necessary that the children suffer, it would not be surprising that he says this; but in fact, when we conquer him, we will gain control of the children at the same time, and thus we will easily take back the children, having rescued them from their hardships there.

[34] My argument, therefore, is that we should defend ourselves against the man who wrongs us, take vengeance for those who have died, show favor to those related to us,[299] welcome our fortune, become allies of the Greeks and enemies of the Barbarians, put our trust in those who benefit us but fear those who do not, consider those who injure us enemies and those who defend us friends, and finally, recognize that facts are more important than suppositions. [35] This, then, is my argument. My opponents have come to such a level of audacity that the force of their argument must be just the opposite: that we should put up with being wronged, help those who wrong us, flee from those who wish to help us, distrust our friends and trust our enemies, fear what is far away and neglect what is close by, [36] and furthermore that we not become allies of the Greeks but of the Barbarians, and indeed of the most hated of these, and again, that the dead be left to have died unavenged, and that those related to us be without honor, and that there be neither constitution nor laws nor justice. [37] This must necessarily be the force of my opponents' argument, for these are the opposite conclusions from those I have reached. If you let yourselves be persuaded by them, you will not fail to achieve these results. But if you eagerly accept the alliance [with Sparta], we will inflict punishment for what we have suffered and we will never suffer such things again.

---

[299] This term apparently designates fellow-Greeks, as opposed to Macedonians, who were considered Barbarians; cf. Thrasymachus, fr. 2.

Lycophron

Very little is known of Lycophron's life. He lived in the late fifth and early fourth centuries and was probably a follower of Gorgias. The following quotations are all from works of Aristotle.

1. *(DK 3)*

Law is the guarantee of just behavior (*dikaia*) among men.

2. *(DK 4)*

The beauty of a high birth (*eugeneia*) is not evident; its nobility exists only in the word.

3. *(DK 1)*

Knowledge is an association between knowing and the soul.

Alcidamas

Alcidamas (from Elaea) was a pupil of Gorgias who taught in Athens in the late fifth and early fourth centuries. Although his writings are probably later than those of the other sophists, we include his writings in this anthology because he shows little or no influence from Socrates or Plato, his concerns are an extension of the fifth-century debates on several issues, and the works are not readily available in English. In addition to these, Alcidamas also wrote a work on Homer, a few papyrus fragments of which have recently been discovered. This was apparently the main source for a later work entitled The Contest of Homer and Hesiod.

1. *(Scholiast on Aristotle,* Rhetoric *1373b6)*

God set all people free; nature has made no one a slave.

2. *On Those Who Write Speeches,*[300] *or On Sophists*

This essay may be a response to Isocrates' Against the Sophists *(Isoc. 13), written c. 391. Isocrates (436–338) was the leading teacher of rhetoric at Athens in the fourth century, but was a notoriously poor speaker himself. There may be a degree of irony in some of the arguments*

---

[300] *Logoi* (lit. "words") can designate (among other things) either an oral "speech" or a written "treatise"; the singular form is *logos*: "word, argument, reason, speech, etc." We have used "speech" throughout, since the written *logoi* in question take the form of speeches.

Alcidamas uses to attack writing – an attack that is itself (as he acknowledges) written.

[1] Some of those who are called sophists are not concerned with inquiry (*historia*) or general education (*paideia*), and they are just as inexperienced in the practice of speaking as ordinary men; but they are proud and boastful about their practice of writing speeches and displaying their own intelligence through their books. Though they possess only a small degree of rhetorical ability, they lay claim to the whole profession (*technē*). Therefore I shall undertake the following criticism of those who write speeches, [2] not because I consider their ability to be foreign to me, but because I have a higher regard for other pursuits and think one ought to practice writing only as an ancillary skill. I suspect that those who spend their life in this pursuit have failed in rhetoric and philosophy, and I think they would more rightly be called poets than sophists.

[3] In the first place, one would despise writing on the grounds that it is exposed to attack, and is an easy undertaking, available to anyone whatever natural ability he happens to have. Now, to speak appropriately, on the spot, on whatever topic is proposed, to be quick with an argument and ready with the right word, and to find just the right speech to match the current situation (*kairos*) and people's desires – all this is not within the natural ability of everyone nor the result of whatever education one happens to have had. [4] On the other hand, to write something over a long period of time, to revise it at one's leisure, to consult the works of earlier sophists and collect from many sources their arguments on the same topic, to imitate passages that happen to be expressed well, and then in some places to make further revisions on the advice of laymen and in others, after investigating the matter thoroughly by oneself, to delete everything and write it over again – all this is naturally easy even for those with no education. [5] But everything good and noble (*kalon*) is scarce and difficult and usually obtained only through hard work, whereas it is easy to possess things that are of low quality and little worth. Thus, since writing is easier for us than speaking, it is reasonable to conclude that the ability to write is of less value.

[6] Furthermore, no sensible person would doubt that those who are skillful (*deinos*) at speaking could write speeches reasonably well

with only a slight change in their mental state, but no one would believe that those who have practiced writing could use the same ability to be able to speak as well. For when those who accomplish difficult tasks turn their mind to easier things, they are likely to complete these tasks easily, whereas for those who train with easy exercises the pursuit of more difficult tasks presents a severe obstacle. This can be understood from the following examples. [7] Someone who can lift a heavy load would easily manage if he switched to a lighter load, whereas someone who applies his strength to the light weights would not be able to lift any of the heavier ones. In addition, a swift runner could easily keep up with slower runners, but the slow man could not run with faster runners. Besides, someone who is accurate with a javelin or a bow at long distance can also easily hit a nearby target, but if someone knows how to hit nearby targets, it is not yet clear whether he can also hit distant ones. [8] A similar argument holds for speeches: it is clear that someone who can make good use of them on the spot will, if he has some leisure time for writing, be a superior writer; but if someone who composes written treatises switches over to extemporaneous speeches, his mind will be full of uncertainty and rambling and confusion.

[9] I also think that in human life speaking is always useful in every matter, whereas only occasionally does the ability to write prove opportune. For who does not know that public speakers and litigants in court and those engaged in private discussions must necessarily speak extemporaneously? Often events unexpectedly present opportunities, and at these times those who are silent will appear contemptible, whereas we observe that those who speak are held in honor by others for having a god-like intelligence. [10] For when one needs to admonish wrongdoers, or comfort the unfortunate, or calm those who are upset, or refute sudden accusations – on these occasions the ability to speak can help people in their need, whereas writing requires leisure and thus takes more time than the occasion allows. People require speedy assistance in their trials (*agōnes*), but writing produces speeches slowly, at one's leisure. Thus, what sensible person would crave this ability, which is so inadequate on such occasions? [11] And surely it would be ridiculous if, when the herald calls out, "what citizen wishes to

address the meeting?"³⁰¹ or when the water-clock is running in court,³⁰² the speaker should turn to his writing tablet, intending to compose and then memorize his speech! True, if we were tyrants of cities, we could convene courts and schedule deliberations about public affairs, so that whenever we wrote speeches, we could summon the rest of the citizens to hear them; but since others are in charge of these matters, would we not be foolish to practice speeches in some other way that is inconsistent with that?³⁰³ [12] In fact, when speeches are fashioned with verbal precision, resembling poems more than speeches, have lost spontaneity and verisimilitude, and appear to be constructed and composed with much preparation, they fill the minds of the listeners with distrust and resentment. [13] The best evidence for this is that people who write speeches for the lawcourts³⁰⁴ avoid great precision of expression and imitate instead the style of extemporaneous speakers; and their writing appears finest when they produce speeches least like those that are written. Now, if even speech-writers have this standard of excellence as their goal, that they imitate extemporaneous speakers, must we not honor most the kind of education that makes us adept at this kind of speech?

[14] I think we should also condemn written speeches because the lives of those who compose them are inconsistent. For it is by nature impossible to know written speeches about all matters; and thus if someone extemporizes some parts of his speech but carefully composes others, he will necessarily be criticized because of the inconsistency of the speech: some parts of it will closely resemble dramatic delivery and poetic recitation, while others will appear base and worthless when compared to the precision of the rest.

[15] It is strange that someone who lays claim to philosophy and undertakes to educate others is able to demonstrate his wisdom when he has a writing tablet or a book but is no better than an

---

³⁰¹ These words opened the proceedings in the Athenian Assembly.

³⁰² Time limits were imposed on speeches in court, and were measured by a water-clock, or jar filled with water that ran out slowly through a small hole at the bottom.

³⁰³ At the end of section 11 and at several points in section 12 the text is doubtful; for the most part we follow Blass.

³⁰⁴ In a legal case plaintiff and defendant had to deliver their own speeches, but they often had these speeches written for them by a "speech-writer" (*logographos*).

uneducated person when he has neither of these; or that he can produce a speech when he is given time but is more speechless than a layman when a topic is proposed for immediate discussion; or that he professes the skill (*technē*) of speeches but appears to have within him not the slightest ability to speak. Indeed, the practice of writing renders a person largely unable to speak. [16] For when someone is accustomed to crafting every detail of his speeches, and composing every phrase with precision and attention to rhythm, and perfecting his expression with slow and deliberate thought, it is inevitable that, when he turns to extemporaneous speeches and does the opposite of what he is accustomed to do, his mind will be filled with uncertainty and confusion, he will be annoyed at everything, he will speak like someone with an impairment, and will never regain the easy use of his native wit or speak with fluent and engaging speeches. [17] Rather, just as those who are freed from bonds after a long period of time are unable to walk like other people but are forced back to the same posture and movements they had to use when they were bound, in the same way writing slows down a person's mental processes and gives him training in habits opposite to those used in speaking; it thereby renders his mind helpless and fettered and blocks completely the easy flow of extemporaneous speech.

[18] I also think that learning written speeches is difficult, remembering them is laborious and forgetting them in trials is disgraceful. For all would agree that it is more difficult to learn and remember small things than large, and many things than few. In extemporaneous speaking you need to keep your mind fixed on the arguments alone and you can supply the right words as you proceed; but in written speeches in addition you must necessarily learn and remember very precisely the words and even the syllables. [19] Now, there are only a few arguments in speeches and they are important, but there are many words and phrases that are unimportant and differ only slightly from one another; moreover, each of the arguments is presented only once, whereas we are compelled to use the same words many times. Thus the arguments are easy to remember but the precise words are hard to remember or to keep in your mind when you have learned them. [20] Furthermore, if you forget something in an extemporaneous speech, your disgrace is not clear to others. For since the expression can be easily broken

up and the wording has not been precisely determined, if a speaker forgets one of the arguments, it is not difficult for him to skip over it and pick up the other arguments in order, thereby keeping the speech free of disgrace. Indeed, the argument you forgot can easily be presented later, if you remember it. [21] But if those who recite written speeches during a trial forget or alter even a small detail, they are inevitably beset by uncertainty and wandering and searching. Then there is a long pause and often complete silence takes hold of the speech. The speaker's helplessness is disgraceful, ridiculous, and hard to remedy.

[22] I also think extemporaneous speakers satisfy the audience's desires better than those who deliver written speeches. For the latter take great trouble over their composition before a trial, but sometimes miss the opportunity (*kairos*): either they irritate the audience by speaking longer than they desire, or they cut short their speech when people still want to hear more. [23] For it is difficult, perhaps even impossible, for human foresight to reach into the future and know precisely what attitude the audience will have toward the length of the speech. In extemporaneous speeches, however, the speaker can note the effect of his words and control them, cutting short some lengthy remarks or extending the presentation of short topics.

[24] Apart from these considerations, we see that both groups cannot make the same use of arguments supplied by the trial itself. If those who speak without a written text take an argument from the opposing litigant or through their own mental effort come up with an idea themselves, they can easily fit it into the order of their speech, since by choosing the words for their exposition on the spot, they produce a speech without any unevenness or roughness, even when they speak longer than they had planned. [25] However, if those who enter such trials with written speeches are given an argument other than what they have prepared, they have difficulty fitting it in harmoniously; for the perfect precision of their diction does not allow for spontaneous additions. Rather, either the speaker must make no use of the arguments provided by chance or, if he uses them, he must break up and destroy the entire edifice of words: by speaking precisely in some places but carelessly in others he will fashion a confused and discordant presentation. [26] But what sensible person would accept a pursuit

like this, that prevents one from using advantages that suddenly present themselves, and at times is less helpful to speakers than simple good luck? Other professions (*technai*) generally improve human life, but this one impedes even those advantages that come spontaneously.

[27] I do not even think it is right to call written texts "speeches" (*logoi*): rather, they are like images or outlines or representations (*mimēmata*)[305] of speeches, and it would be reasonable to view them in the same way as bronze statues or stone sculptures or pictures of animals. Just as these are representations of real bodies – they are a joy to look at but of no real use in people's lives – [28] in the same way a written speech, which has just one form and arrangement, may have some striking effects when viewed in a book, but for a particular occasion is of no help to those who have it because it cannot change. And just as real bodies are less attractive in appearance than beautiful statues, but for practical purposes are many times more helpful, so too a speech spoken extemporaneously from one's own mind is animated and alive and corresponds to actual events, just like a real body, whereas a written text by nature resembles the image of a speech and is totally ineffective.

[29] Perhaps someone might say it is illogical (*a-logos*) that I criticize the ability to write while I present my case by this very means, and that I cast aspersions on that very activity through which one procures a good reputation among the Greeks – and further, that although I do much work in philosophy, I praise extemporaneous speeches and consider luck more important than forethought and speeches spoken offhand more intelligent than those written with care. [30] Let me first say that I have uttered this speech not because I do entirely reject the ability to write but I consider it inferior to the ability to speak extemporaneously and think one should give most of one's attention to being able to speak. Second, I use writing not because I am especially proud of my accomplishment but in order to demonstrate to those who pride themselves on this ability that with little trouble we can overshadow and destroy their speeches. [31] In addition, I also use writing to prepare display pieces for delivery before a large audience. For I urge those who regularly converse with me to test me in that

---

[305] Cf. Plato's criticism of poetry as *mimēsis* in *Republic* 595a–603c.

way, whenever we can speak opportunely and gracefully about any proposed topic; but I try to demonstrate something written for those who have only lately come to hear me speak and have never encountered me before. For they are accustomed to hearing written speeches from others, and if they heard me speak extemporaneously, they might perhaps have a lower opinion of me than I deserve. [32] Aside from these considerations, in written speeches one can most clearly see signs of the probable improvement in someone's thinking. It is not easy to judge whether we are better now at extemporaneous speaking than before, for it is difficult to remember speeches spoken earlier; but by looking at something written one can easily view (as if in a mirror) the improvement of someone's mind. Finally, I try my hand at writing speeches because I am eager to leave behind a memorial of myself and wish to gratify this ambition.

[33] On the other hand, rest assured that in valuing the ability to speak extemporaneously above that of writing I am not recommending that one speak offhandedly. I think public speakers should choose in advance their arguments and overall organization, but the actual words should be supplied at the time of speaking. For the precision obtainable in written speeches gives less benefit than the appropriateness allowed in an extemporaneous display of speech. [34] Thus, whoever desires to become a skillful (*deinos*) public speaker and not just an adequate maker (*poiētēs*) of speeches, and wishes to make best use of his opportunities rather than speak with verbal precision, and is eager to procure the goodwill of the audience on his side rather than its resentful opposition, and who further wishes that his mind be relaxed, his memory quick, his forgetfulness hidden, and is eager to achieve an ability with speeches commensurate with the needs of his life – it would be reasonable for him to practice extemporaneous speaking on every possible occasion. If he practices writing only for amusement[306] and as an ancillary skill, those with good sense will judge him a sensible man.

3. *Odysseus*

Palamedes was known for his intelligence and inventiveness. When the Greeks were gathering their forces for the Trojan expedition, Odysseus

---

[306] Cf. the last word of Gorgias' *Helen* (fr. 1).

*feigned insanity in order to avoid joining it, but Palamedes exposed him
by placing Odysseus' infant son Telemachus in front of his plow. In
revenge, when they reached Troy, Odysseus concocted a charge of treason
against Palamedes and hid a sum of gold in his tent, claiming later that
this was the bribe Palamedes had received. This false accusation was
successful and Palamedes was convicted and put to death.*

*This version of Odysseus' speech at the trial was probably written as
a response to Gorgias' version of Palamedes' speech (fr. 2), with which
it should be compared.*

[1] I have often thought and wondered, gentlemen, about the
intentions of public speakers. Why on earth do they come forth
so readily and give us advice, when they bring no benefit to the
public welfare but offer a great deal of slander against each other
and carelessly throw out arguments that are quite inappropriate to
the present situation? [2] Every one of them says he only wants to
gain a reputation, but some also demand payment and give their
advice to whichever side they think will pay them more. And if
someone in the camp does wrong or harms the public interest
while getting rich himself, we can see that no one thinks anything
of it. Or if one of us gets more than another, by bringing back a
prisoner of war, or earning a reward, this causes us to have great
disputes among ourselves in our great zeal for these things. [3]
My own opinion is that a good (*agathos*) and just (*dikaios*) man
should pay no attention to personal enmities or private friendships,
and should not use his ambition in the service of one man, holding
money in higher regard and not thinking about what would be of
advantage to the mass of people. ⟨ ... ⟩ Rather, I will put aside
old labors and arguments (*logoi*) and will try to ensure that this
man, Palamedes, has a fair trial before you. [4] Let me remind
you that the charge is treason and that the penalty is set at ten
times as great as in other charges. Let me add that, as you all
know, he and I have never fought or quarreled about anything,
not even during wrestling matches or at drinking parties, where
strife and bickering most often occur. But the man I am about to
accuse is a clever intellectual (*deinos philosophos*); thus you ought
to pay close attention and not disregard what I am saying.

[5] I think you yourselves know the danger we faced: some of
our men had already fled to their ships, the rest had taken refuge

inside the trenches, the enemy were launching an attack on our camp, and no one knew where the impending evil would lead. This is what happened: Diomedes and I happened to be stationed in the same place near the gate, and Palamedes and Polypoites were nearby. [6] When we were engaging at close quarters with the enemy, one of their archers ran out and shot at Palamedes, but his arrow missed and hit the ground near me. Palamedes hurled a spear at him and he picked it up and returned to his camp. I picked up the arrow and gave it to Eurybatus to give to Teucer to use. When there was a short lull in the fighting, Teucer showed me that it had some writing under the feathers. [7] I was astounded at this development, and calling Sthenelus and Diomedes I showed them the contents. The writing read as follows: "Alexander to Palamedes. You shall have everything you and Telephus agreed on, and my father will give you Cassandra for your wife, just as you asked. But see to it that you fulfill your part of the bargain quickly." That is what was written. Now those who handled the bow should come forth and testify.

[Witnesses][307]

[8] I would have also shown you the arrow itself, just as it really was, but in the confusion Teucer unknowingly shot it. I should recount the rest of the matter, however, and not accuse an ally of ours of a capital crime for no good reason, imposing this most disgraceful blame on him, especially considering his former high reputation among you. [9] Now, before we launched this expedition, we stayed in the same place for a long time,[308] and no one noticed any sign on Palamedes' shield; but when we had sailed to this place, he inscribed a trident on it. Why? So that this sign would make him conspicuous, and the designated enemy archer would shoot the arrow at him and he would throw a spear back. [10] We should also infer from this evidence a likely explanation for his throwing the spear: for my claim is that it too had writing on it, stating the precise time when he would betray us. These missiles

---

[307] In Athenian law witnesses simply delivered a sworn statement; they were not questioned. In our manuscripts of legal speeches, this testimony is rarely quoted. Instead, the manuscripts simply note, as here, that witnesses testified at this point.

[308] A reference to the delay of the expedition at Aulis before sailing for Troy.

were pledges for each side to send to the other and to confirm their agreement without the use of messengers. [11] Another point to consider is that we had voted that if anyone obtained an arrow from the enemy, he should give it to our leaders, since we had a shortage of them for our own use. Everyone else abided by this decision, but although this man picked up five arrows that had been shot, he clearly did not give a single one over to you. I think this in itself would be sufficient justification for putting him to death. [12] Or do you think this happens to be characteristic of the thinking of this sophist, who in his philosophizing acts against those who deserve it the least? I will show that this man himself and his father are to blame for the entire expedition and related events. To tell what happened will necessarily require a rather long account.

This man had a poor father, whose name was Nauplius and whose trade was fishing. [13] This man has done away with many Greeks, has stolen much money from the ships, and has injured many sailors; in short, there is no villainy he is not involved in. As my speech proceeds, you will learn all this and hear the truth of what hapened. [14] Now, Aleüs, king of Tegea, consulted the oracle at Delphi and was told that if a son was born to his daughter, this son was destined to kill Aleüs' sons.[309] When he heard this, Aleüs quickly went home and made his daughter a priestess of Athena, telling her he would put her to death if she ever slept with a man. As fortune (*tuchē*) would have it, Heracles came by during his campaign against Augeas, king of Elis, [15] and Aleüs entertained him in the precinct of Athena. Heracles saw the girl in the temple, and, in a drunken state, he slept with her. When Aleüs saw she was pregnant, he sent for this man's father, Nauplius, since he knew that he was a boatman and a clever one. When Nauplius arrived, Aleüs gave him his daughter to cast into the sea. [16] He took her away, and when they reached Mt. Parthenius, she gave birth to Telephus. Nauplius then ignored the orders Aleüs had given him and took the girl and her child to Mysia, where he sold them to king Teuthrus, who was childless. Teuthrus made Auge his wife, and giving the child the name Telephus, he adopted him and later gave him to Priam to be educated at Troy.

[309] Aleüs had three sons and a daughter, Auge.

[17] Time passed and Alexander [Paris] wished to visit Greece. He wanted to see the sanctuary at Delphi, but at the same time, it is clear that he had heard about Helen's beauty, and he had also heard about Telephus' birth: where it took place, and how, and who had sold him. And so for all these reasons Alexander took a trip to Greece. Now, at just that moment the sons of Molus arrived from Crete, asking Menelaus to arbitrate their dispute and divide their property. Their father had died and they were quarreling over their patrimony. [18] All right, so what happens then? Menelaus decided to sail to Crete and directed his wife and her brothers [Castor and Pollux] to take care of their guests, making sure they had everything, until he returned from Crete. He then departed. But Alexander, seducing his wife and taking as much as he could from the house, sailed off without any regard for Zeus, god of hospitality, or any other god. These were such lawless and barbarian acts that even many years later no one could believe them. [19] When he had returned to Asia with the money and the woman, did you [Palamedes] at any time try to help, or alert the neighbors, or gather any assistance? You don't have anything to say, but you did ignore the fact that Greeks were being assaulted[310] by Barbarians. [20] When the Greeks became aware of the abduction and Menelaus had been told, he began to gather an army and sent some of us to different cities to ask for troops. He sent this man here [Palamedes] after Oenopion in Chios and Cinyras in Cyprus. Palamedes persuaded Cinyras not to join our expedition, and sailed off with the many gifts Cinyras had given him.[311] [21] He gave Agamemnon only a bronze breastplate, worth nothing, but kept the rest of the money himself. In his report he said Cinyras would send a hundred ships, but you yourselves have seen that not a single ship has arrived from him. I think this too would be sufficient justification for putting him to death – if it is right to punish this sophist, who has clearly been plotting the most disgraceful acts against his friends.

[22] We also deserve to know what attempts at philosophizing lay behind his deception and beguilement of the young men, when he claimed he had invented military strategy, letters of the alphabet,

---

[310] The verb is *hubrizein*, with meanings ranging from "rape" to "insult."
[311] I.e. Palamedes (allegedly) persuaded Cinyras to buy his way out of joining the expedition.

numbers, weights and measures, draughts, dice, music, coinage, and fire-beacons.[312] And he is not the least bit ashamed if I immediately prove to you that he is clearly lying. [23] For Nestor here, who is the oldest of all of us – Nestor himself at the wedding feast of Peirithoüs fought with the Lapiths against the Centaurs drawn up in a phalanx arrangement.[313] And they say Menestheus was the first to arrange military ranks and companies and put them together into phalanxes, when Eumolpus, son of Poseidon, and his Thracians made war against Athens. Thus this is not the invention of Palamedes, but of others before him. [24] Moreover, Orpheus was the first to introduce the letters of the alphabet, having learned them from the Muses, as even the inscription on his tombstone makes clear.

Here the Thracians buried Orpheus, servant of the Muses;
   Zeus who rules on high killed him with his lurid thunderbolt.
He was the son of Oeagrus, the teacher of Heracles,
   And he discovered letters and all human wisdom.

[25] Music was discovered by Linus, son of Calliope, who was killed by Heracles. As for numbers, they were introduced by an Athenian, Musaeus, a member of the Eumolpid clan, as his poems show.

   ... a hexameter verse of twenty-four measures.
   ... so that a hundred men might live in the tenth generation.

[26] And was not coinage discovered by the Phoenicians, who were the most learned and cleverest of the foreigners? For they divided a solid metal bar into equal parts and were the first to stamp an impression on them according to weight, indicating the larger and smaller amounts. This man then returned from visiting the Phoenicians and laid claim to the same system. In sum, it is clear that all these things, which he claims to have invented, are older than he. [27] But he did invent some things: weights and

---

[312] All of these except dice, music, and coinage are claimed by Palamedes in Gorgias' speech (fr. 2). See also Aeschylus, 10–11, and Sophocles, 19–20.

[313] Peirithoüs, king of the Lapiths, married Hippodameia and invited the Centaurs to the wedding. They became drunk and a large battle ensued, representations of which were a very popular subject for Greek sculpture. The Lapith victory was often seen as a victory of order and civilization over the violent, lawless elements of nature.

measures, which let store-keepers and traders cheat and swear false oaths, and draughts so that idle men could quarrel and bicker; and he showed people how to play dice, the greatest evil, which results in pain and punishment for those who lose and ridicule and criticism for those who win; for the winnings from dice games bring no benefit, since most of the proceeds are spent immediately. [28] And he also contrived fire-beacons, but these worked to our detriment (as he intended) and to the advantage of the enemy.[314]

Now, for a man to have *aretē* he must pay attention to his leaders, follow orders, serve the whole community, conduct himself as a good man in every respect, and help his friends and harm his enemies. This man's abilities are the opposite of all these: he helps the enemy and harms his friends.

[29] I ask you, then, to consider the matter carefully in reaching your common decision about this man. Do not let him go, now that you have him in your power. If you let him go because you are moved to pity by his speech, this will be seen as an astonishing violation of army rules. Every soldier will know that Palamedes clearly committed these crimes and was not punished at all, and they will try to commit crimes themselves. Thus, if you give the matter your full attention, you will cast your votes in your own best interest, you will punish this man, and you will set an example for the rest.

---

[314] The Persians used fire-beacons during the Persian Wars (Herodotus 9.3).

Anonymus Iamblichi

The following paragraphs, of unknown authorship, are generally agreed to be from a sophistic treatise of the late fifth or early fourth century. The work gets its title (lit. "The Anonymous Author of Iamblichus") *from the fact that it is embedded in a work by the fourth-century* CE *Neoplatonic philosopher Iamblichus. Iamblichus' work, entitled* Protrepticus *or* Exhortation to Philosophy, *quotes many passages from earlier authors. The style of these paragraphs is typical of the sophistic period and the subject matter also clearly belongs to the same period.*

1. [1] Whatever goal anyone wishes to attain with the very best results – wisdom, courage, eloquence, or *aretē* (either as a whole or in part) – he will be able to succeed given the following conditions. [2] First, one must have natural ability, and this is granted by fortune (*tuchē*). The other things are in the person's own hands: he must be eager for beauty (*kalon*) and goodness (*agathon*) and willing to work hard, beginning his studies very early and seeing them through to the end over a long period of time. [3] If even one of these is absent, it is impossible to reach the highest goal in the end; but if any human being has all these things, he will be unsurpassed in whatever pursuits he undertakes.
2. [1] When someone wishes to acquire a good reputation among men and to appear to others to be such as he is, he must begin immediately at a young age and must apply himself consistently and not vary according to the circumstances. [2] When each of his qualities has been present for a long time, tended to from the very beginning and brought to completion, it will procure him a firm

290

reputation and fame, since he has the unqualified confidence of others. He also avoids envy, which causes men not to praise or give proper credit to some things and to falsify and unjustly criticize other things. [3] People do not find it pleasant to honor someone else, for they think they themselves are being deprived of something. But when they are brought around little by little over a period of time, overcome by sheer necessity, they give praise, though even then only reluctantly. [4] At the same time they do not question whether he is the sort of man he appears to be, or is setting traps, hunting a good reputation by deceit and leading others to give himself more credit. If *aretē* is attended to in the way I have set forth, it convinces others of its own worth and gains a high reputation. [5] For at the point when people are strongly convinced, they can no longer give in to envy, nor do they think they are being deceived. [6] Moreover, when a public or private achievement takes a long time, that strengthens one's endeavor, whereas a short time cannot accomplish this. [7] If someone learned and understood the skill (*technē*) of words, he would be no worse than his teacher in a short time, but the *aretē* that results from many achievements (*erga*) cannot possibly be brought to completion in a short time by someone who begins late; he must be nurtured and grow up with it, keeping away from evil words and habits, and giving himself to the accomplishment of other things over a long time and with much care. [8] At the same time a reputation gained in a short time has the following drawback: those who in a short time become rich or wise or good or courageous are not gladly received by other people.

3. [1] When someone has desired one of these things, whether eloquence, wisdom or strength, and has complete and full mastery of it, he should use it for good and lawful purposes. But if he uses the good he possesses for wrong and unlawful purposes, this is the worst of all things, and it would be better for him to lose it than to continue to have it. [2] Just as the man who has one of these things and uses it for good purposes is perfectly good, so, on the contrary, he who uses it for evil purposes is perfectly evil. [3] We must also consider what word or deed would best enable a man who desires to attain the whole of *aretē*. Such a man would benefit the most people. [4] If someone benefits his neighbors by gifts of money, he will also be compelled to be evil if he collects

the money. Then too, he could not gather such an abundance that, with his grants and donations, it would not run out. And then this second evil is added after gathering the money, when he goes from being rich to being poor, from having money to having none. [5] How then indeed could someone be a benefactor of men not by distributing money but in some other way, and do it not with evil but with *aretē*? And furthermore, if he gives gifts, how can he not exhaust his ability to give? [6] This will happen in the following way: if he supports the laws and justice (*to dikaion*); for this is what brings together and holds together men and cities.

4. [1] Moreover, every man should be especially concerned to exercise the greatest self-control. Someone would best do this if he should be superior to money, which brings all men to ruin, and should show no concern for his own soul (*psuchē*)[315] in his eager pursuit of justice and *aretē*. For most people lack self-control in these two matters.[316] [2] They suffer because they love their souls, which give them life, and therefore they preserve them and cherish them because of their fondness for living and the partnership they have developed with them. And they love money because of things that frighten them. [3] What are these? Diseases, old age, sudden losses – not losses resulting from lawsuits, for it is easy to be careful and protect oneself against these, but losses resulting from such things as fire, the death of household members or livestock, or other misfortunes affecting our bodies or our souls or our material wealth. [4] For all these reasons, every man wants to be rich, so that he will have money to use in case of such misfortunes. [5] And there are other reasons, no less important than those just mentioned, that drive people to make money: competition with others, jealousies, and struggles for political power. Men value money so highly, because it can contribute to these goals. [6] But a man who is truly good does not hunt for a reputation by clothing himself in the splendor of others, but in his own *aretē*.

5. [1] As for loving one's own soul, you might persuade people with the following argument: if the human condition were such

---

[315] The word *psuchē* does not yet seem to have the meaning given to it, perhaps, by Socrates of a person's spiritual and moral self; here it retains some of its original sense of "life force."

[316] I.e. in regard to money and self-preservation.

that someone who was not killed by another person would be unaging and deathless for the rest of time, then a person would have much justification for showing concern for his own soul [2]. But since our condition is such that if a person's life is prolonged, he faces an evil old age and is not immortal, then it is a result of great ignorance and of associating with evil arguments and desires that he seeks to preserve his soul with dishonor, rather than leaving behind, in place of something mortal, that which is immortal, namely eternal and ever-living fame.

6. [1] Furthermore, one should not strive to gain an advantage over others nor think that the mastery (*kratos*) that results from such an advantage is *aretē* while obedience to the laws is cowardice. For this attitude is the worst possible and from it comes everything that is the opposite of good, namely evil and harm. For if humans were by nature incapable of living alone and thus joined together, yielding to necessity (*anankē*), and have developed their whole way of life and the skills required for this end [living together], and cannot be with each other while living in a condition of lawlessness (*anomia*) – for the penalty for lawlessness is even greater than for living alone – because of all these constraints (*anankē*) law (*nomos*) and justice are king among us[317] and will never be displaced, for their strength is ingrained in our nature. [2] Of course, if someone should have the following nature from the beginning – invulnerable flesh, free from disease and suffering, huge and hard as steel in body and soul – one would perhaps think that for such a person the mastery that results from an advantage over others would be sufficient, since he could disobey the law with impunity; but anyone thinking this would be wrong. [3] For if there should be such a person (which there wouldn't be), he would survive by joining with the laws and justice and by strengthening these and using his own strength in support of them and their supporters. Otherwise he would not last. [4] For I think everyone would stand opposed to a person with this nature because of their own need for law and order (*eunomia*), and the multitude, by skill or by power, would overthrow and defeat such a man. [5] Thus it appears that mastery itself – true mastery, that is – is preserved through law and justice.

---

[317] Cf. Pindar, fr. 1 ("custom [*nomos*] is king"); contrast Hippias, fr. 5 ("custom is a tyrant").

7. It is also worth learning how different lawfulness (*eunomia*) and lawlessness (*anomia*) are from each other, and that whereas the former is the best for both the community and the individual, the latter is the worst; for harm results immediately from lawlessness. Let us begin by showing the effects of lawfulness.[318]

[1] The first result of lawfulness is trust, which greatly benefits all people and is among the greatest goods. The result of trust is that property has common benefits, so that even just a little property suffices, since it is circulated, whereas without this even a great amount does not suffice. [2] And lawfulness allows people to manage most usefully the changes of fortune, both good and bad, that affect their lives and property. Those who enjoy good fortune can reap its benefits in safety and without fear of plots by others; whereas those who suffer misfortune are helped by others who are more fortunate, since lawfulness has led to their association with and trust in each other. [3] Another result of lawfulness is that people do not spend their time on public affairs but use it for the work of daily living.[319] [4] In a state of lawfulness people are freed from the most unpleasant concerns, but they enjoy the most pleasant ones; for concern for public affairs is most unpleasant, but concern for one's own work is most pleasant. [5] Moreover, when people go to sleep, which provides a rest from troubles, they go without fear or painful concerns, and when they awake they experience other similar feelings. They are not suddenly full of fear, nor do they after a most pleasant rest await the coming day in a state of fear. Rather, they pleasantly form thoughts without pain about the work of daily living, and they lighten their tasks with confident and well-founded hopes of acquiring benefits in return. And lawfulness is responsible for all this. [6] And the thing that brings people the greatest harm – war, which causes defeat and slavery – this too more readily besets the lawless, and less often the lawful.

[7] Many other goods result from lawfulness, providing assistance in life and consolation for its hardships; but the following are the evils that result from lawlessness. [8] First, people have no time for work but must be concerned with what is most unpleasant: public affairs, not work; and because they have no trust in or

---

[318] This first paragraph of 7 may be Iamblichus' own summary.
[319] The author is implicitly criticizing the Athenian democracy and the large amount of time Athenians spent on public affairs. The criticism continues in 7.8–10.

association with one another, they hoard their possessions and do not share them, so that goods are scarce, even if there are many. [9] The vicissitudes of good and bad fortune have the opposite result in a state of lawlessness: good fortune is not secure but is under attack by others; misfortune, on the other hand, cannot be dispelled but grows stronger for lack of trust or association. [10] Foreign war and internal strife are brought on more frequently for the same reason, and if these did not exist earlier, they now occur. One is continually involved in public affairs because of mutual plotting, which cause people to be continually on guard and to form plots against others in return. [11] When awake their thoughts are not pleasant, and when they enter sleep, they find not a pleasant reception, but a fearful one, where a fearful and terrifying awakening brings a person to the sudden memory of evils. All these as well as the aforementioned evils result from lawlessness.

[12] Tyranny too, that huge and horrible evil, arises from no other source than lawlessness. Some people (who reason incorrectly) think that the installation of a tyrant has some other cause, and that when men are deprived of their freedom, they are not themselves to blame but are overpowered by the established tyrant. This reasoning is not correct. [13] Whoever thinks a king or tyrant arises from any other cause than lawlessness and greed is a fool. This happens only when everyone turns to evil; for people cannot live without laws (*nomoi*) and justice (*dikē*). [14] Thus whenever these two things – law and justice – leave most people, then their protection and oversight fall onto one man; for how else would monarchy devolve upon one man, unless the law, which is beneficial to most people, was banished? [15] For the man who will destroy justice and take away the law, which belongs to and benefits everyone, must be made of steel, if he is going to plunder these from the vast majority of people, one man plundering from many. [16] Someone made of flesh and blood like everyone else would not be able to do this, but he would become a monarch only by re-establishing the opposite qualities, which have disappeared. For this reason some men do not notice this when it happens.

Dissoi Logoi

The Dissoi Logoi *is an anonymous treatise of uncertain date, though most scholars accept a date around 400 (see n. 321 below). It is written in the Doric dialect, a kind of Greek spoken primarily in the Peloponnesus and parts of Sicily and southern Italy. This may indicate the author's provenance, or perhaps that he is writing for an audience that spoke Doric. Speculation about the author's identity has been wide-ranging, but no suggestion has gained much support. The work shows the possible influence of Protagoras (who wrote* Antilogiae *or* Counter-Arguments*), Hippias, Gorgias, Socrates, and others, and may be the work of an unknown student of one of these.*

Good and Bad

1. [1] Double arguments (*dissoi logoi*) are put forward by intellectuals in Greece concerning good and bad. Some say that good is one thing and bad another, while others say that the same thing can be both,[320] and that something may be good for some but bad for others or sometimes good and sometimes bad for the same person.

[2] I myself agree with the latter, and my investigation will begin with human life and its concern with food and drink and sex; for these things are bad for someone sick but good for someone healthy

---

[320] Here and elsewhere in this work (e.g. 2.1) the Greek syntax is ambiguous between "*x* and *y* are the same" and "the same thing is *x* and *y*." The author seems to think these two statements are the same, or at least plays on the ambiguity. We have varied our translation depending on the context.

who needs them. [3] Moreover, lack of control in these things is bad for those who lack control but good for those who sell them and make a profit. Sickness, moreover, is bad for the sick but good for doctors. And even death is bad for those who die but good for undertakers and gravediggers. [4] Farming, when it produces fine crops, is good for farmers but bad for merchants. And when merchant ships are shattered or smashed, it is bad for the ship-owner but good for shipbuilders. [5] Furthermore, if iron is corroded or blunted or shattered, it is bad for others but good for the smith; and if pottery is smashed, it is bad for others but good for the potter; and if shoes wear out or break, it is bad for others but good for the cobbler. [6] In contests in athletics or music or combat, moreover – in a foot race, for instance – a victory is good for the winner but bad for the losers. [7] And the same is true for wrestlers and boxers and all musicians also; lyre-playing, for instance, is good for the winner but bad for the losers. [8] In war (I shall first mention the most recent events) the Spartan victory which they won over the Athenians and their allies[321] was good for the Spartans but bad for the Athenians and the allies; and the victory the Greeks won over the Persians[322] was good for Greeks but bad for foreigners. [9] Moreover, the capture of Troy was good for the Achaeans but bad for the Trojans. And the same is true of the experiences of the Thebans and the Argives.[323] [10] And the battle of the Centaurs and Lapiths[324] was good for the Lapiths but bad for the Centaurs. And indeed, even in the battle reported between the Gods and Giants, victory was good for the Gods but bad for the Giants.

[11] Another argument is made that good is one thing and bad another, and that just as the name is different so too are the things. And I myself also distinguish them in this way. For it seems to me it would not be clear what kind of thing was good and what bad if they were the same thing and not each something different; and that would be remarkable. [12] I think that the person who

---

[321] Usually taken as a reference to the end of the Peloponnesian War in 404. If so, the *Dissoi Logoi* was probably written *c.* 400.

[322] The Persian Wars, 490–479.

[323] Perhaps a reference to the battle between the sons of Oedipus, when Polyneices led an expedition from Argos against Eteocles, who was defending Thebes.

[324] A famous event in Greek myth; see n. 313 to Alcidamas' *Odysseus*, (fr. 3).

makes these arguments would have nothing to say, if someone should ask him, "Tell me, have you ever done your parents any good?" He might say, "Yes, a great deal." "Then ⟨you must think⟩ you owe them a great deal of bad as well, if indeed good is the same thing as bad."³²⁵ [13] "Well then, have you ever done your relatives any good? Then you were doing bad to your relatives. And have you ever done something bad to your enemies? Then you have also done them a great deal of good." [14] "Come now, answer me this. Do you take pity on beggars because they fare very badly and again count them happy because they fare very well, if indeed bad and good are the same thing?" [15] As for the Great King [of Persia], nothing prevents him from being just like a beggar; for his many great goods are many great evils, if indeed good and bad are the same thing. And you can say this about everything. [16] But I will also mention individual cases, beginning with eating and drinking and sex. For if indeed the same thing is good and bad, then it is good for the sick to do these things. And sickness is bad and good for the sick, if indeed good is the same as bad. [17] And the same is true for all the other things mentioned in the earlier argument. And I am not saying what the good is, but I am trying to show that bad and good are not the same thing but each is different.

Proper and Shameful³²⁶

2. [1] Double arguments are also put forth concerning proper and shameful. For some say that proper is one thing and shameful another, and that just as the name is different so too is the thing; but others say that the same thing is proper and shameful. [2] For my part I shall attempt an explanation in the following way: for example, for a boy in the flower of youth to gratify a worthy lover is proper, but to gratify someone who is not a proper lover is shameful. [3] And for women to wash indoors is proper but in the gymnasium is shameful; but for men in the palaestra or the gym-

---

³²⁵ The text may be corrupt here. Some editors change the first question to "Have your parents ever done you any good?"

³²⁶ The terms employed in this section, *kalon* and *aischron*, have a wide range of meanings. *Kalon* can also be translated "beautiful," "fine" or "noble"; *aischron* can also mean "ugly" or "base"; see Glossary.

nasium it is proper. [4] And to have intercourse with one's husband in private is proper, where it is hidden by walls, but outside is shameful, where someone will see them. [5] And to have intercourse with your own husband is proper but with another's is most shameful. And, of course, for a man to have intercourse with his own wife is proper but with another's is shameful. [6] And to adorn oneself and put on makeup and wear gold jewelry is shameful for a man but proper for a woman. [7] To do good to your friends is proper, but to your enemies shameful. And to run away from the enemy is shameful, but from your opponents on the athletic field is proper. [8] And to kill your friends and fellow citizens is shameful but to kill the enemy is proper. And this argument can be made about everything.

[9] But I pass on to what cities and nations think. For example, Spartans think it proper for girls to do athletics and go around with bare arms and without tunics, but Ionians think it shameful. [10] Spartans also think it proper for children not to learn music and letters, but the Ionians think it shameful not to learn all these things. [11] Among the Thessalians it is proper for someone to take horses and mules from the herd and break them himself, and to take an ox and slaughter it, skin it and cut it up himself, but in Sicily this is shameful and the work of slaves. [12] The Macedonians think it proper for girls before they take a husband to love and have intercourse with another man, but when married it is shameful; among the Greeks both are shameful. [13] In Thrace a tattoo is an ornament for a girl, but other people consider the marks a punishment for wrongdoing. The Scythians consider it proper for someone who kills a man in war to scalp him and carry the scalp on his horse's forehead, and to cover the skull with gold or silver and drink and pour libations to the gods from it. Among the Greeks one would not even wish to enter the same house with someone who had done such things. [14] The Massagetai cut up their parents and eat them,[327] and they think the finest tomb is to be buried inside one's children; but in Greece if someone did these things, he would be driven out of Greece and would die wretchedly for having committed such terrible and shameful acts. [15] The Persians think that for men too to be decked out like

---

[327] I.e. when they die. The same example is cited by Herodotus, fr. 3 (3.38).

women is proper, and also to have intercourse with a daughter or mother or sister; but the Greeks think these things are shameful and unlawful. [16] Indeed, it seems proper to the Lydians that girls prostitute themselves and earn money and so get married,[328] but among the Greeks no one would be willing to marry [such a girl]. [17] The Egyptians do not consider the same things proper as others do. For here it is proper for women to do weaving and other work, but there it is proper for men to do this but for women to do what men do here. And for them it is proper to moisten clay with one's hands and flour with one's feet, but for us just the opposite. [18] I think that if you asked all people to bring to one place the things they each thought shameful, and then to take away from this collection the things they each thought proper, there would be nothing left, but all together they would take away everything;[329] for all do not have the same views. [19] I shall also cite a poem in this regard:

For you will see this other law (*nomos*) for mortals
if you make this distinction. Nothing is proper or shameful
in every way, but the occasion (*kairos*) takes the same things
and makes them shameful or changes them into something proper.[330]

[20] One can say in general that everything is proper at the right time (*kairos*) but shameful at the wrong time. What then have I accomplished? I said I would show that the same things are proper and shameful and I have shown this in all these cases.

[21] But it is also said about the shameful and the proper that each is different. For if one should ask those who say that the same thing is shameful and proper if they have ever done anything proper, they will agree they have done something shameful, if indeed the same thing is both shameful and proper. [22] And if they know that some man is proper [i.e. handsome], they know this same man is also shameful [i.e. ugly]; and if he is white the same man is also black. And if it is proper to honor the gods, it is therefore also shameful to honor the gods, if indeed the same thing is shameful and proper.

[23] You may assume that I can make the same point in every case. Let me turn to the argument they give. [24] If it is proper

---

[328] The money is for their dowries; cf. Herodotus 1.93.
[329] For a similar view see Herodotus, fr 3 (3.38).
[330] The author of these verses is unknown; see Other Tragic Fragments, fr. 9.

for a woman to adorn herself, it is shameful for a woman to adorn herself, if indeed the same thing is shameful and proper. And in every other case it is the same: [25] in Sparta it is proper for girls to do athletics, in Sparta it is shameful for girls to do athletics, and similarly for the other examples. [26] They say that if someone collected shameful things from nations everywhere and then called people together and asked them to take away the things each thought proper, everything would be thought proper and taken away. But I would be astonished if things that were collected as shameful will be proper and not remain as they were. [27] Surely if they brought horses or cattle or sheep or humans, they would not take something different away. For if they had brought gold they would certainly not take away bronze, nor if they brought silver would they take away lead. [28] Do they then in place of shameful things take away proper things? Come now, if someone brings an ugly man, does he take him away handsome? And then they cite poets as witnesses, but the purpose of their work is pleasure, not truth.

Right and Wrong [331]

3. [1] Double arguments are also put forth concerning right and wrong; and some say that right is one thing and wrong another, but others that the same thing is right and wrong. And I shall try to support this position. [2] First I shall say that it is right to lie and deceive; one could even assert that it is shameful and wicked to do these things to enemies but not to close relatives.[332] Take parents, for example. If you need to give a drug to your father or mother to eat or drink, and they are unwilling, isn't it right to give it in their porridge or their drink and not tell them it is there? [3] Therefore, to lie to and deceive your parents and indeed to steal your friends' property and use force against friends is right. [4] For example,[333] if a member of the household should be in pain

---

[331] *Dikaios* and *adikos* are usually translated "just" and "unjust," but "right" and "wrong" give a better sense of the wide range of both words in this section. In one case (3.14) we have reverted to the traditional translations.

[332] The author reverses the traditional Greek view, that it is proper to lie, etc. to enemies but not to friends and relatives.

[333] Cf. Plato, *Republic* 1.

or upset about something and is going to kill himself with a sword or a rope or something else, it is right to hide this, if you can; or, if you are late and find him with the implement, to take it by force. [5] And surely it is right to enslave the enemy and, if you can, to capture and sell an entire city into slavery. And to break into public buildings appears right; for if your father has been caught in factional strife (*stasis*) and sentenced to death by his political enemies, isn't it right to break in and save your father by stealing him away? [6] And oath-breaking: if someone is captured by the enemy and swears an oath that if released he will betray his city, would he do the right thing by keeping his oath? [7] I don't think so; but rather he should save his city and his friends and his ancestral temples by breaking his oath. So now oath-breaking is right. And temple-robbery – [8] I say nothing of temples belonging to individual cities; but consider the public shrines of Greece at Delphi and Olympia. When the Barbarian is about to capture Greece[334] and our safety depends on money, isn't it right to take it and use it for the war? [9] And killing one's nearest and dearest is right, since both Orestes and Alcmaeon did it[335] and the god's oracle said they did the right thing.

[10] I shall turn to the arts, and to the art of the poets. For in writing tragedy and in painting the one who deceives the most by creating things similar to the truth, he is the best.[336] [11] I also want to introduce the testimony of older poetry, for instance Cleobuline:[337]

> I saw a man stealing and deceiving by force,
>   and to accomplish this by force was completely right.

[12] Those verses are very old. And these are by Aeschylus:[338]

> A god does not avoid deceit if it is right.
> Sometimes a god respects the right moment (*kairos*) to tell a lie.

[13] And to this too an opposing argument is put forth, that right is one thing and wrong another, and that as the name is

---

[334] Apparently a reference to the Persian invasion of Greece in 480.
[335] Both killed their mothers to avenge a crime against their fathers.
[336] Cf. Gorgias, fr. 10.
[337] Very little is known about this sixth-century poet. It's not certain what her riddle refers to; perhaps a wrestling match.
[338] The two lines appear not to belong together; we don't know which plays they are from.

different so too is the thing; since if someone should ask those who say that the same thing is right and wrong if they have ever done anything right for their parents, they will agree. But then they have done wrong too; for they agree that the same thing is wrong and right. [14] Take another point: if you know that some man is just, then you know the same man is also unjust (and by the same reasoning he is also large and small), and he should die for all the wrongs he has committed.

[15] That is enough about these things. I turn now to what they say when they think they are showing that the same thing is both right and wrong. [16] For the fact that stealing the property of the enemy is right also shows that the same thing is wrong, if their argument is true, and it's the same for the other things. [17] And they bring in the arts, in which there is no right and wrong. And poets compose their poetry not for the truth but for people's pleasure.

Truth and Falsehood

4. [1] Double arguments are also put forth concerning truth and falsehood. One of them says a false statement is one thing and a true statement another, but others say that on the contrary, they are the same. [2] I say the latter. First, they are spoken with the same words; second, whenever a statement is made, if things turn out just as was stated, then the statement is true, but if they do not turn out, the same statement is false. [3] For example, a statement accuses someone of temple-robbery: if the act took place, the statement is true, but if it didn't take place, it is false, and the same for the statement of the defendant. In fact, the courts judge the same statement both false and true. [4] Furthermore, if we sit in a row and say "I am an initiate,"[339] we shall all be saying the same thing, but only I will be truthful, since in fact I am. [5] Thus it is clear that the same statement, whenever falsehood is present in it, is false, but whenever truth is present, is true, just as a person is the same as a boy and a youth and a man and an old man.

---

[339] There were several "mystery" cults in Greece at the time. Initiates (*mystoi*) were supposed to keep details about membership and rites secret.

[6] But it is also said that a false statement is one thing and a true statement another, and that just as the name is different, so is the thing. But if someone should ask those who say the same statement is false and true, which of these their statement is, if they say "false," it is clear that they are two different things, but if they answer "true," then this same statement is also false. And if he ever said anything true or presented any true testimony, then these same things would also be false. And if he knows that some man is truthful, he knows that the same man is also a liar. [7] In their argument they say that when the deed took place, the statement is true, but when it didn't, it's false; [but[340] in these cases the thing is different and] therefore [the name too] is different. [8] Again, [they are wrong to ask] jurors what their judgment is, for they were not present at the deed. [9] And they too agree that that in which falsehood is mixed is false but that in which truth is mixed is true. And this is completely different.

5.[341] [1] Those who are mad and those of sound mind and the wise and the foolish both say and do the same things. [2] First, they use the same names: "earth" and "person" and "horse" and "fire" and all the other things. And they do the same things: they sit down, eat, drink, lie down, and do other things in the same way. [3] And indeed the same thing is also both greater and smaller, and more and less, and heavier and lighter. For in this way all things are the same. [4] A talent is heavier than a *mina* and lighter than two talents.[342] Thus the same thing is both lighter and heavier. [5] And the same man lives and does not live and the same things are and are not. For things that are here are not in Libya, and the things in Libya are not in Cyprus. And the same argument applies to other things too. Therefore, things both are and are not.

[6] Those who say these things – that those who are mad and the wise and the foolish do and say the same things, and the other consequences of this argument – do not argue correctly. [7] For if someone should ask them if madness differs from a sound mind and wisdom from foolishness, they say, "Yes." [8] For it is readily

---

[340] There are gaps in the syntax here and in the next sentence; we supply a possible line of argument.

[341] It is possible that a section title and introductory sentence similar to those of the first four sections has dropped out.

[342] See Glossary, *s.vv. "mina"* and "talent."

apparent that they would agree, judging from the actions of each group. So even if they do the same things, it's not true that the wise are mad or the mad wise or that all things are confounded. [9] And the point must be raised whether those of sound mind or those who are mad speak when they ought to; for they say that these say the same thing when you ask them, but the wise when they ought to and those who are mad when they ought not. [10] And in saying this they seem to add this little "when they ought or ought not," and so it's no longer the same thing. [11] But I think things are altered not just by the addition of such a thing but even by an accent changing. For example,[343] *Glaúcus* and *glaucús* ("white"), or *Xánthus* and *xanthús* ("blond"), or *Xúthus* and *xuthús* ("nimble"). [12] These changed because of the accent changing, but the following because of being spoken with a long or short vowel: *Turos* ("Tyre") and *tūros* ("cheese"), or *sakos* ("shield") and *sākos* ("enclosure"), and others by transposing letters: *kártos* ("strength") and *kratós* ("head"), or *onos* ("ass") and *noös* ("mind"). [13] Since, then, there is so much change when nothing is removed, what if you either add something or take it away? And I'll show how this is. [14] If you take one away from ten, it's no longer ten or one, and the same for other things. [15] As for the same person both existing and not existing, I ask, "Is it with respect to something or with respect to all things that he exists?" Therefore, if someone says that he does not exist, he is lying if he means in respect to all things. All these things, then, exist in some way.

On Whether Wisdom and *Aretē* are Teachable[344]

6. [1] A certain position is put forth, neither true nor new, that wisdom (*sophia*) and *aretē* are neither teachable nor learnable. Those who maintain this give the following reasons. [2] If you give something to someone else, it is not possible that you will still have it yourself. That is one argument. [3] Another is that, if they were teachable, there would be recognized teachers, as in the case of music. [4] A third is that those in Greece who became wise men (*sophoi*) would have taught their own children and their friends.

---

[343] In the following examples the capitalized forms are all proper names.
[344] Several issues in this section are also discussed in Plato's *Protagoras*.

[5] A fourth is that some people have already gone to sophists and have not been helped at all. [6] A fifth is that many people who have not associated with sophists have become noteworthy.

[7] I myself think this argument is extremely simple-minded. For I know that teachers teach letters, which they happen to know themselves, and lyre-players teach lyre-playing. As for the second argument, that there are no recognized teachers, what then do the sophists teach, if not wisdom and *aretē*? [8] And what were the followers of Anaxagoras and Pythagoras?[345] As for the third, Polycleitus taught his son to make statues.[346] [9] Even if someone does not teach, this is no indication that teaching is not possible; but if there is one example of teaching, this is proof that teaching is possible. [10] As for the fourth, if some do not become wise from studying with wise sophists, many have also not learned their letters despite studying them. [11] There is in fact a certain natural ability (*phusis*), by which someone who does not study with the sophists becomes competent, if he is truly well-endowed, to grasp most things easily once he has learned a few things from those from whom we also learn our words. And these, to a greater or lesser extent, we learn either from a father or a mother. [12] And if someone is not convinced that we learn our words, but thinks we are born already knowing them, let him learn from the following: if someone should send a newborn child to Persia and raise it there, without hearing any Greek, it would speak Persian; if someone brought a child from there to here, it would speak Greek. In this way we learn words, and we don't know who our teachers are.

[13] So, the position is stated and you have the beginning, middle, and end. I don't say that they are teachable, but those arguments [that they are not teachable] do not satisfy me.

7. [1] Some of the popular orators say that public offices should be assigned by lot,[347] but this opinion is not the best. [2] What if you should ask him, "Why do you not assign your servants their

---

[345] Anaxagoras of Clazomenae (*c.* 500–*c.* 428) and Pythagoras of Samos (flourished around 530).

[346] Cf. Plato, *Protagoras* 328a (Protagoras, fr. 10).

[347] Assigning public offices by lot was a characteristic of Athenian democracy; see Introduction. A notable exception was the office of general, which was filled by popular election.

jobs by lot, so that if the ox-leader drew the job of cook, he would cook, and the cook would lead the oxen, and similarly with the other jobs? [3] And how come we didn't assemble the smiths and the cobblers and the carpenters and the jewelers and draw lots and compel them each to practice the craft he was assigned by lot and not the one he knew?" [4] In the same way we could also draw lots for competitors in music contests, and each person would compete in whatever contest he was assigned by lot, a flute-player perchance competing on the lyre and a lyre-player on the flute. And in war an archer and an infantryman will ride in the cavalry and the cavalryman will shoot a bow. Thus all will be doing jobs for which they have neither knowledge nor competence. [5] They say that this method is both a good thing and very democratic, but I don't think it is democratic at all. For in these cities there are those who hate the common people (*dēmos*), and if their lot happens to be selected, they will destroy the people. [6] The people themselves, however, should watch closely and in all cases choose those who are sympathetic toward their interests, and choose as generals those suited for commanding troops, others suited to be guardians of the law, and so forth.

8. [1] I think it is a quality of the same man and the same profession (*technē*) to be able to engage in short question-and-answer discussions, and to know the truth of things (*pragmata*), and to plead a case correctly in court, and to be able to address a public body, and to know the craft (*technē*) of words, and to teach others about the nature of all things, how things are and how they came to be. [2] First, if someone knows the nature of all things, how can he possibly not act correctly in every respect? [3] Furthermore, someone who knows the craft of words will speak correctly (*orthōs*) about everything. [4] For someone who is going to speak correctly must speak about things that he knows; therefore, it seems, he will have knowledge of everything. [5] For he knows the craft of all words, and all words cover all subjects. [6] And someone who is going to speak correctly must know about whatever it is that he speaks of, ... and to teach the city correctly to accomplish good things and prevent them from doing bad things. [7] And in knowing these things, he will also know things different from these, for he will know everything. For these things belong

to all things and, if necessary, he will accomplish the other things that need to be done.[348] [8] Even if he does not know flute playing, he will be able to play the flute if it should be necessary to do so.

[9] And someone who knows how to plead a case in court must understand justice (*to dikaion*) correctly; for this is what trials are about. And if he knows this, he will also know its opposite and things different from these. [10] He must also know all the laws; and yet if he does not understand the facts (*pragmata*), he will not understand the laws either. [11] For who is it who understands the law of music?[349] It is the person who understands music; and whoever does not understand music, also does not understand the laws of music. [12] At any rate, it is a simple argument that someone who knows the truth of things (*pragmata*) knows everything. [13] And someone who can engage in short ⟨question-and-answer discussions⟩ must, when asked, give answers concerning everything; and therefore he must know everything.[350]

9. [1] The greatest and finest discovery that has been made for our lives is memory; it is useful for everything, for intellectual pursuits (*philosophia*)[351] and for wisdom (*sophia*). [2] This is what it is: if you pay close attention, in this way your mind will tend to perceive what you have learned as a whole. [3] Second, if you hear something, you must go over it; for by hearing and saying the same thing many times, it becomes part of your memory. [4] Third, if you hear something, associate it with something you already know; for example, you must remember the name, Chrysippos: associate it with *chrysos* ("gold") and *hippos* ("horse"). [5] Another example: Pyrilampe; associate it with *pyr* ("fire") and *lampein* ("shining"). This advice applies to names. [6] For things, do this: associate courage with Ares[352] and Achilles, bronzeworking with Hephaestus, cowardice with Epeius,[353] . . .

---

[348] There is much uncertainty about the correct text and interpretation of this sentence.

[349] There is a pun here on *nomos*, which can mean "tune" as well as "law."

[350] Cf. Plato, *Protagoras* 334c–338e; Hippias, fr. 5.

[351] *Philosophia* (lit. "love of wisdom") had not developed the specialized sense of "philosophy" at this time.

[352] Ares is the god of war; Achilles, the greatest warrior in the *Iliad*; Hephaestus, the smith-god. Epeius is a minor mythological figure, whose name was a byword for cowardice.

[353] Our manuscripts indicate that the text originally continued beyond this point, but we do not know how much is lost.

From unknown authors

In this section are two passages that cannot be assigned with certainty to any particular historical figure. They reflect teachings that have been associated with various sophists.

1. The social contract (Plato, Republic 358e3–359b5)

Hoping that Socrates will be able to refute the view, Glaucon tells him what is being said about the nature and origin of justice. We do not know who first proposed the contract theory of the origin of justice, or who first inferred from the theory that justice is not an intrinsic good. Although the language of the passage is Platonic, it probably reflects the views of an earlier thinker connected with some of the sophists.

As far as nature goes, they say that doing injustice is good, while suffering injustice is bad; the badness of suffering injustice, however, outweighs the goodness of doing it to such an extent that after people have been doing injustice to each other and suffering it, once they've had a taste of both, then those who lack the power 359a to avoid the one while choosing the other decide that it is in their interests to make a mutual agreement neither to do nor to suffer injustice. And so (they say) people start making their own laws (*nomoi*) and agreements (*sunthēkai*) at that point, and they use the words "lawful" (*nomimon*) and "just" (*dikaion*) for what these laws require. This, they say, is the origin and essence of justice lying in between what is really best – doing injustice without paying the penalty – and what is worst – suffering injustice without the power to take revenge. People welcome justice as an intermediate between these things, not because it is really good, but because of the value 359b it draws from their being too weak to do injustice. Anyone who did have the power to do this, however, and was truly a man, would never make an agreement with anyone to refrain from doing and suffering injustice. He would be crazy to do that. So that is the nature of justice, Socrates; that is what it is like, and those are the circumstances in which it is born, according to this view (*logos*).

2. The law of nature (Plato, Gorgias 483a7–484c3)

*Callicles (who may or may not have been an historical figure) accuses Socrates of cheating in his arguments by not correctly observing the distinction between nature and custom (*phusis and nomos*).*

By nature whatever is worse, such as suffering injustice, is more shameful; and it is only by custom (*nomos*) that doing injustice is worse. That is not a man's fate, to suffer injustice, but a slave's; 483b it's for someone who is better off dead than alive, since once a person has suffered injustice and been thoroughly abused he's unable to come to his own defense or that of anyone else for whom he cares. In fact, I think it is people who are weak – common people (*hoi polloi*) – who make the laws (*nomoi*). It's for themselves and their own advantage that they make the laws they make, praise what they praise, and blame what they blame. They 483c are afraid of the people who are stronger and have the power to take more than their share, and so to keep them from taking more than their share they say that taking more than one's share (*pleonexia*) is shameful (*aischron*) and unjust (*adikon*). Since they are weaker, I believe they are pleased to have an equal share (*to ison*). That is why people say, by custom, that it is unjust and shameful to try to have a bigger share than the common people, and they call this "doing injustice."

But I believe that nature itself reveals that it is just for the better 483d man to have a larger share than the worse, and the more powerful than the less powerful. This is clearly shown to be so everywhere, both for the other animals and for whole cities and tribes of human beings: that justice has been decided in this way, for the better

man to rule the worse and to have a larger share. What other kind
of justice did Xerxes plead when he invaded Greece, or his father,
when he invaded Scythia?[354] And one could name any number of 483e
similar examples. Now I believe that it was in accordance with the
nature of justice that these men acted thus, and yes, by Zeus, in
accordance with the law of nature[355] – though probably not in
accordance with this law that *we* make. We take our own best and
strongest when they are young like lions,[356] and we mold them
into slaves, bewitching them with incantations, saying that [everyone] 484a
should have an equal share and that this is what justice and nobility
require. I believe, however, that if a man is born with a nature
that is good enough he will shake all this off and burst through
and escape.[357] He will trample on our written stuff and magic tricks
and incantations and on all those laws that are against nature. The
slave will rise and show himself our master, and the light of natural 484b
justice (*to tēs phuseōs dikaion*) will shine from him. Pindar, I think,
makes just this point in his ode when he says,

> Custom, king of all
> of mortals and immortals. . . .

And this it is, he says, that

> takes up and justifies what is most violent
> with a supremely high hand. As evidence
> I cite the deeds of Heracles, since . . . without paying. . .[358]

He says something like that – I don't really know the poem – he
says that he drove off the cattle of Geryon though he did not pay
and Geryon did not give them to him, on the grounds that, by 484c
the nature of justice, the cattle and other possessions of those who
are worse and weaker all belong to the better and stronger man.

---

[354] Xerxes invaded Greece in 480; his father, Darius, invaded Scythia in 512. Both
expeditions fared badly in the event.

[355] An untranslatable particle in Greek makes it clear that "the law of nature" is a
novel expression.

[356] Probably an allusion to the fable of the lion's whelp who is tamed at first by the
family who raises him, but who afterwards turns violent (Aeschylus, *Agamemnon*
717–736).

[357] Cf. Antiphon's contention that the advantages of law are "bonds of nature" (fr.
7b, col. 4).

[358] These five lines are from Pindar, fr. 1. We translate the entire fragment above.

Index

A reference such as 169.25 denotes lr. 25 on p. 169. For authors whose works are known by conventional numbering systems: see also the table of equivalents, p. l. For explanations of Greek words and proper names, consult the glossary, p. xliv.

Index

land reform, 6.3, 27
language, 68–9, 156–7, 184, 306;
origin of, 177; Antiphon on,
244.5; Gorgias on, 208–9;
Protagoras on, 188–9
Lapiths, 288n., 297
laughter: in rhetoric, 204.9
lawgivers, 19.18, 23, 146.4.
183
laws, xi–xiii, 127, 146.4, 160.18,
161.25, 194, 310; Athenian
law, 27, 137, 142; common law
(*koinos nomos*), 68.13, 70.20;
divine law, 152.6–8; law of
nature, 310–11; legal
procedure, 6.2, 19–20, 81,
246–7; origin of law, 80–1,
260–2, 309–10; unwritten law,
95; written law, 65, 201; in
civil war, 108; and common
good, 273–4; *dēmos* and, 152.7;
in education, 183–4; and ethics,
103–4, 160.21–3; force and,
91, 109; human nature and,
115–16; opposed to nature,
245; precision of, 203; relativity
of, 70.20; respect for, 94–5;
rule of, 229; slaves and, 75.11;
tyranny and, 70.18, 83;
Anonymus Iamblichi on, 292,
293, 295; Antiphon on, 245–7;
Critias on, 259–60; *Dissoi Logoi*
on, 300, 307–8; Lycophron on,
275.1; sophists on, xxii
lawsuits: in Athens, 91, 142
Leontini, 125
Leucippus, 156
liberty, 85, 92, 124, 129; see also
freedom
likelihood: see *eikos*
likemindedness: see *homonoia*
lion and dolphin (fable), 148
lions and hares (fable), 145
liturgia (sponsorship), 136n., 142–
3, 224n.
logos, logoi (speech, speeches),
xxviii, 105, 149.13, 181, 204.8,
259–60; and peace, 58.33; as
reason, 188.28; and
responsibility, 192–3; and
women, 160.20; Heraclitus on,
151.1, 151.3; opposed *logoi*: see

opposed speeches; see also
rhetoric; speech; speeches
logos–ergon (contrast of word with
action), 93, 96, 97, 98, 105,
110, 168–9, 196, 202, 209,
232, 291; in Thucydides, xxx,
88
lot: selection by, in democracy,
xiii–xiv, 83, 94n., 118, 134,
306–7
love (as motive), 191, 193–4
Lycophron, 275
Lycurgus, xi, 23, 215.2
lying, 19.7, 48.13, 48.14, 54.16,
154.24, 301, 302, 304

Macedonia, 267–74
madness, 30
magistrates, 159.14–16
man–measure doctrine, 186.15
marriage, 1, 56, 60–1, 62, 248–9
meaning, 209, 244.5
Medical writers, xix, 164–6; *Airs,
Waters, Places*, 164–5; *On
Human Nature*, 166
Megabyxos (defender of
oligarchy), 84
Melian dialogue, 118–25
Melissus, 206, 207
memory, 45, 253.37, 308
Meno (of Plato), 205.12, 205.15
metaphor, 203n.
metics (foreign residents), 135–6
miasma (defilement, pollution),
155.26, 218, 220, 221, 224,
226; from homicide, 237, 239–
40, 241, 243–4; from
unintentional homicide, 229,
234
middle class, 63.5
Miletus, 144
mimēsis (imitation), 282
mind–body, 247.8
mob rule, 64
moderation, 32.3, 57.29, 162.31,
263.18; see *sôphrosunē*
monarchy, xv, 65; criticized, 63,
83; defended, 4, 64; and
sophia, 55–6; Heraclitus on,
152.8–10, 153.13; see also
kings; tyrants
Muses, 19–20, 29–30, 45, 288

Index

Index

Cambridge Texts in the History of Political Thought

Titles published in the series thus far

Aristotle *The Politics and The Constitution of Athens* (edited by Stephen Everson)
   0 521 48400 6 paperback
Arnold *Culture and Anarchy and other writings* (edited by Stefan Collini)
   0 521 37796 x paperback
Astell *Political Writings* (edited by Patricia Springborg)
   0 521 42845 9 paperback
Augustine *The City of God against the Pagans* (edited by R.W. Dyson)
   0 521 46843 4 paperback
Austin *The Province of Jurisprudence Determined* (edited by Wilfrid E. Rumble)
   0 521 44756 9 paperback
Bacon *The History of the Reign of King Henry VII* (edited by Brian Vickers)
   0 521 58663 1 paperback
Bakunin *Statism and Anarchy* (edited by Marshall Shatz)
   0 521 36973 8 paperback
Baxter *Holy Commonwealth* (edited by William Lamont)
   0 521 40580 7 paperback
Bayle *Political Writings* (edited by Sally L. Jenkinson)
   0 521 47677 1 paperback
Beccaria *On Crimes and Punishments and other writings* (edited by Richard Bellamy)
   0 521 47982 7 paperback
Bentham *Fragment on Government* (introduction by Ross Harrison)
   0 521 35929 5 paperback
Bernstein *The Preconditions of Socialism* (edited by Henry Tudor)
   0 521 39808 8 paperback
Bodin *On Sovereignty* (edited by Julian H. Franklin)
   0 521 34992 3 paperback
Bolingbroke *Political Writings* (edited by David Armitage)
   0 521 58697 6 paperback
Bossuet *Politics Drawn from the Very Words of Holy Scripture*
(edited by Patrick Riley)
   0 521 36807 3 paperback
The British Idealists (edited by David Boucher)
   0 521 45951 6 paperback
Burke *Pre-Revolutionary Writings* (edited by Ian Harris)
   0 521 36800 6 paperback
Christine De Pizan *The Book of the Body Politic* (edited by Kate Langdon Forhan)
   0 521 42259 0 paperback
Cicero *On Duties* (edited by M. T. Griffin and E. M. Atkins)
   0 521 34835 8 paperback
Cicero *On the Commonwealth and On the Laws* (edited by James E. G. Zetzel)
   0 521 45959 1 paperback
Comte *Early Political Writings* (edited by H. S. Jones)
   0 521 46923 6 paperback
Conciliarism and Papalism (edited by J. H. Burns and Thomas M. Izbicki)
   0 521 47674 7 paperback
Constant *Political Writings* (edited by Biancamaria Fontana)
   0 521 31632 4 paperback
Dante *Monarchy* (edited by Prue Shaw)
   0 521 56781 5 paperback
Diderot *Political Writings* (edited by John Hope Mason and Robert Wokler)
   0 521 36911 8 paperback

The Dutch Revolt (edited by Martin van Gelderen)
  0 521 39809 6 paperback
Early Greek Political Thought from Homer to the Sophists
(edited by Michael Gagarin and Paul Woodruff)
  0 521 43768 7 paperback
The Early Political Writings of the German Romantics
(edited by Frederick C. Beiser)
  0 521 44951 0 paperback
The English Levellers (edited by Andrew Sharp)
  0 521 62511 4 paperback
Erasmus *The Education of a Christian Prince* (edited by Lisa Jardine)
  0 521 58811 1 paperback
Fenelon *Telemachus* (edited by Patrick Riley)
  0 521 45662 2 paperback
Ferguson *An Essay on the History of Civil Society* (edited by Fania Oz-Salzberger)
  0 521 44736 4 paperback
Filmer *Patriarcha and Other Writings* (edited by Johann P. Sommerville)
  0 521 39903 3 paperback
Fletcher *Political Works* (edited by John Robertson)
  0 521 43994 9 paperback
Sir John Fortescue *On the Laws and Governance of England*
(edited by Shelley Lockwood)
  0 521 58996 7 paperback
Fourier *The Theory of the Four Movements* (edited by Gareth Stedman Jones and
Ian Patterson)
  0 521 35693 8 paperback
Gramsci *Pre-Prison Writings* (edited by Richard Bellamy)
  0 521 42307 4 paperback
Guicciardini *Dialogue on the Government of Florence* (edited by Alison Brown)
  0 521 45623 1 paperback
Harrington *The Commonwealth of Oceana* and *A System of Politics*
(edited by J. G. A. Pocock)
  0 521 42329 5 paperback
Hegel *Elements of the Philosophy of Right* (edited by Allen W. Wood and
H. B. Nisbet)
  0 521 34888 9 paperback
Hegel *Political Writings* (edited by Laurence Dickey and H. B. Nisbet)
  0 521 45979 3 paperback
Hobbes *On the Citizen* (edited by Michael Silverthorne and Richard Tuck)
  0 521 43780 6 paperback
Hobbes *Leviathan* (edited by Richard Tuck)
  0 521 56797 1 paperback
Hobhouse *Liberalism and Other Writings* (edited by James Meadowcroft)
  0 521 43726 1 paperback
Hooker *Of the Laws of Ecclesiastical Polity* (edited by A. S. McGrade)
  0 521 37908 3 paperback
Hume *Political Essays* (edited by Knud Haakonssen)
  0 521 46639 3 paperback
King James VI and I *Political Writings* (edited by Johann P. Sommerville)
  0 521 44729 1 paperback
Jefferson *Political Writings* (edited by Joyce Appleby and Terence Ball)
  0 521 64841 6 paperback
John of Salisbury *Policraticus* (edited by Cary Nederman)
  0 521 36701 8 paperback

Kant *Political Writings* (edited by H. S. Reiss and H. B. Nisbet)
    0 521 39837 1 paperback
Knox *On Rebellion* (edited by Roger A. Mason)
    0 521 39988 2 paperback
Kropotkin *The Conquest of Bread and other writings* (edited by Marshall Shatz)
    0 521 45990 7 paperback
Lawson *Politica sacra et civilis* (edited by Conal Condren)
    0 521 39248 9 paperback
Leibniz *Political Writings* (edited by Patrick Riley)
    0 521 35899 x paperback
The Levellers (edited by Andrew Sharp)
    0 521 62511 4 paperback
Locke *Political Essays* (edited by Mark Goldie)
    0 521 47861 8 paperback
Locke *Two Treatises of Government* (edited by Peter Laslett)
    0 521 35730 6 paperback
Loyseau *A Treatise of Orders and Plain Dignities* (edited by Howell A. Lloyd)
    0 521 45624 x paperback
Luther and Calvin on Secular Authority (edited by Harro Höpfl)
    0 521 34986 9 paperback
Machiavelli *The Prince* (edited by Quentin Skinner and Russell Price)
    0 521 34993 1 paperback
de Maistre *Considerations on France* (edited by Isaiah Berlin and Richard Lebrun)
    0 521 46628 8 paperback
Malthus *An Essay on the Principle of Population* (edited by Donald Winch)
    0 521 42972 2 paperback
Marsiglio of Padua *Defensor minor* and *De translatione Imperii*
(edited by Cary Nederman)
    0 521 40846 6 paperback
Marx *Early Political Writings* (edited by Joseph O'Malley)
    0 521 34994 x paperback
Marx *Later Political Writings* (edited by Terrell Carver)
    0 521 36739 5 paperback
James Mill *Political Writings* (edited by Terence Ball)
    0 521 38748 5 paperback
J. S. Mill *On Liberty*, with *The Subjection of Women* and *Chapters on Socialism*
(edited by Stefan Collini)
    0 521 37917 2 paperback
Milton *Political Writings* (edited by Martin Dzelzainis)
    0 521 34866 8 paperback
Montesquieu *The Spirit of the Laws* (edited by Anne M. Cohler,
Basia Carolyn Miller and Harold Samuel Stone)
    0 521 36974 6 paperback
More *Utopia* (edited by George M. Logan and Robert M. Adams)
    0 521 40318 9 paperback
Morris *News from Nowhere* (edited by Krishan Kumar)
    0 521 42233 7 paperback
Nicholas of Cusa *The Catholic Concordance* (edited by Paul E. Sigmund)
    0 521 56773 4 paperback
Nietzsche *On the Genealogy of Morality* (edited by Keith Ansell-Pearson)
    0 521 40610 2 paperback
Paine *Political Writings* (edited by Bruce Kuklick)
    0 521 66799 2 paperback
Plato *The Republic* (edited by G. R. F. Ferrari and Tom Griffith)
    0 521 48443 x paperback